GRAMMAR IN CONTEXT

FIRST CANADIAN EDITION

SANDRA N. ELBAUM

PATRICIA MUNRO CONWAY

 I(T)P Nelson

an International Thomson Publishing company

Toronto • Albany • Bonn • Boston • Cincinnati • Detroit • London • Madrid • Melbourne
Mexico City • New York • Pacific Grove • Paris • San Francisco • Singapore • Tokyo • Washington

I(T)P® International Thomson Publishing
The ITP logo is a trademark under licence
www.thomson.com

Published in 1999 by
I(T)P® Nelson
A division of Thomson Canada Limited
1120 Birchmount Road
Scarborough, Ontario M1K 5G4
www.nelson.com

ISBN-13: 978-0-17-607334-3
ISBN-10: 0-17-607334-5

Canadian Cataloguing in Publication Data
Elbaum, Sandra N.,
    Grammar in context, Book 1

1st Canadian ed.
Includes index.
ISBN 0-17-607334-5

1. English language – Textbooks for second language learners.*
2. English language – Grammar – Problems, exercises, etc.
I. Conway, Patricia Munro. II. Title

PE1112.E42 1998   428.2'4   C98–930955-X

Publisher and Team Leader   Michael Young
Acquisitions Editor   Nicole Gnutzman
Project Editor   Jenny Anttila
Production Editor   Tracy Bordian
Production Coordinator   Brad Horning
Marketing Manager   Kevin Smulan
Art Director   Sylvia Vander Schee
Cover Design   Sylvia Vander Schee
Senior Composition Analyst   Daryn DeWalt

Printed and bound in Canada

2 3 4 5 (WC) 09 08 07 06

CONTENTS

PREFACE

Grammar in Context, Book One is the first part of a three-part grammar series for adult students of English as a Second Language. This series of work-texts is designed for the high beginning to low advanced instructional levels.

As ESL teachers know, presenting English in a meaningful context allows for a better understanding of the grammar point. *Grammar in Context* is unique among grammar texts in its use of culturally rich, informative readings to present and illustrate the target grammar, and to stimulate interest in the topic.

Grammar in Context is organized as follows:

Lesson Focus The lessons begin with an overview and brief explanation of the grammar points covered. The Lesson Focus also includes sentences that illustrate the grammar point(s) being addressed.

Pre-Reading Questions These questions stimulate student interest in the topic of the reading that follows.

Introductory Readings A short reading illustrates each new grammar point in a natural, authentic context. These high-interest readings about culturally rich topics engage the student's attention and help focus on the grammar points. The real-life subject matter provides practical information about Canadian life and customs, stories about famous people and events, and contemporary issues that are of concern to Canadians as well as to recently arrived residents. These readings can be used as springboards for lively classroom discussions, as well as inspiration for out-of-class activities.

Since *Grammar in Context* is not a reader, the readings are written at a simple, accessible level, for their primary goal is to exemplify the target grammar. The practical vocabulary and idioms that are needed to understand the passage are anticipated and explained in footnotes or illustrations.

Grammar Boxes and Language Notes This book anticipates difficulties that most students have—for example, count and noncount nouns, contracted verb forms, modal auxiliaries, and question formation. Also, a great deal of attention is given to word order.

The grammar boxes use simple language in grammar explanations, illustrative example sentences, and charts with a clear graphic overview. Because *Grammar in Context* does not rely on a knowledge of linguistic jargon, fine points of grammar are often placed in a footnote so as not to overwhelm students who do not need so much detail.

The Language Notes provide the students with additional information on the functions of language, level of formality/informality, appropriate usage, spelling, and pronunciation. At times they include information on the differences between Canadian English and British English.

Exercises There is a great variety of exercise types. The change of pace from one exercise to another reduces boredom in the classroom and offers challenges to different types of language learners as well as language teachers. Exercises include traditional fill-ins, cloze tasks, pair work, editing exercises, and combination exercises that review previous material in the context of the new or integrate several subskills from within the lesson. Many of the exercises allow students to personalize their remarks to reflect their own observations about Canadian life, their opinions on cultural matters, and their feelings.

Expansion Activities These activities, grouped at the end of each lesson, allow students to use the grammar points covered in more communicative ways. Expansion Activities include pair work; group discussions; writing; poetry, proverbs, famous quotes and sayings; and outside activities. These activities give subjects for debate and discussion, topics for written reflection, and ideas for further research on the context of the lesson or on a related topic (including suggestions for interviewing Canadians and bringing the findings back to share with the class). The poems, proverbs, famous quotes and sayings not only illustrate the grammar items, but also provide an opportunity for a rich cross-cultural interchange.

Because they are progressively more challenging, the Expansion Activities lead away from a mechanical manipulation of grammar toward situations in which students put their recently learned grammatical knowledge to immediate practical use.

The teacher may choose to have students do Expansion Activities after a related grammar point has been thoroughly studied, or may assign them after the lesson has been completed.

Editing Advice Potentially troublesome issues with the grammar points covered in the lesson are presented, showing students common errors and ways to correct them.

Summary The end-of-lesson summary encapsulates all of the grammar presented in the chapter in a simple graphic format.

Cultural References Visual aids, illustrations, and charts support the vocabulary in the readings and the content of the exercises. Maps of Canada and references to provinces and territories, major cities, and regions familiarize the students with names they will frequently hear. Articles about well-known Canadians, both past and present, or people who have contributed to the growth of Canada are included in order to provide an appropriate cultural context.

Test/Review Each lesson ends with a test/review section that allows both the teacher and the students to evaluate the mastery of concepts. Different formats—editing, fill-ins, and multiple choice questions—are used.

Appendices This book includes appendices that provide useful information in list or chart form. The appendices are cross-referenced throughout the text.

How to Use the *Grammar in Context* Series

Book One can be used for a high beginning class, Book Two for an intermediate class, and Book Three for a low advanced class. However, users should note that grammar points often overlap books in the series. Since students rarely master a point after only one presentation and practice, there is a repetition at the next level, as well as added complexity.

Grammar in Context provides thorough coverage of the grammar and a variety of exercise types, and anticipates student problems, thereby freeing the teacher from excessive class preparation. By providing grammar practice in the context of relevant and stimulating ideas, the *Grammar in Context* series eases the transition to Canadian life, both linguistically and culturally.

ACKNOWLEDGMENTS

First, I would like to thank Michael Young and Andrew Livingston at ITP Nelson for appreciating the need for a Canadian edition of *Grammar in Context* and for having faith in my ability to do justice to the project. I have been particularly fortunate in the excellent production team at ITP Nelson: Nicole Gnutzman, Acquisitions Editor; Jenny Anttila, Project Editor; Tracy Bordian, Production Editor; Brad Horning, Production Coordinator; Laurie MacLean, Designer; Sylvia Vander Schee, Art Director; Lynne Missen, Copy Editor; and Daryn DeWalt, Sr. Composition Analyst. Their support, help, and encouragement sustained me throughout development of the adaptation.

In addition, I would like to extend a particular thank-you to Nasneen (Virginia) Wallis, who proofread the manuscript of the Canadian material with interest and perspicacity.

Finally, my students deserve special mention for their curiosity regarding the geography and culture of their adopted land, which prompted much of the Canadian material. Their difficulties with English pronunciation, grammar, and vocabulary have challenged me to explore my own language in new ways. I am immensely grateful for all they have taught me.

Patricia Munro Conway
Montreal, 1998

GRAMMAR IN CONTEXT

Montreal

LESSON ONE

GRAMMAR

Be—Affirmative and Negative
Statements

CONTEXT

Canada
Postcard from Ottawa

Lesson Focus *Be*—Affirmative and Negative Statements

Be is an irregular verb. It has three forms in the present: *am, is, are.*

Most of the United States is south of Canada.
Alaska isn't south of Canada.

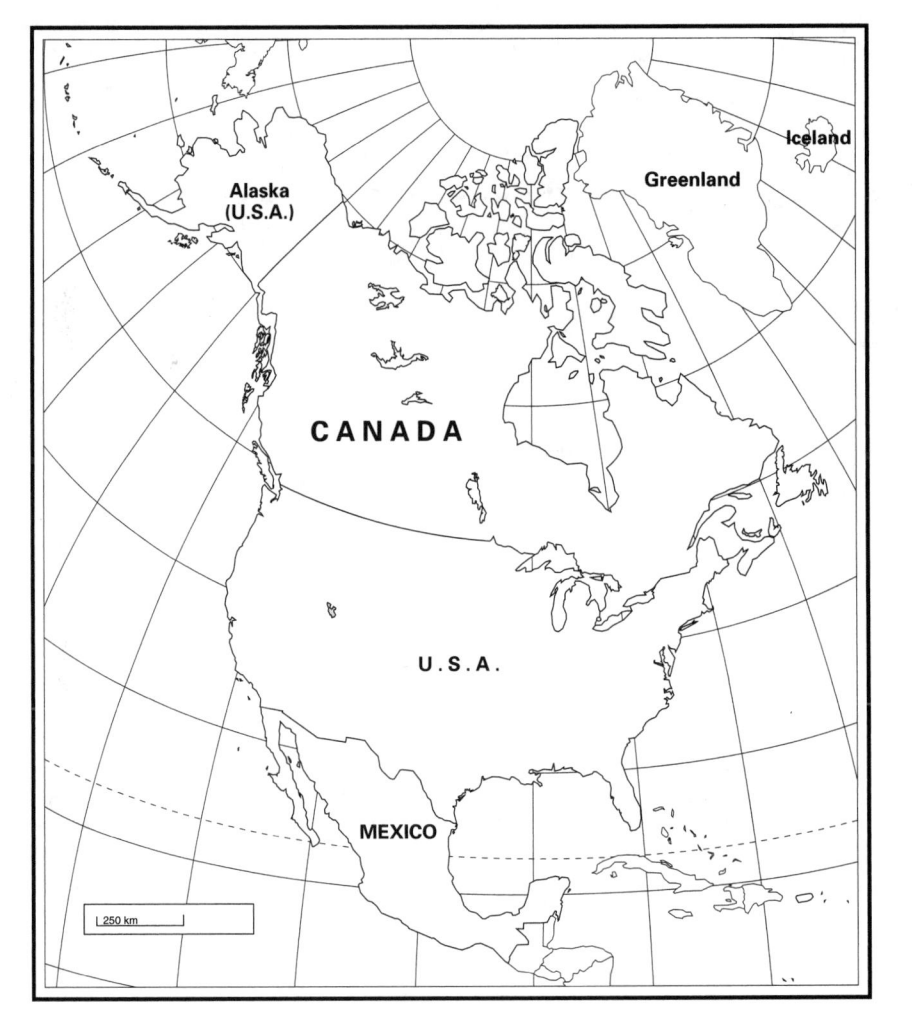

Before you read:

1. Look at the map of North America. Find Alaska, Greenland, and Iceland.
2. Look at the map of Canada. Find the province where you live.

Read the following article. Pay special attention to the forms of the verb *be.*

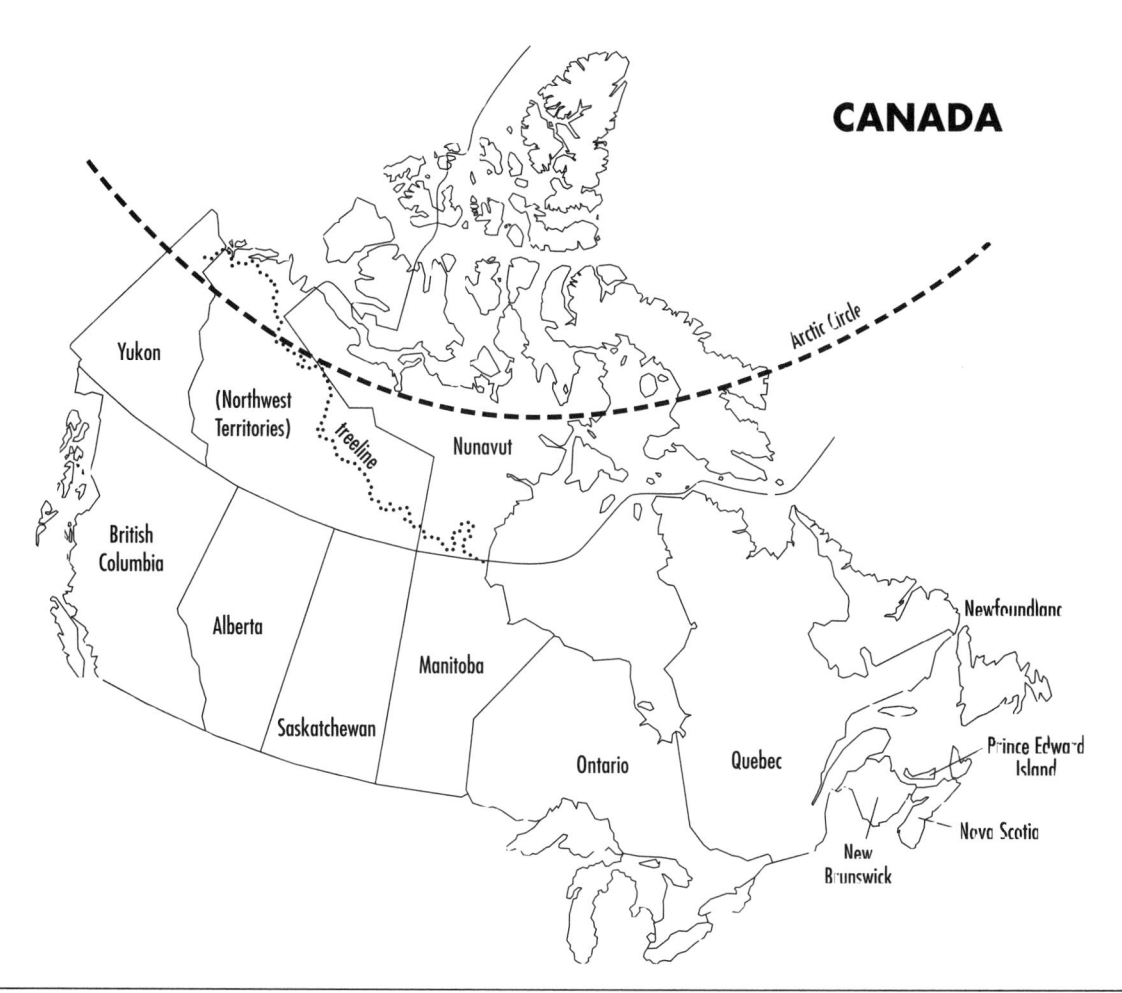

CANADA

Abbreviation	Province/Territory	Capital	Population*
NF	Newfoundland	St. John's	564,929
PE	Prince Edward Island	Charlottetown	137,715
NS	Nova Scotia	Halifax	945,839
NB	New Brunswick	Fredericton	762,760
QC	Quebec	Quebec	7,413,944
ON	Ontario	Toronto	11,361,578
MB	Manitoba	Winnipeg	1,148,251
SK	Saskatchewan	Regina	1,025,086
AB	Alberta	Edmonton	2,828,189
BC	British Columbia	Victoria	3,915,898
YT	Yukon Territory	Whitehorse	31,627
NT	Northwest Territories	Yellowknife	45,057
NV	Nunavut (April 1, 1999)	Iqaluit	22,000 (approx.)
CA	Canada	Ottawa	30,202,873

*Statistics Canada population figures are postcensus estimates, as of April 1, 1997.

CANADA

Canada **is** a big country. It **is** the second largest country in the world. Russia **is** the biggest. There **are** five geographical regions in Canada: the Pacific Region (British Columbia), the Prairie provinces (Alberta, Saskatchewan, and Manitoba), Central Canada (Ontario and Quebec), the Atlantic provinces (the three Maritime provinces of New Brunswick, Nova Scotia, and Prince Edward Island, and the province of Newfoundland), and the North or Arctic Region (the Yukon and the Northwest Territories).

There **are** ten provinces. One province **is** an island: Prince Edward Island. It **is** in the Gulf of St. Lawrence, in eastern Canada. It **is** Canada's smallest province. Newfoundland **is** the most easterly province in Canada. There **are** two parts to this province: the island of Newfoundland and the mainland portion of Labrador.

Ottawa **is** the capital of Canada. It **is** in Ontario, on the border with Quebec. The federal Parliament Buildings **are** in Ottawa. The homes of the prime minister and the Governor General of Canada **are** also in Ottawa.

Most of Canada's cities **are** in the southern part of Canada. About 75 percent of the population of Canada **is** urban. The largest city in Canada **is** Toronto. Other big cities **are** Montreal, Vancouver, and Winnipeg.

In addition to the ten provinces, there **are** two territories: the Yukon and the Northwest Territories. In 1999, the Northwest Territories will be divided into two territories. The eastern part of the Northwest Territories will be called Nunavut. However, Nunavut **is** not a territory yet. It **is** still part of the Northwest Territories until April 1999.

There **are** two official languages in Canada: English and French. Most of the population of Quebec **is** French-speaking. Most of the other provinces **are** English-speaking. However, there **are** French-speaking communities throughout Canada.

1.1   Forms and Uses of *Be*

I	*am*	in Ottawa now.
My father		in Winnipeg.
He		a mechanic.
My sister		in Prince Edward Island.
She	*is*	married.
Prince Edward Island		a Maritime province.
It		small.
We		students.
You		a teacher.
Newfoundland and Labrador	*are*	part of one province.
Montreal and Vancouver		cities.
They		big.

Language Notes

We use the verb *be* for the following:

Definition	British Columbia *is* a province.	*Description*	British Columbia *is* beautiful.
Location	British Columbia *is* on the Pacific Coast.	*Place of origin*	I *am* from British Columbia.
		Age	I *am* 25 years old.

EXERCISE I   Fill in each blank with *is, are,* or *am.*

> **EXAMPLE: Canada ___*is*___ a big country.**

1. Quebec _____ the largest province in Canada.

2. The Yukon and the Northwest Territories _____ in Canada's North.

3. Prince Edward Island _____ small.

4. Newfoundland and Labrador _____ one province.

5. Canada _____ the second largest country in the world.

6. English and French _____ the official languages of Canada.

7. We _____ in Canada.

8. I _____ a student in Canada.

1.2   The Subject

A sentence always has a subject. The subject is usually before the verb.

Subject	*Be*	Complement[1]
English and French	are	the two official languages.
Prince Edward Island	is	the smallest province.
Quebec	is	very large.
Russian	is	my native language.

The subject pronouns are *I, you, we, they, he, she, it.* The subject pronouns can take the place of the subject noun.

---

[1]The *complement* finishes, or completes, the sentece.

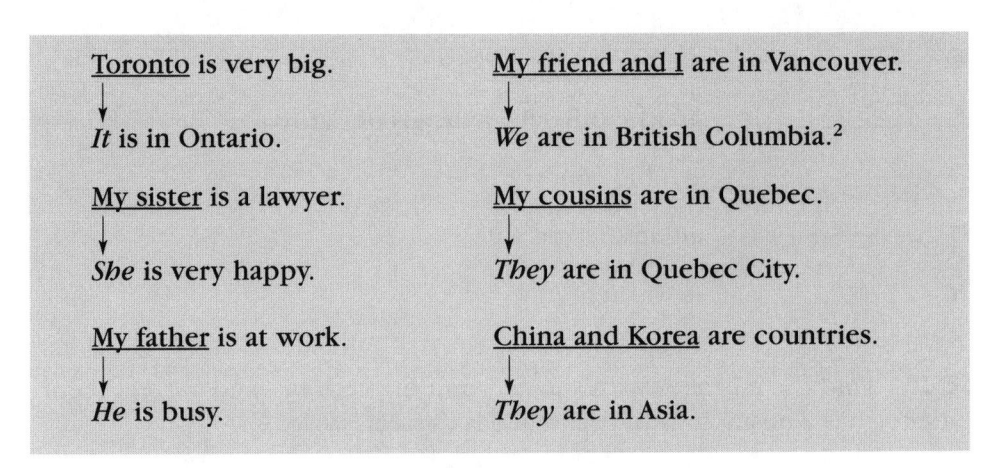

Toronto is very big.
↓
It is in Ontario.

My sister is a lawyer.
↓
She is very happy.

My father is at work.
↓
He is busy.

My friend and I are in Vancouver.
↓
We are in British Columbia.[2]

My cousins are in Quebec.
↓
They are in Quebec City.

China and Korea are countries.
↓
They are in Asia.

NOTE: Use *they* for plural people or things.

1. Singular means one. Plural means more than one. A plural noun usually ends in -s.

SINGULAR: The language of the U.S. *is* English.
PLURAL: The languages of Canada *are* English and French.

2. *You* can be singular or plural.
I am from Nova Scotia.
You are a Maritimer.
We are from Peru.
You are from South America.

3. Do not use the subject noun and the subject pronoun together.

The prime minister ~~he~~ is in Ottawa.
Ottawa ~~it~~ is the capital of Canada.

4. We use the subject *it* to talk about time and weather.

It is cold today.
It is six o'clock now.

5. The United States (the U.S.) is a singular noun.

The *U.S.* is a big country. *It* is in North America.

NOTE: Always use *the* before United States or U.S.

6. Use the correct word order. Put the subject at the beginning of the sentence.

Switzerland is a small country. NOT: Is a small country Switzerland.

EXERCISE 2   Fill in each blank with a subject.

EXAMPLE: _____*Montreal*_____ **is a big city.**

1. _____ is in the Central Region of Canada.

2. _____ are Canada's northern territories.

3. _____ is the capital of Canada.

---

[2]Canadians often say *B.C.* for British Columbia.

4. _____ are two of the largest cities in Canada.

5. _____ are the official languages of Canada.

6. _____ is a big country.

7. _____ am in Canada.

8. _____ is warm in July.

EXERCISE 3   Find the mistakes with subjects and the verb *be*, and correct them. Not every sentence has a mistake. If the sentence is correct, write **C**.

> **EXAMPLES: My daughter ~~she~~ is in Alberta.**
>
> **Alberta is a province.** *C*

1. Is a nice day.

2. Manitoba and Ontario are provinces. Its big.

3. The president he is a busy man.

4. Is very big Quebec.

5. You a very nice teacher.

6. You are very nice students.

7. Is cold in the Yukon.

8. The teacher is from Canada. You is from Vietnam.

9. My cousins they very nice people.

10. We students. You are a teacher.

11. The U.S. are big.

12. Is hot today.

Before you read

1. Name a place in Canada that you want to visit.
2. What is the capital of your country? Is it an interesting city?

Read the following postcard. Pay special attention to the contractions.

POSTCARD FROM OTTAWA

Dear Cousins,

I'm on vacation now. I'm in Ottawa. It's the capital of Canada. It's a beautiful city. This is a picture of the Parliament Buildings. The government representatives meet there, but they're not in session now.

My daughter's with me. She's very happy here. We're both happy. The weather's nice now. It's sunny and warm. It's spring, and the trees are beautiful.

How are you? Are you on vacation now? How's the family? I hope you're all fine.

Goodbye for now.

Love,

Maria

I.3   Contractions of *Be*

Full Forms	Contracted Forms
I am	I'm in Ottawa.
You are	You're in Italy.
The prime minister is	The prime minister's in Mexico now.
He is	He's very busy.
My daughter is	My daughter's with me.
She is	She's very happy.
Ottawa is	Ottawa's the capital of Canada.
It is	It's a beautiful city.
We are	We're very happy.
You are	You're at home.
They are	They're on vacation.

Language Notes

1. We usually say a contraction when we speak. We sometimes write a contraction in informal writing.

2. We can make a contraction with a subject pronoun and *am, is,* and *are.* To make a contraction, we take out the first letter of *am, is,* or *are* and put an apostrophe (') in place of the missing letter. We can also make a contraction with most nouns and *is.*

   Vancouver<u>'s</u> big.

   <u>It's</u> in the West.

3. We don't make a contraction with *is* if the noun ends in these sounds: *s, z, sh, dz* or *ch.*

   Whitehor<u>se is</u> the capital of the Yukon.

   Fran<u>ce is</u> in Europe.

   Niagara Fall<u>s is</u> a beautiful city.

   Lethbri<u>dge is</u> in Alberta.

   Englis<u>h is</u> one of Canada's official languages.

   Wasaga Bea<u>ch is</u> in Ontario.

4. We don't make a contraction with a plural noun and *are.*

   The trees *are* beautiful.

EXERCISE 4   Fill in each blank with the correct form of *be.* Make a contraction whenever possible. Not every sentence can have a contraction.

> EXAMPLE: Canada _____*is*_____ a big country. It _____'s_____ north of the
> United States.

1. The United States and Mexico _____ countries. They _____ in North America.

2. British Columbia _____ a big province in Canada. It _____ in the Pacific Region.

3. Ottawa _____ the capital of Canada. It _____ the home of the prime minister. He _____ busy now.

4. Ontario and Quebec _____ the biggest provinces in Canada.

5. Edmonton _____ a big city. It _____ in Alberta.

6. English _____ one of the official languages of Canada. French _____ the other. German _____ the language of Germany. Chinese (Cantonese) _____ the language of Hong Kong.

7. Most people in Quebec _____ French-speaking. Many Canadians _____ bilingual.

8. My daughter and I _____ in Ottawa. We _____ happy here.

EXERCISE 5 Fill in each blank. Make a contraction whenever possible. Not every sentence can have a contraction.

I *'m* _____ a student of English at Macdonald College. _____'m happy in Canada
 (1)

My teacher _____ Canadian. His name _____ Charles Hudson. Charles
 (2) (3)

_____an experienced teacher. _____'s patient with foreign students.
 (4) (5)

My class _____big. _____'s interesting. All the students _____
 (6) (7) (8)
immigrants, but we _____ from many different countries. Five students
 (9)

_____from Asia. One woman _____from Poland. _____from Warsaw,
 (10) (11) (12)
the capital of Poland. Many students _____from South America.
 (13)

We _____ready to learn English, but English _____a difficult language.
 (14) (15)
I sometimes tell Charles, "You _____a very kind teacher." Charles says,
 (16)
"_____all good students, and I _____ happy to teach you English."
 (17) (18)

1.4 *Be* with Descriptions

Subject	*Be*	(Very)	Adjective	Complement
Ottawa	is		beautiful	in the spring.
My daughter and I	are		interested	in Ottawa.
I	am	very	tired.	

Language Notes

1. We use a form of *be* with words that describe the subject. We use adjectives to describe. Descriptive adjectives have no plural form.

 Toronto is *big*. Toronto and Montreal are *big*.

2. Some words that end with *-ed* or *-ing* are adjectives: marri*ed*; tir*ed*; interest*ing*; bor*ing*.

 I'm *worried* about you.

 He's *tired*.

 She's *bored*.

3. We use a form of *be* with a physical or mental condition.

 He's *hungry*.

 I'm *thirsty*.

 We're *afraid*.

 They're *angry*.

EXERCISE 6   Complete each statement with a subject and the correct form of *be*. Write a contraction wherever possible. Make a **true** statement. Use both singular and plural subjects.

EXAMPLES: *My parents are* _____ intelligent.

The teacher's very _____ patient.

Many people in my country are poor.

1. _____ red.
2. _____ expensive.
3. _____ cheap.
4. _____ new.
5. _____ rich.
6. _____ lazy.

7. _____ big.
8. _____ wonderful.
9. _____ difficult.
10. _____ beautiful.
11. _____ famous.
12. _____ young.

EXERCISE 7   Work with a partner. Write a form of *be* and an adjective to describe each of the following nouns. Report one of your answers to the class.

EXAMPLES: **This classroom** *is clean.* _____

Quebec City *is interesting.* _____

1. The teacher _____

2. This city _____

3. This school _____

4. Today's weather _____

5. Canadians _____

6. Canadian food _____

1.5   *Be* with Nouns

Singular Subject	*Be*	*A(n)*	(Adjective)	Singular Noun
Newfoundland	is	an		island.
Toronto	is	a	big	city.

Plural Subject	*Be*		(Adjective)	Plural Noun
They	are			teachers.
We	are		overseas	students.

1. A noun is a person, place, or thing. We use *be* with nouns to classify or define the subject.

   Fredericton is *a* city. New Brunswick is *a* province.

2. We use the article *a* or *an* before a singular noun. We use *an* before a vowel sound. The vowels are *a, e, i, o,* and *u.*

   Vietnamese is *a* language. Newfoundland is *an* island.

3. We don't use the article *a* or *an* before a plural noun.

   Toronto and Vancouver are *cities.*
   Ontario and British Columbia are *provinces.*

4. We can put an adjective before the noun.

   Winnipeg is a *big* city.

EXERCISE 8   Fill in each blank with a form of *be* and a definition of the subject.

EXAMPLE: **Manitoba** *is a province.*

Alaska *is an American state.*

1. Canada _____

2. Nunavut _____

3. Blue _____

4. Wednesday _____

5. New Year's Day _____

6. Saturday and Sunday _____

7. Christmas and Hanukkah _____

8. White and red _____

9. January and February _____

10. Alberta, Saskatchewan, and Manitoba _____

EXERCISE 9   Add an adjective to each statement. Be careful to use *a* before a consonant and *an* before a vowel sound.

      EXAMPLE: **July 1 is a holiday.**

                  July 1 is an important holiday.

   1. August is a month.
   2. Australia is an island.
   3. Burger King is a restaurant.
   4. I'm a student.
   5. St. John's and Edmonton are cities.
   6. John is a name.

EXERCISE 10   Fill in each blank with the correct form of *be*. Add *a* or *an* for singular nouns only. Don't use an article with plural nouns.

      EXAMPLES: **Canada ____*is a*____ big country.**

               Canada and the U.S. ____*are*____ big countries.

   1. Saskatchewan _____ province.

   2. Toronto and Ottawa _____ cities in Ontario.

   3. Montreal, Toronto, and Vancouver _____ big cities.

   4. Newfoundland _____ island.

   5. Newfoundland _____ large island.

   6. Newfoundland and Australia _____ islands.

   7. Thanksgiving _____ Canadian holiday.

   8. French and Spanish _____ languages.

9. France and Spain _____ countries.

10. Coke (Coca-Cola) _____ soft drink.[3]

11. Coke, Pepsi, and 7-Up _____ soft drinks.

EXERCISE 11   Work with a partner. Complete each statement. Give a subject and the correct form of *be*. Add *a* or *an* for singular nouns only. Don't use an article with plural nouns. Read some of your sentences to the class.

EXAMPLES: *Russia is a* _____ **big country.**

Canada and Brazil are _____ **big countries.**

1. _____ nice person.

2. _____ good student.

3. _____ big company.

4. _____ expensive item.

5. _____ exciting sport.

6. _____ Canadian holiday.

7. _____ warm months.

8. _____ small countries.

9. _____ European countries.

10. _____ big cities.

11. _____ famous people. (NOTE: *people* is plural.)

12. _____ Asian languages.

_____

[3]A *soft drink* has no alcohol.

EXERCISE 12   Work with a partner. Fill in each blank to talk about your city. Make **true** statements. Remember to add *a* or *an* for a singular noun. Read some of your sentences to the class.

> EXAMPLES: *Chez Paul is an* _____ **expensive restaurant in the city.**
>
> *January and February are* _____ **cold months in this city.**

1. _____ interesting place.

2. _____ popular tourist attractions.

3. _____ big stores.

4. _____ beautiful month.

5. _____ beautiful park.

6. _____ inexpensive restaurant.

7. _____ wide streets.

8. _____ good school.

9. _____ historic area.

10. _____ tall buildings.

EXERCISE 13   Fill in each blank to make a **true** statement about your country. Put in a subject and a form of *be*. Find a partner from another country, if possible, and read your answers to each other. The teacher can fill in the blanks about Canada and read his or her answers to you.

> EXAMPLES: *Rock and roll music is* _____ **popular in my country.**
>
> *Politicians are* _____ **rich in my country.**

1. _____ the biggest city in my country.

2. _____ rich.

3. _____ expensive.

4. _____ the language(s) of my country.

5. _____ necessary for a good life.

6. _____ a popular sport.

7. _____ hard to find.

8. _____ very common.

9. _____ a beautiful place.

EXERCISE 14   Work with a partner. Describe a famous person (an actor, a singer, an athlete, a politician). Report your description to the class.

     EXAMPLE: **Céline Dion is beautiful.**
                   She's a singer.
                   She's famous.
                   She's a French Canadian.

1.6 *Be* with Location and Origin

Subject	*Be*	Preposition	Place
I	am	near	the door.
My book	is	on	the floor.
The teacher	is	from	England.

Language Notes

We use prepositions to show location and origin. Study the following prepositions and their meanings.

A. *On*

The book is *on* the table.
The cafeteria is *on* the first floor.

B. *At* shows general area or place:

The students are *at* school.
My brother is *at* home.

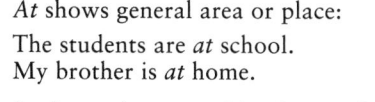

C. *In* shows that something is completely or partially enclosed:

Calgary is *in* Alberta.
The wastebasket is *in* the corner.

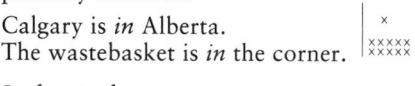

D. *In front of*

The chalkboard is *in front of* the students.

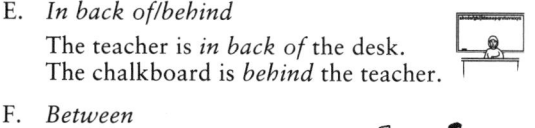

E. *In back of/behind*

The teacher is *in back of* the desk.
The chalkboard is *behind* the teacher.

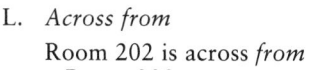

F. *Between*

The empty desk is *between* the two students.

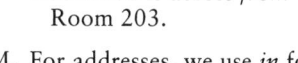

G. *Above/over*

The exit sign is *over* the door.
The clock is *above* the exit sign.

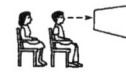

H. *Under/below*

The textbooks are *below* the desk.
The dictionary is *under* the textbooks.

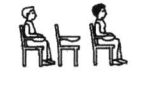

I. *Near/by/close to*

The sharpener is *by* the window.
The bulletin board is *near* the sharpener.
The desk is *close* to the window.

J. *Next to*

The light switch is *next to* the door.

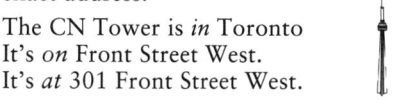

K. *Far from*

Halifax is *far from* Victoria.

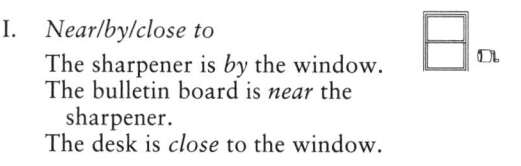

L. *Across from*

Room 202 is across *from* Room 203.

M. For addresses, we use *in* for a city, province, or country; *on* for a street; and *at* for an exact address.

The CN Tower is *in* Toronto
It's *on* Front Street West.
It's *at* 301 Front Street West.

N. We say *in* the East and *on* the East Coast.

Montreal is *in* the East.
British Columbia is *on* the West Coast.

O. We use the present tense of *be* and the preposition *from* to talk about place of origin.

Mario is *from* Brazil. He's *from* São Paolo.
Sofia and Alex are *from* Russia. They're *from* Moscow.

NOTE: We can also use *come from* with place of origin. (See Lesson Three.)

I *come from* China. You *come from* Iran.

EXERCISE 15. Use a form of *be* and a preposition to tell the location of these things or people in your classroom or school.

> **EXAMPLES: My dictionary** *is in my backpack.*
>
> **The students** *are in front of the teacher.*

1. This classroom _____

2. The clock _____

3. The teacher _____

4. The wastebasket _____

5. The chalk _____

6. The light switch _____

7. The chalkboard _____

8. I _____

9. My books _____

10. The cafeteria _____

11. The school _____

12. The school library _____

13. We _____

chalk

EXERCISE 16 Talk to the student next to you. Find out where he or she is from. Find out the country, the city, the location, and other information. Report to the class.

> **EXAMPLES: Kim is from Korea. He's from Seoul. It's a big city. It's the capital of Korea. It's a beautiful city.**
>
> **Maria's from Spain. She's from Lugo. It's a small town. It's in the northwest corner of Spain. It's near Portugal.**

1.7   **This, That, These, Those**

We can use *this, that, these,* and *those* to identify objects or people.

	Near	Not Near/Far
Singular	This is my pen.	That is my pen.
Plural	These are my pens.	Those are my pens.

Language Notes

1. After we identify a noun, we can use subject pronouns.

   This is my school. *It's* on Laurier Avenue.
   Those are tall buildings. *They're* downtown.
   That's my cousin. *He's* a good student.

2. Only *that is* can form a contraction in writing: *that's.*

EXERCISE 17   Look at the pictures. Imagine that you are showing a new student the school cafeteria. Point out each part of the cafeteria. Use *this, that, these,* or *those,* and a form of *be* to complete each sentence.

EXAMPLES: *This is* _____ **the school cafeteria.**

   Those are _____ **the clean dishes.**

1. _____ the trays.

2. _____ today's special.

3. _____ the napkins.

4. _____ the forks, knives, and spoons.

5. _____ the cashier.

6. _____ the vending machines.

7. _____ the change machine.

8. _____ the garbage cans.

9. _____ the recycle bin.

10. _____ the staff room.

1.8 Negative Statements with *Be*

We put *not* after a form of *be* to make a negative statement.

Subject	*Be*	*Not*	Complement
I	am	not	married.
Peter	is	not	from the U.S.
We	are	not	late.

We can make contractions for the negative. There is only one contraction for *I am not*. There are two negative contractions for all the other combinations:

I am not	I'm not	—
you are not	you're not	you aren't
he is not	he's not	he isn't
she is not	she's not	she isn't
it is not	it's not	it isn't
we are not	we're not	we aren't
they are not	they're not	they aren't
Tom is not	Tom's not	Tom isn't

EXERCISE 18 Fill in each blank with a pronoun and a negative verb. Practise using both negative forms.

　　EXAMPLE: The classroom is clean and big.

　　　　　　It isn't _____ **dirty.** *It's not* _____ **small.**

1. We're in the classroom.

   _____ in the library. _____ in the cafeteria.

2. Today's a weekday.

   _____ Saturday. _____ Sunday.

3. I'm a student. _____ a teacher.

4. The students are busy.

   _____ lazy. _____ tired.

5. You're on time.

   _____ early. _____ late.

6. My classmates and I are in an English class.

   _____ in the cafeteria. _____ in the library.

7. The teacher's in the classroom.

   _____ in the hall. _____ in the library.

8. This lesson is fine.

   _____ easy. _____ hard.

EXERCISE 19   Fill in each blank with a form of *be* to make a **true** affirmative statement or negative statement about Canada.

   EXAMPLES: Canada ____*is*____ in North America.

   Canada ____*isn't*____ a small country.

1. Quebec _____ a province.

2. Montreal _____ the capital of Quebec. It _____ on the East Coast.

3. Nova Scotia and Prince Edward Island _____ big.

4. Alberta and Manitoba _____ in the Pacific Region.

5. The CN Tower _____ Calgary.

6. Montreal _____ a big city.

7. Labrador and British Columbia _____ islands.

8. The Yukon _____ a province of Canada.

9. Labrador and New Brunswick _____ on the mainland.

10. The Northwest Territories _____ cold in the winter.

EXERCISE 20   Fill in each blank with a form of *be* to make an affirmative statement or negative statement about you, your country, or your hometown. Find a partner from a different country, if possible. Compare answers with your partner.

EXAMPLES: I *'m*_____ **from the capital city.**

I *'m not*_____ **from a small town.**

1. I _____ happy with the government of my country.

2. I _____ from the capital city.

3. My city _____ noisy.

4. North American cars _____ common in my country.

5. Teachers _____ strict.[4]

6. Most people _____ rich.

7. Gas _____ cheap.

8. Apartments _____ expensive.

9. Bicycles _____ popular.

10. Public transportation _____ good.

11. My country _____ rich.

12. A postsecondary education _____ free.

13. The prime minister (president) _____ a woman.

14. My hometown _____ in the mountains.

15. My hometown _____ very big.

16. It _____ very cold in the winter in my hometown.

---

[4]A *strict* teacher has a lot of rules.

EXERCISE 21   Use the words in parentheses ( ) to change each sentence into a negative statement.

      EXAMPLE: **My teacher is Canadian. (American)**

           He isn't American. _____

1. Winnipeg and Edmonton are cities. (provinces)

   _____

2. I'm from Russia. (Canada)

   _____

3. Canada is a big country. (Germany)

   _____

4. Quebec is a big province. (Nova Scotia and Prince Edward Island)

   _____

5. We're in class now. (in the library)

   _____

6. You're an English teacher. (a math teacher)

   _____

EXERCISE 22   Fill in each blank with the affirmative or negative of the verb *be* to make a **true** paragraph.

      My name ___*is*___ _____ . I _____ from an English-speaking country.
              EXAMPLE   YOUR NAME   (1)

I _____ a student at Pearson College. I _____ in my English class now.
   (2)   (3)

The class _____ big. My teacher _____ a man. He/She _____ very
          (4)   (5)   (6)

young. The classroom _____ very nice. It _____ clean. My classmates
                 (7)   (8)

_____ all very young students. We _____ all from the same country. We
   (9)   (10)

_____ all immigrants. I _____ happy to learn English. English _____
   (11)   (12)   (13)

very easy for me. It _____ a useful language.
               (14)

EXPANSION ACTIVITIES

WRITING   Write a paragraph using Exercise 22 as a model. For every negative statement that you write, add an affirmative statement. You may add other
information, too.

EXAMPLE:

> My name is Mohammad. I'm
> not from an English - speaking country.
> I'm from Iran. I'm not a
> student at Pearson College. I'm a
> student at Dalhousie University.
> I'm in an English class now....

PROVERBS   The following proverbs contain a form of the verb *be*. Discuss the meaning
of each proverb. Do you have a similar proverb in your language?

Love is blind.
Beauty is only skin deep.
Silence is golden.

POEM   This is a common poem of love or friendship:

> Roses are red.
> Violets are blue.
> Sugar is sweet
> And so are you.

Work with a partner. Write your own poem. Read your poem to the class.

OUTSIDE   1. Do you have a postcard from your city? Bring it to the class and tell
ACTIVITIES   about the picture.

2. Buy a postcard of this city. Write to a friend, giving some information
   about the picture or about this city. Read your postcard to the class.

SUMMARY OF LESSON ONE

1. Uses of *Be*
   - With a description (adjective):
        Toronto *is* big.
   - With a classification, definition, or identification of a noun:
        This *is* Toronto. Toronto *is* a city. It*'s* a big city.
   - With a location:
        Toronto *is* in Ontario.
   - With a place of origin:
        The teacher *is* from Toronto.
   - With age:
        I*'m* 25 (years old).
   - With physical or mental conditions:
        He*'s* hungry.
        I*'m* thirsty.
        She*'s* worried.

2. Subject Pronouns
        I   we   he/she
        you   they   it

3. Contractions
   - Subject Pronouns with a Form of *Be:*
        I*'m*   you*'re*   he*'s*
   - Subject Nouns with *Is*:
        the teacher*'s*   Carlo*'s*   Suzanne*'s*
   - A Form of *Be* with *Not*:
        he isn*'t*   you aren*'t*   they aren*'t*

4. *This/That/These/Those*
        This is an English book.
        These are pencils.
        That's a pen.
        Those are notebooks.

5. Articles *A/An*
   - Use *a/an* before a singular noun to give a definition.
        Toronto is *a* big city. Newfoundland is *an* island.
   - Don't use *a/an* before plural nouns.
        Toronto and Vancouver are big cities.

6. Word Order = Adjective + Noun
        Toronto is a *big city*.
        A *good teacher* is popular.

7. Word Order = Noun/Pronoun + *Be* + Adjective
        Toronto is big.
        They are happy.

LESSON ONE TEST/REVIEW

Part 1   Write a contraction of the words shown. If it's not possible to make a contraction, put an **X** in the blank.

> **EXAMPLE:** she is ___*she's*___   **EXAMPLE:** **English is** ___*X*___

1. we are _____   5. this is _____

2. you are not _____   6. Niagara Falls is _____

3. I am not _____   7. She is not _____

4. they are _____   8. Bruce is not _____

Part 2   First read the affirmative statement. Then write a negative statement with the new subject given. Make any necessary changes.

> **EXAMPLE: Canada is a big country. (Switzerland)**
>
> _____*Switzerland isn't a big country.*_____ .

1. Winnipeg is a big city. (Churchill)

   _____

2. Winnipeg and Churchill are in Manitoba. (Saint John)

   _____

3. January is a cold month. (July and August)

   _____

4. We're newcomers. (the teacher)

   _____

5. You're Canadian. (I)

   _____

Part 3   Fill in each blank with the correct preposition.

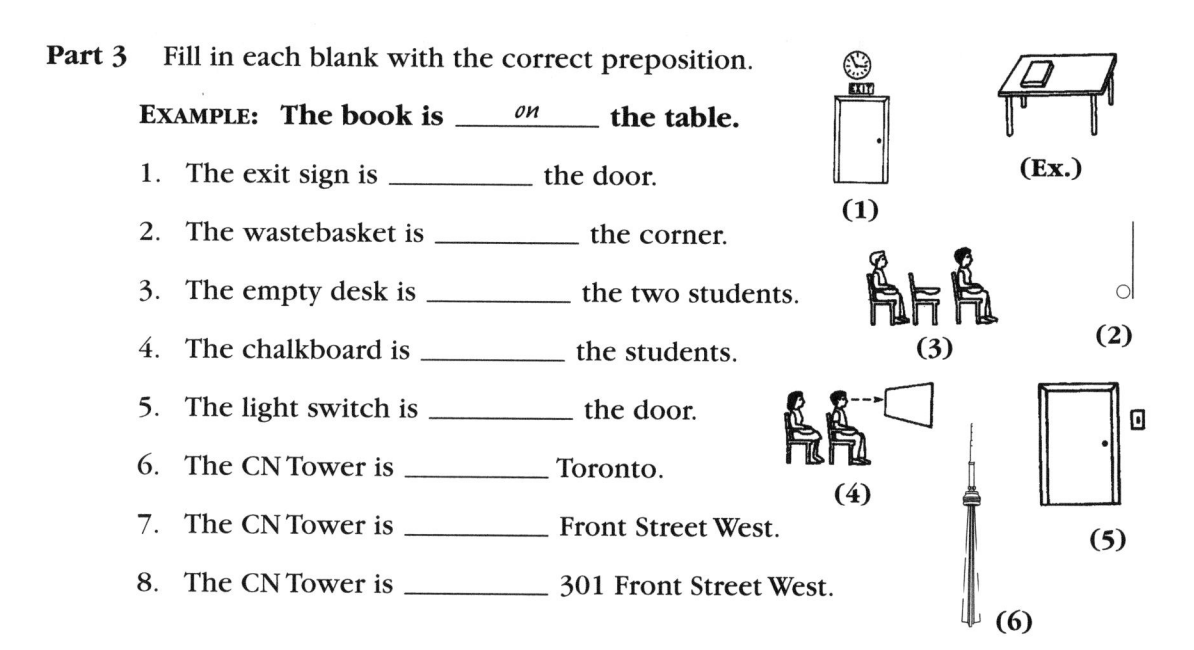

EXAMPLE: **The book is _____on_____ the table.**

1. The exit sign is _____ the door.

2. The wastebasket is _____ the corner.

3. The empty desk is _____ the two students.

4. The chalkboard is _____ the students.

5. The light switch is _____ the door.

6. The CN Tower is _____ Toronto.

7. The CN Tower is _____ Front Street West.

8. The CN Tower is _____ 301 Front Street West.

(Ex.)

(1)

(2)

(3)

(4)

(5)

(6)

Part 4   Find the mistakes in the following sentences and correct them. Not every sentence has a mistake. If the sentence is correct, write **C**.

EXAMPLES: **My teacher ~~she~~ is very strict.**

         We aren't bored.   *C*

1. Vancouver and Montreal are a big cities.

2. The teacher's not here today.

3. She is'nt in the library.

4. I amn't from Pakistan.

5. The students they are very smart.

6. Quebec and Ontario are bigs provinces.

7. They're not hungry. They aren't thirsty.

8. It's warm today.

9. I'm from Ukraine. My wife from Poland.

10. Is very long this book.

CN Tower

LESSON TWO

GRAMMAR

Questions and Answers
with *Be*

CONTEXT

Questions about
Canada

Lesson Focus   Questions and Answers with *Be*

To ask a question with the verb *be,* we put a form of *be* before the subject.

Is Russia a big country?   Where is Russia?

R
E
A
D

N
G

Before you read:

1. What is the biggest city in your country? Is it the capital of your country?
2. Look at the map of Canada on page 4. Where are the small provinces? Where are the large provinces?

Read the following questions and answers about Canada. Pay special attention to questions with the verb *be.*

QUESTIONS ABOUT CANADA

A. **What is the biggest province in Canada?**
B. Quebec is the biggest province in land area, but Ontario is the largest province in population.

A. **Is the Yukon a province?**
B. No. It is a territory. Both the Yukon and the Northwest Territories are in the Arctic Region, north of Canada's ten provinces.

A. **Is the Northwest Territories larger than Quebec?**
B. Yes, it is. The Northwest Territories is more than twice the size of Quebec and about one-third the size of the whole of Canada. However, the population is small. The climate in winter is very cold.

A. **Where is Prince Edward Island?**
B. It isn't on the mainland. It's an island just northeast of New Brunswick and Nova Scotia.

A. **Is Labrador a province?**
B. No, it isn't. It's part of the province of Newfoundland.

A. **Where is Labrador?**
B. It's northeast of Quebec. Labrador is the mainland portion of the province of Newfoundland, and Newfoundland, the island a few kilometres southeast off the coast of Labrador, is the island section of the province.

A. **What are the biggest cities in Canada?**
B. The two biggest cities are Toronto and Montreal.

A. **Is Montreal near Vancouver?**

B. No, it isn't. Montreal is in eastern Canada. Vancouver is on the West Coast. Montreal is about 3670 kilometres from Vancouver.

A. **We say Quebec City, but we don't say Toronto City. Why not?**

B. Quebec is the name of a city and also the name of the province.

A. **Where is St. John's?**

B. St. John's is on the southeast coast of the island of Newfoundland. It is the capital of the province of Newfoundland. However, there is another city with a similar name. It is Saint John, a city in New Brunswick.

2.1 *Be* in *Yes/No* Questions and Short Answers

To ask a *yes/no* question with the verb *be*, we put a form of *be* before the subject. We usually answer a *yes/no* question with a short answer. Compare statements, *yes/no* questions, and short answers with *be*.

Statement	*Yes/No* Question	Short Answer
I am a student.	Am I a good student?	Yes, you are.
You are from France.	Are you from Paris?	No, I'm not.
He is late.	Is he absent?	No, he isn't.
Kathy is a Canadian.	Is Kathy from Alberta?	No, she isn't.
She is employed.	Is she happy?	Yes, she is.
It is cold today.	Is it windy?	Yes, it is.
We are here.	Are we late?	No, you aren't.
They are new students.	Are they confused?	Yes, they are.

Language Notes

1. A short answer contains a pronoun.

   Is the teacher here today? Yes, *she* is.
   Are your parents in Canada? No, *they* aren't.

2. We don't use a contraction for a short affirmative answer.

   Is British Columbia a big province? *Yes, it is.*
   NOT: Yes, it's.

3. We usually end a *yes/no* question with a rising intonation. Listen to your teacher pronounce the statements and questions in the above box.

EXERCISE I   Look at the map of Canada on page 4 and answer these questions.

> EXAMPLES: **Is Whitehorse in the Yukon?**
> **Yes, it is.**
>
> **Is Toronto the capital of Canada?**
> **No, it isn't.**

1. Is Quebec a big province?
2. Is Labrador part of Quebec?
3. Is Vancouver near the Atlantic Ocean?
4. Is Prince Edward Island near New Brunswick?
5. Is Edmonton the capital of Alberta?
6. Is Winnipeg a big city?
7. Is Newfoundland an island?

EXERCISE 2   The teacher will ask you some questions. Answer with a **true** short answer. If the answer is negative, you may add more information.

> EXAMPLE: **Is your book new?**
> **Yes, it is.** OR **No, it isn't. It's a used book.**

1. Is your country big?
2. Is Chinese your native language?
3. Is English hard for you?
4. Are you from South America?
5. Are you a citizen of Canada?
6. Are you married?
7. Are you a lazy student?
8. Is my pronunciation clear to you?
9. Am I a strict teacher?
10. Are all of you from the same country?
11. Are all of you the same age?
12. Are all of you immigrants?
13. Are you tired of my questions?

EXERCISE 3   Ask and answer questions about this school and class with the words given.

> EXAMPLE: **school/big**
> **A. Is this school big?**
> **B. Yes, it is.**

1. this school/near your house
2. it/near public transportation
3. the cafeteria/on this floor
4. it/open now
5. the library/in this building
6. it/closed now
7. this course/free
8. the textbooks/free
9. the teacher/strict
10. this room/clean
11. it/big
12. the chalkboard/black
13. the chairs/in a circle
14. the windows/open
15. these questions/difficult

EXERCISE 4   Ask and answer questions with the words given. Use the correct form of *be*.

EXAMPLE: **you/a new student**
            A. Are you a new student?
            B. Yes, I am. OR **No, I'm not. This is my second term here.**

1. you/from Asia
2. you/a new student
3. your country/big
4. you/from the capital city
5. you/an immigrant
6. you/happy in Canada

7. hockey/popular in your country
8. Japanese cars/popular in your country
9. teachers/strict in your country
10. education/free in your country
11. medical care/free in your country

EXERCISE 5   Ask and answer questions about Canada with the words given. If no one knows the answer, ask the teacher.

EXAMPLE: **movie stars/rich**
            A. Are Canadian movie stars rich?
            B. Yes, they are. They're very rich.

1. Canadian teachers/rich
2. a high school education/free
3. a postsecondary education/free
4. medical care/free
5. doctors/rich
6. blue jeans/popular
7. houses/expensive

8. Canadians/friendly
9. English/one of the official languages
10. Japanese cars/popular
11. fast-food restaurants/popular
12. theatre tickets/cheap
13. public schools/closed on New Year's Day

EXERCISE 6   Read each statement. Then write a *yes/no* question about the words in parentheses ( ). Write a short answer.

EXAMPLE: **The post office is closed on Sunday. (this school) (yes)**
            Is this school closed on Sunday? Yes, it is.

1. July and August are warm months. (January and February) (no)

2. Montreal is a big city. (Toronto) (yes)

3. Ontario is a big province. (British Columbia and Quebec) (yes)

4. Coke and Pepsi are soft drinks. (7-Up) (yes)

5. New Brunswick is in the east. (Alberta) (no)

_____

6. Halifax is on the East Coast. (Victoria) (no)

_____

7. Regina isn't a province. (Saskatchewan) (yes)

_____

EXERCISE 7   By going around the room and asking questions, find one person for each of the items below, if possible. Write that person's name in the blank. Then tell the class about something you and another person have in common.

> EXAMPLES: **Tsering and I are both religious. He's a Buddhist, and I'm a Hindu.**
> **Gabriel and I are both from Africa. He's from Ethiopia, and I'm from Sudan.**

1. athletic _____

2. shy _____

3. from Asia _____

4. from Europe _____

5. from Africa _____

6. interested in politics _____

7. a grandparent _____

8. under 20 years old _____

9. lazy _____

10. religious _____

11. (a) Christian _____

12. hungry _____

13. afraid to speak English _____

14. in love _____

15. an only child[1] _____

16. from the capital of your country _____

17. a Canadian citizen _____

_____

[1]An _only child_ has no sisters or brothers.

2.2   *Wh-* Questions

A *wh-* question asks for information. The question words are *who(m), when, why, what, which, where,* and *how.* To form a *wh-* question, we put the question word first, then a form of *be,* followed by the subject. Compare these statements and questions.

Wh-Word	*Be*	Subject	*Be*	Complement	Short Answer
		Vancouver	is	a city.	
	Is	Vancouver		on the West Coast?	Yes, it is.
Where	is	Vancouver?			
		Calgary	is	the capital of Alberta.	
	Is	Calgary		in northern Alberta?	No, it isn't.
Where	is	Calgary?			

Study the different question words:

Question Word	Example

Who asks about a person.	Who's your teacher?
	    My teacher is Ms. Weiss.
	        OR
	    Ms. Weiss is my teacher.

What asks about a thing.	What's your name?
	    Linda Tran.
	What's Canada Day?
	    It's a holiday.

When asks about time.
    Use *in* for months and years.
    Use *on* for days and dates.
	When is Canada Day?
	    It's in July.
	    It's on July 1.

Why asks for a reason.	Why's Mr. Park absent? He's absent because he's sick.

Where asks about a place.
    The answer contains a
    preposition. Review
    prepositions on page 18.
	Where's China?
	    It's in Asia.
	Where are your books?
	    They're on the floor.
	Where are you from?
	    I'm from Hong Kong.

1. In conversation, the *wh-* word + *is* can make a contraction.

   Where's your father?   *How's* the weather now?

EXCEPTIONS:

- We can't make a contraction for *which is*.

   Which is your book?

- There is no contraction for a *wh-* word and *are*.

   Who are they?   Why are they late?

2. We usually end a *wh-* question with a falling intonation. Listen to your teacher say the questions in the box on page 35.

EXERCISE 8   Answer these questions.

>   EXAMPLE: **Who's your best friend?**
>   **David Orlov is my best friend.**

1. Who's your advisor or counsellor?
2. Who's the leader of your country?
3. Who's your best friend?
4. Who's absent today? (The answer may be plural.)
5. Who's near the door? (The answer may be plural.)

EXERCISE 9   Answer these questions.

>   EXAMPLE: **Where's Poland?**
>   **It's in eastern Europe.**

1. Where's Beijing?
2. Where's Bolivia?
3. Where's Ethiopia?
4. Where's Ottawa?
5. Where are Victoria and Vancouver?
6. Where are Ecuador and Peru?
7. Where are Nigeria and Cameroon?
8. Where are Spain and Portugal?
9. Where are Madrid and Barcelona?

EXERCISE 10   Answer these questions about this classroom and your school. Use the correct preposition. (Your school may not have all of these things.)

>   EXAMPLE: **Where's the light switch?**
>   **It's next to the door.**

1. Where's the library?
2. Where's the computer lab?
3. Where's the parking lot?
4. Where's the coffee machine?

5. Where's the men's washroom?
6. Where's the women's washroom?
7. Where's the water fountain?
8. Where's the teacher's office?

EXERCISE 11   Answer these questions. Use *in* for months and years. Use *on* for days and dates.

>   EXAMPLE: **When's Christmas?**
>   **In December.   OR   On December 25.**

1. When's your birthday?
2. When's summer vacation?
3. When's winter vacation?

4. When's Labour Day in your country?
5. When's the last day of this term?
6. When's spring break?

2.3   Questions with *What*

Study these common questions with *what*.

What (Noun)	*Be*	Complement	Answer
What	is	your name?	My name is Sandy.
What	is	your profession?	I'm a teacher.
What	is	your phone number?	555-3696
What	is	your favourite TV show?	*W5*
What nationality	is	the teacher?	She's Canadian.
What kind of class	is	this?	It's an English class.
What day	is	today?	It's Friday.
What time	is	it?	It's four o'clock.

Language Notes

1. Questions with *what* ask about things.

   What's your major? It's math.
   What's the capital of British Columbia? It's Victoria.

2. Questions with *what* can ask for a definition.

   What is the Yukon? It's a territory of Canada.
   What are Ontario and New Brunswick? They're provinces.

3. A noun can follow *what*.

   What colour is the Canadian flag? It's red and white.

EXERCISE 12   Answer these *what* questions.

> EXAMPLE: **What's your major?**
> **Computer science.**

1. What's your name?
2. What's your date of birth?
3. What time is it now in your hometown?
4. What nationality is the teacher?
5. What's the capital of your country?
6. What colour is the flag of your country?
7. What's your major?
8. What's your favourite TV show?
9. What kind of words are *big, tall, old, new,* and *good*?
10. What kind of names are Charles, Elizabeth, and Andrew?

EXERCISE 13   Answer these *what* questions with a definition. Remember to use the article *a* or *an* before a singular noun.

> EXAMPLES: **What's Nova Scotia?**
> **It's a province.**
>
> **What are English and French?**
> **They're languages.**

1. What's Regina?
2. What's Canada Day?
3. What's a rose?
4. What's a cat?
5. What are Burger King and McDonald's?
6. What are Spanish and Italian?
7. What are Spain and Italy?
8. What are hockey and baseball?

2.4 Questions with *How*

Study these common questions with *how*.

How	Be	Subject	Answer
How	are	you?	I'm fine.
How	is	the weather?	It's sunny and warm.
How old	is	your brother?	He's 16 (years old).
How tall	are	you?	I'm 1.58 metres tall.
How big	is	your apartment?	It has four rooms.
How long[2]	is	this course?	It's 10 weeks long.
How long	is	the race?	It's 2½ kilometres.
How much	is	that painting?	It's $800.

1. *How* can ask an opinion or a description.

   How's your life in Canada? It's difficult, but interesting.

2. *How* can ask about health.

   How's your mother today? She's sick.

3. *How* can ask about the weather.

   How's the weather today? It's cold and windy.

4. Another word[3] can immediately follow *how*.

   How much is that painting? It's $800.
   How tall is your father? He's 1.7 metres tall.   OR   He's 1.7 metres.

   NOTE: Although Canada uses the metric system, many Canadians use feet (') and inches (") for height: 5'8" tall. We say "five feet, eight inches tall" or simply "five-eight."

5. We use the verb *be* to talk about age. It is not usually polite to ask an adult Canadian his or her age.

EXERCISE 14   Write a question with how.

EXAMPLE: _How old is your son?_   **My son is 10 years old.**

1. _____   It's sunny and warm in Toronto today.

2. _____   My brother is 1.8 metres tall.

3. _____   My parents are fine, thank you.

4. _____   I'm 25 years old.

5. _____   That car is $15,000.

6. _____   This course is six weeks long.

---

[2]*How long* can ask about either time or distance.

[3]These words are adjectives or adverbs.

EXERCISE 15   Fill in each blank to make **true** statements about yourself. Then find a partner from a different country, if possible, and interview your partner by asking questions with the words in parentheses ( ).

> **EXAMPLE: I'm from** _____*Turkey.*_____   **(Where)**
> > **A. I'm from Turkey. Where are you from?**
> > **B. I'm from Taiwan.**

1. My name is _____. (What)

2. I'm from _____. (Where)

3. The prime minister/president of my country is _____. (Who)

4. The prime minister/president of my country is about _____ years old. (How)

5. The flag from my country is _____. (What colour)

6. My country is in _____. (Where)
   (continent or region)

7. I'm _____ metres tall. (How tall)

8. I'm _____ today. (How)
   (fine/sick)

9. My birthday is in _____. (When)
   (month)

10. My favourite TV show is _____. (What)

11. My favourite colour is _____. (What)

12. My address is _____. (What)

EXERCISE 16   Read each statement. Then write a *wh-* question with the words in parentheses ( ). Answer with a complete sentence.

> **EXAMPLE: Victoria is in British Columbia. (St. John's)**
> > *Where is St. John's? It's in Newfoundland.*

1.   Paris is in France. (Ottawa)

_____

2. The capital of England is London. (the capital of Canada)

    _____

3. Calgary and Edmonton are in Alberta. (Winnipeg and Churchill)

    _____

4. Ontario is a province. (Whitehorse)

    _____

5. The U.S. is in North America. (Peru)

    _____

6. Poland is in Europe. (Ethiopia and Nigeria)

    _____

7. Korea and Japan are in Asia. (Colombia)

    _____

8. The Mexican flag is green, white, and red. (what colour/the Canadian flag)

    _____

9. Igor and Boris are Russian names. (what kind of names/James and William)

    _____

EXERCISE 17   Read the following telephone conversation between Cindy (C) and Maria (M). Fill in each blank.

C. Hello?

M. Hi, Cindy. This is Maria.

C. Hi, Maria. *How are you?* _____

M. I'm fine. This is a long-distance call. I'm not home now.

C. Where _____?
                      (1)

M. I'm in Ottawa. I'm on vacation. I'm a tourist.

C. _____?
                      (2)

M. Oh, yes. It's very interesting. The Peace Tower and the Parliament Buildings are here.

C. How _____?
                          (3)

M. It's sunny and warm. The trees and flowers are beautiful now.

C. _____?
                    (4)

M. No, I'm not alone.

C. Who _____?
                        (5)

M. My daughter is with me.

C. _____?
                    (6)

M. She's 12. She's very interested in Canadian government.

C. It's six-thirty in Vancouver. _____ in Ottawa.
                                                  (7)

M. It's nine-thirty.

C. I'm happy to hear from you. Thanks for calling.

M. I'll see you when I get home.

EXPANSION ACTIVITIES

OUTSIDE ACTIVITIES

Interview a Canadian (a neighbour, a co-worker, another student, or a teacher at this institution). Ask him or her these questions:

1. What city are you from?
2. Are your parents or grandparents from another country? Where are they from?
3. Is most of your family in this city?
4. Are you happy with this city? Why or why not?
5. What are your favourite places in this city?

Report this person's answers to the class.

EDITING ADVICE

1. Be careful to use the correct word order.

   Toronto is very big.
   ~~Is very big Toronto.~~

   Where ~~he is~~ from? *is he*

2. Use *be* before the complement.

   He ^ angry. *is*

   I ~~have~~ 25 years ^. *am* *old*

   She ~~has~~ hungry. *is*

3. Use *it* before *is* to introduce time or weather.

   It's
   ~~is~~ ten o'clock.

   It's
   ~~is~~ very hot today.

4. Don't confuse *your* and *you're*.

   You're
   ~~Your~~ a nice person.

5. Don't confuse *this* and *these*.

   This
   ~~These~~ is my coat.

   These
   ~~This~~ are my shoes.

6. Use an apostrophe ('), not a comma (,) for a contraction. Put the apostrophe in place of the missing letter.

   He's
   ~~He,s~~ late.

   She ~~is'nt~~ here today. *isn't*

7. Use the article *a* before a singular noun.

   Toronto is ^ big city. *a*

8. Don't use the article *a* before a plural noun.

   Toronto and Montreal are ~~a~~ big cities.

9. Don't put the article *a* before an adjective with no noun.

   Toronto is ~~a~~ big.

10. Don't make a contraction after *s, z, sh, dz,* or *ch* sounds.

    Niagara Falls is
    ~~Niagara Falls's~~ a beautiful place.

    Bridge is
    Okanagan Lake ~~Bridge's~~ Canada's longest floating bridge.

11. Don't make an adjective plural.

    Winnipeg and Vancouver are ~~bigs~~.

12. For age, use a number only or number + *years old*.

    He's 12 years ^. *old*   or   *He's 12.*

13. Don't use a contraction for a short *yes* answer.

    Are you from Korea? Yes, ~~I'm~~. *I am*

SUMMARY OF LESSON TWO

1. Statements and Questions with *Be*

Affirmative	New Brunswick *is* a province.
Negative	Fredericton *isn't* a province.
Yes/No *Question*	*Is* Fredericton in New Brunswick?
Short Answer	Yes, it *is.*
Wh- *Question*	Where *is* Charlottetown?
Long Answer	It *is* in Prince Edward Island.

2. Contractions
   - Pronoun + *Am, Is, Are* (except in a short *yes* answer)
            I'm   she's   we're
   - *Is, Are + Not*
            isn't   aren't
   - Question Word + *Is* (except *which is*)
            who's   what's   where's

3. Word Order
   Compare statements and questions:

Wh-Word	*Be*	Subject	*Be*	Complement	Answer
		Winnipeg	is	a big city.	
	Is	Winnipeg		in Alberta?	No, it isn't.
Where	is	Winnipeg?			
		You	are	from Asia?	
	Are	you		from China?	Yes, I am.
What city	are	you	from?		

4. Common Questions with *Be*
   - What's your name? My name is Daniel.
   - What time is it? It's six-thirty.
   - What colour is the flag? It's red and white.
   - What kind of class is this? It's an English class.
   - What's this? It's a pencil sharpener.
   - What's Lisbon? It's a city.
   - How are you? I'm fine.
   - How old are you? I'm 24 OR I'm 24 years old.
   - How tall are you? I'm 1.65 metres tall OR I'm 1.65 metres.
   - Where are you from? I'm from Guatemala.

LESSON TWO TEST/REVIEW

Part 1 Find the mistakes and correct them.

> EXAMPLE: A. Where <u>you are</u> from?   *are you*
>   B. I'm from Russia.

A. Are you happy in Canada?

B. Yes, I'm. Canada is great country!

A. Are you from a big city?

B. Yes. I'm from Leningrad. It's a city very big. These city is a big and beautiful too. But is cold in the winter.

A. Is from Leningrad your roommate too?

B. No, he from Taiwan. My roommate is'nt happy. He,s homesick.

A. Why he's homesick?

B. His parents is in Taiwan. He's alone here.

A. How is he old?

B. He's very young. He's only 17 years.

Part 2 Read the conversation between two students, Sofia (S) and Danuta (D). They are talking about their classes and teachers. Fill in the blanks.

D. Hi, Sofia. How's your English class?

S. Hi, Danuta. It'<u>s</u>_____ wonderful. I _____ very happy with it.
                                                (1)

D. _____ 'm in level 3. What level _____ in?
            (2)   (3)

S. I'_____ in level 2.
          (4)

D. My English teacher _____ Ms. Kathy James. _____ a
                              (5)   (6)

very good teacher. Who _____?
                              (7)

S.   Mr. Bob Kane is my English teacher. _____ very good, too.
                                                    (8)

D.   _____ an old man?
            (9)

S.   No, he _____. He's _____ young man. He
                    (10)   (11)

     _____ about 25 years _____. How
            (12)   (13)

     _____ ?
            (14)

D.   Ms. James _____ about 50 years old.
                        (15)

S.   How _____ ?
                (16)

D.   She's about 1.6 metres tall.

S.   Is she Canadian?

D.   Yes, she _____. She's from Ottawa.
                    (17)

S.   _____ ?
            (18)

D.   Yes. My class is very big. The students _____ from many
                                                        (19)

     countries. Ten students _____ from Asia, six students
                                    (20)

     _____ from Europe, one student _____ from
            (21)   (22)

     Africa, and five are _____ South America. Is your class big?
                                (23)

S.   No, it _____.
                (24)

D.   Where _____ ?
                (25)

S.   The students _____ all from the same country. We
                         (26)

_____ from Russia.
        (27)

D.   _____ Russian?
            (28)

S.   No. Mr. Kane isn't Russian. He's from the U.S., but he's _____
                                                                                              (29)

Canadian citizen now.

D.   _____?
            (30)

S.   No. That's not Mr. Kane. That _____ my brother. I
                                                      (31)

_____ late! See you later.
        (32)

LESSON THREE

Simple Present Tense

English Spelling

Lesson Focus   Simple Present Tense

We use the simple present tense to talk about general truths and regular activities (habits).

Students have difficulty with English spelling. We often use our dictionaries.

Before you read:

1. Is spelling easy in your language?
2. Name some words that are hard to spell in English.

Read the following article. Pay special attention to simple present tense verbs.

ENGLISH SPELLING

The English language **has** a difficult spelling system. Students of English as a second language often **complain** about English spelling. One vowel often **has** several pronunciations. For example, the "ou" in the following three words is different: "out," "thought," "through."

There are also some confusing differences between Canadian and American spelling. For example, Americans **don't include** "u" in the spelling of such words as "favour," "colour," and "neighbour." Instead, they **spell** these words as "favor," "color," and "neighbor." American English always **spells** the word "license" with an "s" and "practice" with a "c." In Canadian English, "license" and "practise" are verbs, but "licence" and "practice" are nouns.

Silent letters also **cause** problems. In the word "through," the "gh" is silent. However, in the word "enough," we **pronounce** "gh" like "f." Many people **think** that this **doesn't make** sense.

Some words **sound** the same, but they **have** different spellings and meanings. For example, "know" and "no," "meat" and "meet," and "ate" and "eight."

Why **does** English **have** such a difficult system? The answer is simple: We **pronounce** in modern English, but we **continue** to spell in older English.

Even Canadians **have** difficulty with spelling. We often **hear** Canadians say, "How **do** you **spell** 'receive'?" or "**Does** 'occasion' **have** one s and two c's or double s and one c?" Canadians often **need** to use a dictionary to check their spelling. Many people **consult** the *ITP Nelson Canadian Dictionary of the English Language* or the *Gage Canadian Dictionary* to find the correct Canadian spelling of confusing words.

3.1   Simple Present Tense—Affirmative Statements

We use the base form when the subject is *I, you, we, they,* or a plural noun.

Subject	Base Form	Complement
I You We They Animals Trees	need	water.

We use the _-s_ form when the subject is _he, she, it,_ or a singular noun.

Subject	_-S_ Form	Complement
He She It A plant A person	needs	water.

1. We use the _-s_ form with _everyone, everybody, everything, no one, nobody,_ and _nothing._

   Everyone _needs_ water.

   Nobody _knows_ the answer.

2. Three verbs have an irregular _-s_ form:

   have—has   I _have_ a European car.

                She _has_ a Japanese car.

   go—goes   I _go_ to a city college.

                He _goes_ to a local university.

   do—does   I _do_ exercises in the morning.

                She _does_ exercises in the afternoon.

3. We use the simple present tense in the following cases:

   - With general truths, to show that something is consistently true.

     English _has_ a difficult spelling system.

     We _pronounce_ in modern English, but we _spell_ in older English.

   - To show regular activity (a habit) or repeated action.

     I sometimes _use_ my dictionary.

     People often _complain_ about English spelling.

   - To show a place of origin.

     Many English words _come from_ French. I _come from_ Hungary.

   NOTE: We can also use _be from: I'm from_ Hungary.

EXERCISE 1   Fill in each blank with the correct form of the verb.

    EXAMPLE: English _____*has*_____ **a difficult spelling system.**
                         (have/has)

  1. "Knife" _____ a silent "k."
                 (have/has)

  2. Canadians _____ difficulty with spelling.
                    (have/has)

  3. Some words _____ hard to spell.
                 (is/are)

4. We _____ one way, but we spell another way.
      (pronounce/pronounces)

5. A dictionary _____ with spelling.
            (help/helps)

6. The teacher _____ our spelling.
           (correct/corrects)

7. A dictionary _____ spelling and meaning.
           (show/shows)

8. Everybody _____ about English spelling.
        (complain/complains)

3.2 Spelling of the -*S* Form

The chart below shows the spelling of the -*s* form. Fill in the last examples.

Rule	Base Form	-*S* Form
Add *s* to most verbs to make the -*s* form.	hope	hopes
	eat	eats
	run	*runs*
	live	_____
When the base form ends in *s, z, sh, ch,* or *x,* add *es* and pronounce an extra syllable /Iz/.	miss	misses
	buzz	buzzes
	wash	_____
	catch	_____
	tax	_____
When the base form ends in a consonant + *y*, change the *y* to *i* and add *es.*	carry	carries
	worry	worries
	study	_____
	hurry	_____
When the base form ends in a vowel + *y*, do not change the *y*.	pay	pays
	obey	obeys
	play	_____
	enjoy	_____

Language
Notes

1. We pronounce /s/ if the verb ends in a voice-less sound: /p, t, k, f/. Listen to your teacher pronounce these examples.

hope—hopes   pick—picks
eat—eats   laugh—laughs

2. We pronounce /z/ if the verb ends in a voiced sound. Listen to your teacher pronounce these examples.

live—lives   run—runs
grab—grabs   borrow—borrows
read—reads   sing—sings

3. When the base form ends in *s, z, sh, ch, x, ge, ce,* or *se,* we pronounce an extra syllable /ɪz/. Listen to your teacher pronounce these examples.

miss—misses   watch—watches
buzz—buzzes   fix—fixes
wash—washes   dance—dances
change—changes   use—uses

4. These verbs have a change in the vowel sound. Listen to your teacher pronounce these examples.

do/du/—does/dʌz/
say/sei/—says/sɛz/

EXERCISE 2   Write the *-s* form of the following verbs. Say each word out loud.

ᴇxᴀᴍᴘʟᴇs: **eat** *eats* _____

study *studies* _____

watch *watches* _____

1. try _____

2. play _____

3. have _____

4. go _____

5. worry _____

6. finish _____

7. do _____

8. push _____

9. enjoy _____

10. think _____

11. say _____

12. change _____

13. brush _____

14. obey _____

15. reach _____

16. fix _____

17. work _____

18. raise _____

19. change _____

20. see _____

EXERCISE 3   Fill in each blank with the *-s* form of the verb in parentheses ( ). Pay attention to the spelling rules. Then pronounce each sentence.

> **Example: A teacher** _____*tries*_____ **to help students learn.**
> (try)

1. A pilot _____ an airplane.
    (fly)

2. A dishwasher _____ dishes.
    (wash)

3. A babysitter _____ children.
    (watch)

4. A soldier _____ an officer.
    (obey)

5. A citizen _____ taxes.
    (pay

6. A mechanic _____ machines.
    (fix)

7. A student _____.
    (study)

8. A student _____ homework.
    (do)

9. A homemaker _____ a home.
    (manage)

10. A secretary _____ a word processor.
    (use)

11. A teacher _____ students.
    (teach)

EXERCISE 4   Find a partner. Tell him or her about your profession or future profession. Tell what someone in this profession does.

> **EXAMPLE: I'm a car mechanic. A mechanic tries to find the problem in a car. Then he or she fixes the problem. A mechanic also changes parts, such as tires, oil, and brakes. A mechanic charges for his or her services by the hour.**

3.3 **Simple Present of *Be* and Other Verbs**

Compare *be* and other verbs in affirmative statements:

I'm a student.	You're right.	We're immigrants.
I speak English.	You know the answer.	We come from Laos.
They're kind.	The teacher's Canadian.	He's late.
They help people.	She teaches grammar.	He works hard.

Language Notes

Avoid making these mistakes with the simple present tense.
    Wrong: I'm work hard   Wrong: He's comes from Italy.
    Wrong: I working hard.   Right: He comes from Italy.
    Right: I work hard.   Right: He's from Italy.

EXERCISE 5   A student is comparing himself to his friend. Fill in each blank with the correct form of the underlined verb.

> EXAMPLES: **My friend and I are very different. I g<u>et</u> up at 7 a.m.**
>
> **He _____*gets*_____ up at 10.**
>
> **<u>I'm</u> a good student. He 's_____ a lazy student.**

1. I <u>study</u> every day. He _____ only before a test.

2. I always <u>get</u> A's on my tests. He _____ C's.

3. I <u>have</u> a scholarship. He _____ a government loan.

4. <u>I'm</u> a good student. He _____ an average student.

5. He <u>lives</u> in a residence.[1] I _____ in an apartment.

6. He<u>'s</u> from Japan. I _____ from the Philippines.

7. He <u>studies</u> with the radio on. I _____ in a quiet room.

8. He <u>watches</u> a lot of TV. I _____ TV only when I have free time.

---

[1] A *residence* is a building where students live.

3.4   Negative Statements with the Simple Present Tense

We use the base form of the verb for all negative statements.

I You We They The students	work. don't work.	He She It My father The telephone	works. doesn't work.

1. We use *don't* (*do not*) + a base form when the subject is *I, you, we, they,* or a plural noun.

2. We use *doesn't* (*does not*) + a base form when the subject is *he, she, it,* or a singular noun.

3. Compare the affirmative and negative statements below:

We *say* the "b" in "lumber."
We *don't say* the "b" in "plumber."
She *writes* English well.
She *doesn't write* Spanish well.

4. In Canadian English and British English, the negative of the verb *have* is different. Compare:

CANADIAN: He doesn't have a dictionary.
BRITISH: He hasn't a dictionary. (formal)
                OR He hasn't got a dictionary. (informal)

EXERCISE 6   Tell if this school has or doesn't have the following.

> EXAMPLES: **ESL courses**
> **This school has ESL courses.**
>
> **classes for children**
> **It doesn't have classes for children.**

1. a library
2. a cafeteria
3. copy machines
4. a parking lot
5. a swimming pool
6. a gym
7. a student newspaper
8. a theatre
9. residences
10. classes for children
11. _____ [2]
12. _____

---

[2]Where you see a blank space in this book, you can add your own item to the list.

EXERCISE 7   Make an affirmative statement or a negative statement with the words given to state facts about the teacher.

> EXAMPLE: **speak Arabic**
> **The teacher speaks Arabic.**
> OR
> **The teacher doesn't speak Arabic.**

1. talk fast
2. speak English well
3. speak my language
4. give a lot of homework
5. give tests

6. pronounce my name correctly
7. wear glasses
8. wear jeans to class
9. _____
10. _____

EXERCISE 8   Fill in each blank with the negative form of the underlined verb.

> EXAMPLES: **We <u>study</u> English spelling.**
>
> **We** _*don't study*_ **the history of English.**
>
> **The teacher <u>speaks</u> English in class.**
>
> **He/She** _*doesn't speak*_ **another language in class.**

1. Australians <u>speak</u> English.

   The people in China _____ English.

2. English <u>uses</u> the Roman alphabet.

   Chinese _____ the Roman alphabet.

3. Spanish <u>has</u> an easy spelling system.

   English and French _____ easy spelling systems.

4. The word "know" <u>has</u> a silent "k."

   The word "keep" _____ a silent "k."

5. "Know" and "no" <u>sound</u> the same.

   "Know" and "now" _____ the same.

6. We <u>have</u> trouble with English pronunciation.

   The teacher _____ trouble with English pronunciation.

7. We <u>pronounce</u> the "t" in "mister."

   We _____ the "t" in "listen."

8. The teacher <u>teaches</u> grammar and pronunciation.

   The teacher _____ the history of the English language.

9. I <u>need</u> a grammar book in this course.

   I _____ a history book.

10. We <u>study</u> Canadian English.

    We _____ British English.

EXERCISE 9   Check (✔) the items that describe you and what you do. Work with a partner. Find out what you and your partner have or don't have in common. Report some of your differences to the class.

> EXAMPLES: ___4___   **have children**
> **I have two children. Ly doesn't have children.**
>
> ___4___   **like cold weather**
> **Ly doesn't like cold weather. He comes from Vietnam.**
> **I like cold weather. I come from Moscow.**

1. _____ speak Chinese

2. _____ live alone

3. _____ live near school

4. _____ walk to school

5. _____ speak Arabic

6. _____ write with my left hand

7. _____ smoke

8. _____ own a car

9. _____ like coffee

10. _____ like cold weather

11. _____ _____

12. _____ _____

3.5 **Negative Statements with the Simple Present of *Be* and Other Verbs**

Compare *be* and other verbs in the negative.

I'm not from Hong Kong.	They're not sure.
I don't speak Cantonese.	They don't know the answer.
You aren't sick.	We aren't confused.
You don't need a doctor.	We don't need help.
She isn't hungry.	He's not cold.
She doesn't want dinner.	He doesn't want a sweater.

EXERCISE 10 Check (✓) the items that describe you. Work with a partner. Find out what you and your partner have or don't have in common. Report some of your differences to the class.

EXAMPLES: ___✓___ be an immigrant
I'm an immigrant. Reiko comes from Japan.
She isn't an immigrant. She's an exchange student.

___✓___ have a computer
I don't have a computer. Reiko has a computer.

1. _____ be married

2. _____ have children/a child

3. _____ have a computer

4. _____ be a Canadian citizen

5. _____ like this city

6. _____ have a job

7. _____ be a full-time student

8. _____ have a pet[3]

9. _____ be an immigrant

10. _____ be unhappy in Canada.

11. _____ _____

12. _____ _____

_____

[3]A *pet* is an animal that lives in someone's house. Dogs and cats are common pets. Pets are also called *companion animals*.

EXERCISE 11   Read each statement. Then make a negative statement with the words in parentheses ( ).

> **EXAMPLES:** **English is a European language (Korean)**
>
> _Korean isn't a European language._
>
> **I speak my language fluently. (English)**
>
> _I don't speak English fluently._

1. English has a difficult spelling system. (Spanish)

   _____

2. "Ate" and "eight" sound the same. ("hate" and "height")

   _____

3. Spanish is a Romance[4] language. (English)

   _____

4. Colombians speak Spanish. (Brazilians)

   _____

5. Colombia is in South America. (Spain)

   _____

6. A, E, I, O, and U are vowels. (B, C, D, F, and G)

   _____

7. We pronounce the "b" in "combine." (the "b" in "comb")

   _____

8. I speak English in class. (my native language)

   _____

9. I'm from _____ (Canada)

                  (your country)

   _____

---

[4]A *Romance* language comes from Latin. Spanish, Italian, and French are Romance languages.

3.6   *Yes/No* Questions and Short Answers with the Simple Present Tense

Yes/no questions in the simple present tense are formed with *do/does*. We use the base form for all *yes/no* questions.

Do/Does	Subject	Verb (Base Form)
Do	I you we they the students	work?
Does	he she it the phone everyone	

Language Notes

1. We usually answer a *yes/no* question with a short answer.

Short Answer:

YES, + PRONOUN SUBJECT + DO/DOES.

NO, + PRONOUN SUBJECT + DON'T/DOESN'T.

Do Australians speak English? Yes, they do.
Do you speak Polish? No, I don't.
Does the school have a library? Yes, it does.
Does the teacher speak your language? No, she doesn't.

2. Compare affirmative statements, questions, and short answers.

English *has* a difficult spelling system.
Does Spanish *have*[5] a difficult spelling system? No, it doesn't.

You *use* a textbook in class.
Do you *use* a dictionary in class? Yes, we do.

I *speak* my native language well.
Do I *speak* English well? Yes, you do.

The teacher *speaks* English well.
Does the teacher *speak* your language? No, she doesn't.

---

[5]CANADIAN: Does he have a car? Yes, he does.

BRITISH: Has he a car?/Has he got a car? Yes, he has.

EXERCISE 12   Ask your teacher a question with "Do you ... ?" and the words given. Your teacher will respond with a short answer.

> **EXAMPLE:** **drive to school**
>
> > **A. Do you drive to school?**
> >
> > **B. Yes, I do.** OR **No, I don't.**

   1. like your job
   2. teach in the summer
   3. have another job
   4. speak another language
   5. teach English to Canadians
   6. know my language
   7. like to read students' homework
   8. live far from the school
   9. have a fax machine
   10. have trouble with English spelling
   11. _____

EXERCISE 13   Two students are comparing teachers. Fill in each blank to complete this conversation.

A. Do you _____*like*_____ your English class?
                         (like)

B. Yes, I _____*do*_____ . I _____ a very good teacher. Her
                                              (1 have)

   name is Ms. Lopez.

A. _____ Spanish?
                    (2)

B. No, she doesn't. She comes from the Philippines. She _____
                                                                    (3 speak)

   English and Tagalog.

A. My teacher is very good too. But he _____ fast, and sometimes
                                              (4 talk)

   I _____ him. He _____ a lot of
                (5 not/understand)   (6 give)

   homework. _____ a lot of homework?
                         (7)

B. Yes, she does. And she _____ a test once a week.
                              (8 give)

A. My teacher _____ jeans to class. He's very informal.
                      (9 wear)

    _____ jeans to class?
                  (10)

B. No, she doesn't. She always wears a dress.

A. My class meets three days a week: Mondays, Wednesdays, and Fridays.

    _____ three days a week too?
                      (11)

B. No, it _____ on Tuesdays and Thursdays.
                (12 meet)

EXERCISE 14   Find a partner from a different country, if possible. Tell your partner about differences between classes and teachers in this institution and a postsecondary institution in your country. Ask your partner about his or her country.

> EXAMPLES: **In my university back home, students stand up when they speak. Do they stand up in your country?**
>
> **This class has some older people. In my country, only young people study at university. Do older people go to university in your country?**

EXERCISE 15   Read each statement. Then write a *yes/no* question about the words in parentheses ( ) . Write a short answer.

> EXAMPLES: **You know the present tense. (the past tense)**
>
> *Do you know the past tense? No, I don't.*
>
> **The school has computer classes. (gym classes)**
>
> *Does it have gym classes? Yes, it does.*

1. The teacher uses the chalkboard. (a map)

    _____

2. You bring your textbook to class. (your dictionary)

    _____

3. We need practice with grammar. (with spelling)

    _____

4. The teacher speaks English. (another language)

    _____

5. I understand the teacher. (you)

    _____

6. "Know" has a silent "k." ("knife")

    _____

7. The past tense has a lot of irregular verbs. (the present tense)

    _____

8. The teacher speaks English fluently. (the students)

    _____

3.7   Questions with *Be* and Other Verbs

Compare *be* and other verbs in *yes/no* questions and short answers.

Are you confused?	No, I'm not.	Am I right?	Yes, you are.
Do you need help?	No, I don't.	Do I have the right answer?	Yes, you do.
Are they from Haiti?	Yes, they are.	Is the teacher from your country?	No, he isn't.
Do they speak French?	Yes, they do.	Does the teacher have an accent?	No, he doesn't.

Avoid making these mistakes with short answers to these questions.

Are you hungry?	Wrong: Yes, I do.
	Right: Yes, I *am*.
Do you like movies?	Wrong: Yes, I am.
	Right: Yes, I *do*.

EXERCISE 16   Read each statement. Then write a *yes/no* question about the words in parentheses ( ). Write a short answer.

> EXAMPLES: **English is a Germanic language. (Spanish)**
>
> *Is Spanish a Germanic language? No, it isn't.*
>
> **Students of English complain about spelling. (students of Spanish)**
>
> *Do students of Spanish complain about spelling? No, they don't.*

1. Children learn a language easily. (adults)

    _____

2. Americans speak English. (Australians) (answer: yes)

    _____

3. "Butter" has two "t's." ("later")

    _____

4. English spelling is hard. (Spanish spelling) (answer: no)

    _____

5. Newcomers make mistakes with English spelling. (Canadians) (answer: yes)

    _____

6. The "g" in "sign" is silent. (the "g" in "signature") (answer: no)

    _____

7. You know Canadian English. (British English)

    _____

8. The teacher speaks English well. (you)

    _____

9. Some languages use the Roman alphabet. (Spanish) (answer: yes)

    _____

10. You're interested in the English language. (Canadian history)

_____

11. French is a Romance language. (Italian) (answer: yes)

_____

EXERCISE 17   Put a check (✓) next to customs from your country. Find a partner from another country, if possible. Tell your partner about customs in your country. Ask your partner if these are customs in his or her country. Tell the class about one custom from your partner's country that surprises you.

> **EXAMPLE:** ___4___ **Russians usually take off their shoes before they enter a house.**

1. People take off their shoes before they enter a house.

2. People bow when they say hello.

bow

3. People shake hands when they say hello.

4. People bring a gift when they visit a friend's house.

5. People eat with chopsticks.

chopsticks

6. On the bus, people stand up to let an older person sit down.

7. Women cover their faces.

8. A smoker offers a cigarette to other people.

9. Men open doors for women.

10. Men give flowers to women for their birthdays.

11. People celebrate children's day.

12. High school students wear a uniform.

13. Students stand up when the teacher enters the room.

14.

3.8 *Or* Questions

An *or* question gives you a choice of answers.

Do/Does	Subject	Verb	Choice 1	Or	Choice 2	Answer
Do	you	study	English	or	French?	I study English.
Does	"better"	have	one t	or	two t's?	It has two t's.

Be	Subject		Choice 1	Or	Choice 2	Answer
Is	Vancouver		on the East Coast	or	the West Coast?	It's on the West Coast.

The first part of an *or* question has a rising intonation; the second part has a falling intonation. Listen to your teacher pronounce the questions above.

EXERCISE 18   Find a partner. Ask your partner these questions, using the correct intonation.

> **EXAMPLE:** **Do you drink coffee or tea in the morning?**
> **I drink coffee.**

1. Do you speak English or your native language at home?

2. Do you prefer classical music or popular music?

3. Are you a resident of Canada or a visitor?

4. Are you married or single?

5. Do you live in a house, an apartment, or a residence?

6. Do you write with your left hand or your right hand?

7. Are you from a big city or a small town?

8. Do you prefer morning classes or evening classes?

9. Is this exercise easy or hard?

3.9 *Wh-* **Questions with the Simple Present Tense**

When we make *wh-* questions, we use the following word order.

Wh- Word	*Do(n't)* *Does(n't)*	Subject	Verb (Base Form)
Where	do	they	study?
What kind of car	do	you	have?
Why	don't	we	eat?
When	does	the class	begin?
How many sisters	does	he	have?
Why	doesn't	your brother	work?
What	does	*complain*	mean?

Compare statements and questions with the simple present tense.

Wh- Word	*Don't/Doesn't*	Subject	Verb	Complement	Short Answer
		He	lives	in Ontario.	
	Does	he	live	in Ontario?	No, he doesn't.
Where	does	he	live?		
Why	doesn't	he	live	in Toronto?	

When the *wh-* question has a preposition, we use the following word order.

Preposition	*Wh-* Word	*Do/Does*	Subject	Verb (Base Form)	Preposition
With	whom	do	you	live?	
	Who	do	you	live	with?
On	what floor	does	he live?		
	What floor	does	he	live	on?

1. It is very formal to put the preposition before a question word. In conversation, we often put the preposition at the end of the question. We almost always say: Where do you come *from?*

2. Remember, we can talk about a person's country of origin with *be* or *come.*

Where *are* you from? *I'm* from Poland.

Where *do* you *come* from? I *come* from Poland.

EXERCISE 19   Fill in each blank with the missing word.

> EXAMPLE: **Where** _____*do*_____ **you live? I live in Calgary.**

1. Where _____ your brother live? He lives in Montreal.

2. How _____ children do you have? I have two children.

3. _____ _____ you study? I study in the library.

4. Why _____ you study at home? I don't study at home because it's too noisy.

5. How many languages _____ your teacher _____? He speaks two languages.

6. Where do you _____? I work downtown.

7. _____ do you live _____ ? I live with my sister.

8. _____ does he come from? He _____ from Thailand.

EXERCISE 20   Ask and answer questions with the words given. First ask a *yes/no* question. Then use the words in parentheses ( ) to ask a *wh-* question, if possible.

> EXAMPLE: **live near school (where)**
> **A. Do you live near the school?**
> **B. Yes, I do.**
> **A. Where do you live?**
> **B. I live on Maple and College.**

1. speak Spanish (what language)
2. need English in your country (why)
3. have Canadian friends (how many)
4. like this city (why)
5. live near the school (where)
6. plan to go back to your country (when or why)
7. live alone (with whom or who ... with)
8. practise English outside of class (with whom or who ... with)
9. bring your dictionary to class (why)
10. have an answering machine (why)

EXERCISE 21   Ask the teacher. First, ask the teacher a *yes/no* question. After you get the answer, use the words in parentheses ( ) to ask a *wh-* question, if possible. Your teacher will answer.

> EXAMPLE: **teach summer school (why)**
>> **A. Do you teach summer school?**
>> **B. No, I don't.**
>> **A. Why don't you teach summer school?**
>> **B. Because I like to travel in the summer.**

1. have an office mate (what/he or she/teach)
2. get paid on the first of the month (when)
3. have a computer (what kind of computer)
4. speak another language (what language)
5. teach summer school (why)
6. work in another school (what other school … in)
7. correct the homework in school (where)
8. prefer evening classes (why)
9. drive to school (how … get[6] to school)
10. like to teach English (why)
11. come from this city (what city … from)
12. have children (how many)
13. _____

EXERCISE 22   Ask and answer questions about another teacher with the words given. First ask a *yes/no* question. Then use the words in parentheses ( ) to ask a *wh-* question, if possible.

> Example: **speak your language (what languages)**
>> **A. Does your teacher speak your language?**
>> **B. No, he doesn't.**
>> **A. What languages does he speak?**
>> **B. He speaks English and French.**

1. give a lot of homework (why)
2. write on the chalkboard (when)
3. use a tape recorder in class (why)
4. come to class late (what time)
5. call you by your first name (why)
6. pronounce your name correctly (how)
7. use a textbook (what textbook)
8. wear jeans to class (what)

_____

[6]*Get* means arrive.

Language Notes

1. We can use the simple present tense to ask questions about the meaning and spelling of a word.

How do you say "knife" in Spanish?   "Cuchillo."
What does "knife" mean?   It means an instrument for cutting.
How do you spell "knife"?   K-N-I-F-E.

2. *Cost* is a verb. We can use the simple present tense to ask questions about cost.

How much does a new car *cost*?   It *costs* over $15,000.
How much do bananas *cost*?   They *cost* $1.49 a kilo.

EXERCISE 23   Answer these questions. Practise the *-s* form.

1. How much does postage[7] to your country cost?
2. How much does a phone call to your country cost?
3. What does "postage" mean?
4. What does "10 bucks"[8] mean?
5. How do you spell your last name?
6. How do you spell your first name?
7. How do you say "hello" in your language?
8. How do you say "goodbye" in your language?

EXERCISE 24   Read each statement. Then ask a *wh-* question about the words in parentheses ( ). Answer with a complete sentence.

EXAMPLES: Vietnam has 50 provinces. (Canada)

A. *How many provinces does Canada have?*

B. *It has 10 provinces.*

Haitians speak French. (Canadians)

A. *What language do Canadians speak?*

B. *Canadians speak English and French.*

1. The British prime minister lives in London, England. (Canadian prime minister)

A. _____

B. _____

---

[7]*Postage* means the price to mail a letter.

[8]*Buck* is slang for *dollar*.

2. Filipinos speak Tagalog. (Americans)

    A. _____

    B. _____

3. A local phone call costs _____¢. (a stamp)

    A. _____

    B. _____

4. "P.E.I." means Prince Edward Island. ("B.C.")

    A. _____

    B. _____

5. You spell "knife" K-N-I-F-E. ("enough")

    A. _____

    B. _____

6. China has more than 1 billion people. (Canada) (answer: about 30 million)

    A. _____

    B. _____

7. Chinese people celebrate the New Year in February. (Canadians)

    A. _____

    B. _____

8. I don't know the word "large." ("large"/mean)

    A. _____

    B. _____

9. We say "book" in English. ("book" in Spanish) (answer: "libro")

    A. _____

    B. _____

10. The teacher doesn't speak a foreign language in class. (why)

    A. _____

    B. _____

11. Argentina has cold weather in July. (when/Canada)

    A. _____

    B. _____

12. Germans celebrate Labour Day in May. (Canadians) (answer: September)

    A. _____

    B. _____

13. "Fall" means autumn. ("automobile")

    A. _____

    B. _____

14. The school year usually starts in September. (when/end)

    A. _____

    B. _____

 **3.10** *Wh-* **Questions with** *Be* **and Other Verbs**

Compare *wh-* questions with questions that have *be* and other verbs.

Where are they from? What language do they speak?	How are they? How do they feel?
Where am I? What do I need?	Where are we? Where do we go now?
Who is she? Where does she live?	What's a stamp? What does "postage" mean?

EXERCISE 25 Read this conversation between two new students, Meilan (M) and Alexander (A). Fill in each blank with the missing word.

M. Hi. My name '*s* Meilan. What _____?
(1)

A. Alexander.

M. Nice to meet you, Alexander. Where _____?
(2)

A. I _____ from Ukraine.
(3)

M. What languages _____?
(4)

A. I speak Ukrainian and Russian.

M. _____ a new student?
(5)

A. Yes, I am. What about you? Where _____ from?
(6)

M. I _____ from Hong Kong.
(7)

A. Where _____?
(8)

M. It's in Asia. We speak Chinese in Hong Kong. I want to learn English and then go back to my country.

A. Why _____ to go back to Hong Kong?
(9)

M. Because my family has an export business there, and I want to work with them.

A. What _____?
(10)

M. "Export" means to sell your products in another country.

A. Why _____ to know English?
(11)

M. I need to know English because we have many Canadian customers.

A. How many languages _____?
                              (12)

M. My father speaks four languages: English, French, Japanese, and Chinese, of course.

A. Tell me about your English class. _____
                                              (13)

    your English teacher?

M. Oh, yes. I like her very much.

A. Who _____ your English teacher?
                (14)

M. Barbara Nowak.

A. _____?
                (15)

M. N-O-W-A-K. It's a Polish name.

A. How many students _____?
                                    (16)

M. It has about 35 students. The classroom is very big.

A. What floor _____?
                          (17)

M. It's on the second floor.

A. When _____ your class _____?
              (18)   (19)

M. It begins at 6 o'clock. I'm late. See you later.

A. _____ "see you later" in Chinese?
              (20)

M. We say "zaijian."

EXPANSION ACTIVITIES

DISCUSSION   Find a partner who speaks the same language, if possible. Talk about some differences between your language and English.

EXAMPLES: **In Spanish, we use almost the same alphabet as English. We have some different letters: ll and ñ. Some words sound the same—"casa" and "caza"—but they don't have the same meaning. We don't pronounce the "h" in Spanish words.**

Russian uses a different alphabet. Russian doesn't have so many verb tenses. We sometimes put the verb before the subject in Russian.

WRITING   Write a list of differences between your language and English. Write about the alphabet, grammar, spelling, accent marks, and pronunciation.

GAME   One student comes to the front of the room. He or she thinks of an animal and writes the name of this animal on a piece of paper. The other students try to guess which animal it is by asking questions. The person who guesses the animal is the next to come to the front of the room.

EXAMPLE: **lion**

Does this animal fly? No, it doesn't.

Does it live in water? No, it doesn't.

What does it eat? It eats meat.

Does this animal live in Africa? Yes, it does.

What colour is this animal?

lion

PROVERBS   The following proverbs contain the simple present tense. Discuss the meaning of each proverb. Do you have a similar proverb in your language?

Every cloud has a silver lining.

A stitch in time saves nine.   — stitch

Practice makes perfect.

OUTSIDE ACTIVITIES   Interview a Canadian. Ask this person to tell you about difficulties he or she has with English spelling. Tell the class what this person said.

SUMMARY OF LESSON THREE

Forms of the Simple Present Tense

1. The simple present has two forms: the base form and the -s form:

I You We They (Plural noun)	eat.	He She It (Singular noun)	eats.

2. Simple present tense patterns with the -s form:

Affirmative	The prime minister *lives* in Ottawa.
Negative	He *doesn't live* in Toronto.
Yes/No *Question*	*Does* he *live* at 24 Sussex Drive?
Short Answer	Yes, he *does*.
Wh- *Question*	Where *does* the Queen *live*?
Negative Question	Why *doesn't* the Queen *live* in Ottawa?

3. Simple present tense patterns with the base form:

Affirmative	We *study* English in class.
Negative	We *don't study* Canadian history in class.
Yes/No *Question*	Do we *study* grammar?
Short Answer	Yes, we *do*.
Wh- *Question*	Why *do* we *study* grammar?
Negative Question	Why *don't* we *study* history?

4. Present tense patterns with the verb *be*:

Affirmative	The teacher *is* absent.
Negative	She *isn't* here today.
Yes/No *Question*	*Is* she sick?
Short Answer	No, she *isn't*.
Wh- *Question*	Where *is* she?
Negative Question	Why *isn't* she here?

Uses of the Simple Present Tense

General Truths	Customs	Habits
English *has* a difficult spelling system. Many English words *have* silent letters. Many Canadians *speak* English. Mexicans *speak* Spanish.	Japanese people *eat* with chopsticks. A lot of Canadians *use* credit cards.	Canadians often *complain* about English spelling. They sometimes *spell* a word wrong.

LESSON THREE TEST/REVIEW

Part 1   Write the *-s* form of the following verbs. Use correct spelling.

      EXAMPLE: take _____*takes*_____

    1. go _____

    2. carry _____

    3. mix _____

    4. drink _____

    5. play _____

    6. study _____

    7. catch _____

    8. say _____

Part 2   Fill in the first blank with the affirmative form of the verb in parentheses ( ). Then write the negative form of this verb.

      EXAMPLES: A monkey _____*lives*_____ **in a warm climate.**
                           (live)

        It _____*doesn't live*_____ **in a cold climate.**

        Brazil _____*is*_____ **a big country.**
                (be)

        Haiti _____*isn't*_____ **a big country.**

    1. The English language _____ the Roman alphabet.
                                 (use)

        The Chinese language _____ the Roman alphabet.

    2. We _____ English in class.
            (speak)

        We _____ our native languages in class.

    3. March _____ 31 days.
              (have)

        February _____ 31 days.

4. Mexico and the U.S. _____ in North America.
   (be)

   Colombia and Ecuador _____ in North America.

5. You _____ the "k" in "bank."
   (pronounce)

   You _____ the "k" in "knife."

6. The teacher _____ the English language.
   (teach)

   He/She _____ Canadian history.

7. A green light _____ "go."
   (mean)

   A red light _____ "go."

8. I _____ from another country.
   (come)

   I _____ from Canada.

9. English _____ hard for me.
   (be)

   My language _____ hard for me.

Part 3   Write a *yes/no* question about the words in parentheses ( ). Write a short answer.

    EXAMPLES: January has 31 days. (February)

        Does February have 31 days? No, it doesn't.

    China is in Asia. (Korea)

        Is Korea in Asia? Yes, it is.

1. "Occasion" has a double "c." ("occupation")

   _____

2. The English language uses the Roman alphabet. (the Russian language) (answer: no)

_____

3. Victoria is in British Columbia. (Nanaimo) (answer: yes)

_____

4. McDonald's sells hamburgers. (Tim Hortons) (answer: no)

_____

5. January and March have 31 days. (April and June) (answer: no)

_____

6. The prime minister lives in Ottawa. (the Queen) (answer: no)

_____

7. Americans speak English. (Australians) (answer: yes)

_____

8. We come to class on time. (the teacher)

_____

9. England and Switzerland are small countries. (Canada)

_____

Part 4   Read each statement. Then write a _wh-_ question about the words in parentheses ( ). You don't need to answer.

    EXAMPLES: **February has 28 days. (March)**

          How many days does March have?
          ————————————————————————

          Mexico is in North America. (Venezuela)

          Where is Venezuela?
          ————————————————————————

1. Filipinos speak Tagalog. (Americans)

_____

2. Canada has 10 provinces. (Vietnam)

   _____

3. You say "book" in English. (in Polish)

   _____

4. The prime minister lives in Ottawa. (the Queen)

   _____

5. Thanksgiving is in October. (Labour Day)

   _____

6. You spell "occasion" O-C-C-A-S-I-O-N. ("tomorrow")

   _____

7. "Occupation" means job or profession. ("occasion")

   _____

8. English doesn't have a simple spelling system. (why)

   _____

9. Marek comes from Poland. (you)

   _____

LESSON FOUR

GRAMMAR

Singular and Plural
Articles and Quantity Words
There + *Be* + Noun

CONTEXT

Facts About Canadians
Finding an Apartment
Calling About an Apartment

Lesson Focus   Singular and Plural

- Nouns can be singular or plural. Plural nouns usually end in -s.

    I have a *brother.*   I have three *sisters.*

    (NOTE: Some nouns have no plural form. These are "noncount" nouns. See Lesson Eleven for noncount nouns.)

- We can use the indefinite articles (*a/an*) with singular nouns. We can use quantity words with plural nouns.

    I have *a cousin* in Edmonton.   I have *some cousins* in Halifax.
    I have *an aunt* in Ottawa.   I don't have *any relatives* in Vancouver.

- We can introduce a noun with *there* + a form of *be.*

    There's an apple in the refrigerator.   *There are* some peaches on the table.

Before you read:

1.   What questions do you have about Canadians and Canadian life?
2.   What surprises you about life in Canada?

Read the following facts and statistics about Canadians. Pay special attention to plural nouns.

FACTS ABOUT CANADIANS

1. There are just under 30 million **people** in Canada.
2. The average household has 2.61 **people.**
3. More than 57 percent of Canadian **women** work for pay.
4. **Canadians** spend an average of $112.09 a week for food. They spend about 72 percent in **stores** and 28 percent in **restaurants.**
5. Over 40 percent of all **marriages** end in divorce.
6. The average Canadian lives about 78 **years. Women** live longer than **men** (81 years compared with 75 years).
7. Sixty-two percent of Canadian **families** own their own **homes.**
8. The average Canadian moves up to a dozen **times.**
9. Sixty-five percent of **Canadians** have high school **diplomas.**
10. Sixty-eight percent of high school **graduates** attend postsecondary **institutions.** More **women** than **men** go to college or university.

4.1   Regular Plural Nouns

We form the plural of most nouns by adding -s at the end of the word. The chart shows regular plural -s endings. Fill in the last examples for each spelling.

Word Ending	Example Words	Plural Addition	Plural Addition	Word Ending	Example Words	Plural Addition	Plural Addition
Vowel	bee	+ s	bees	Vowel + o	patio	+ s	patios
	banana		bananas		radio		radios
	pie		*pies*		stereo		_____
	name		_____		video		_____
Consonant	bed	+ s	beds	Consonant + o	mosquito	+ es	mosquitoes
	card		cards		tomato		tomatoes
	pin		_____		potato		_____
	month		_____		hero		_____
				(Exceptions: photos, pianos, solos, altos, sopranos, autos, avocados)			
s, ss, sh, ch, x, z	church	+ es	churches				
	dish		dishes				
	box		boxes	f or fe	knife	f̷ + ves	knives
	watch		_____		leaf		leaves
	class		_____		calf		_____
					life		_____
Vowel + y	boy	+ s	boys	(Exceptions: beliefs, chiefs, roofs, chefs)			
	day		days				
	toy		_____				
	monkey		_____				
Consonant + y	lady	y̷ + ies	ladies				
	story		stories				
	party		_____				
	cherry		_____				

Language Notes

The regular plural form (with -*s*) has three pronunciations. Listen to your teacher pronounce these examples.

1. After voiceless sounds /p, t, k, f, θ/, -*s* sounds like /s/.

lip—lips	cat—cats	rock—rocks
cuff—cuffs	month—months	

2. After voiced sounds /b, d, g, v, ð, m, n, ŋ, l, r/ and all vowels, -*s* sounds like /z/.

cab—cabs	lid—lids	bag—bags
stove—stoves	lathe—lathes	sum—sums
can—cans	thing—things	bill—bills
car—cars	bee—bees	toe—toes

3. After these sounds /s, z, ʒ, ʃ, ʤ, ʧ/, -*es* sounds like /Iz/ and is a separate syllable.

bus—buses	cause—cause	garage—garages
dish—dishes	beach—beaches	bridge—bridges

EXERCISE I   Write the plural form of each noun, then pronounce each plural form.

EXAMPLES: **leaf** _____ *leaves* _____

 toy _____ *toys* _____

1. dish _____
2. country _____
3. half _____
4. book _____
5. boy _____
6. girl _____
7. bench _____
8. box _____
9. table _____
10. stereo _____
11. knife _____
12. story _____
13. sofa _____
14. key _____
15. movie _____
16. bath _____
17. mosquito _____
18. lion _____
19. fly _____
20. cow _____
21. shark _____
22. cockroach _____
23. fox _____
24. horse _____
25. turkey _____
26. chicken _____
27. wolf _____
28. dog _____
29. squirrel _____
30. pony _____
31. duck _____
32. moth _____

4.2   **Irregular Plural Nouns**

Some plural nouns are not formed by adding *-s.*

Language Notes

1. Some nouns have the same singular and plural form.

fish	I have one *fish*.
	He has three *fish*.
sheep	One *sheep* is here.
	Three *sheep* are there.

2. Some nouns change a vowel to make the plural.

man—men	One *man* speaks French.
woman—women	Three *men* speak
mouse—mice	German.
tooth—teeth	One *woman* is tall.
foot—feet	Two *women* are short.
goose—geese	

3. Some nouns have different words for their plural forms.

child—children	One *child* is hungry.
person—people	Two *children* are tired.
(or persons)	One *person* is late.
	Three *people* are absent.

4. Some words only have a plural form.

pyjamas	
clothes	Your *clothes* are dirty.
pants	The *pants* are blue.
(eye)glasses	My *glasses* are broken.
slacks	
scissors	

EXERCISE 2   The following nouns have an irregular plural form. Write the plural.

EXAMPLE: **man** _____*men*_____

1. foot _____

2. woman _____

3. tooth _____

4. child _____

5. fish _____

6. mouse _____

7. sheep _____

8. person _____

EXERCISE 3   Use the plural of each noun to ask "How many ... do you have?" Another student will answer. For a zero answer, say, "I don't have any <plural form>."

Example: sister

  A. How many sisters do you have?

  B. I have two sisters.   OR   **I don't have any sisters.**

1. child	7. telephone
2. brother	8. watch
3. sister	9. television
4. niece	10. radio
5. nephew	11. _____
6. aunt	12. _____

4.3   Using the Plural to Make a Generalization

Study two ways to make generalizations:

No Article	Plural Subject	Verb	Complement
	Dogs	are	faithful animals.
	Children	need	love from their parents.
	Immigrants	have to learn	a new language.
Indefinite Article	**Singular Subject**	**Verb**	**Complement**
A	dog	is	a faithful animal.
A	child	needs	love from his or her parents.
An	immigrant	has to learn	a new language.

Language Notes

1. We often use the plural form of nouns to make generalizations. We say that something is true about all members of a group. We don't use an article with plural nouns to make a generalization.

2. We can also use the singular form of nouns to make generalizations. We use the indefinite article (*a* or *an*) with singular nouns.

3. After the verb, we usually use the plural form with no article to make a generalization.
   I like *apples*.
   I don't like *peaches*.
   I don't understand Canadian *customs*.

EXERCISE 4   Change the subject from plural to singular. Make other necessary changes. (Both singular and plural give a generalization.)

> **EXAMPLE: Immigrants have to learn English or French.**
>
> *An immigrant has to learn English or French.*

1. Adults have a lot of responsibilities.

_____

2. Children like to play.

   _____

3. Single parents have a hard job.

   _____

4. Women live longer than men.

   _____

5. Cars are expensive.

   _____

6. Houses cost a lot of money.

   _____

EXERCISE 5   Change the subject from singular to plural. Make other necessary changes. (Both singular and plural give a generalization.)

   EXAMPLE: **An immigrant has many problems.**

   Immigrants have many problems.
   _____

1. A child needs love.

   _____

2. An egg has protein.

   _____

3. A banana is yellow.

   _____

dolphin

4. A dolphin is intelligent.

   _____

5. A dolphin doesn't live on land.

   _____

6. A mouse is small.

   _____

EXERCISE 6   Work with a partner. Use the plural form of the word in parentheses ( ) to make a generalization. Remember, don't use an article with the plural form to make a generalization.

   EXAMPLES: (child)

   Children like to watch cartoons.

   Canadian (highway)

   Canadian highways are in good condition.

   1. (Canadian)

   _____

   2. Canadian (child)

   _____

   3. big (city) in Canada

   _____

   4. (teacher) at this institution

   _____

   5. (student) at this institution

   _____

   6. Canadian (doctor)

   _____

   7. old (person) in Canada

   _____

EXERCISE 7   Find a partner from a different country, if possible.[1] Use the noun in parentheses ( ) to give your partner general information about your country. Use the singular form with an article or the plural form with no article.

> EXAMPLE: **(woman)**
>
>   **Generally, women don't work outside the home in my country.**
>
>   OR
>
>   **Generally, a woman doesn't work outside the home in my country.**

1. (person)	5. (house)	9. (_____)
2. old (person)	6. poor (person)	10. (_____)
3. (woman)	7. (car)	11. (_____)
4. (man)	8. (doctor)	12. (_____)

EXERCISE 8   Use the plural form of each noun to tell if you like or don't like the following:

> EXAMPLE: **apple**
>
>   **I like apples.**   OR   **I don't like apples.**

1. tomato	6. peach
2. orange	7. radish
3. strawberry	8. pear
4. grape	9. potato
5. banana	10. cherry

EXERCISE 9   Ask "Do you like" + the plural form of the noun. Another student will answer.

> EXAMPLES: **child**
>
>   **A. Do you like children?**
>   **B. Yes, I do.**
>
>   **dog**
>   **A. Do you like dogs?**
>   **B. No, I don't.**

_____

[1]If you and your partner are from the same country, see if you agree about your generalizations.

1. cat
2. dog
3. Canadian doctor
4. Canadian car
5. Canadian TV show

6. fashion magazine
7. comic book
8. computer game
9. strict teacher
10. _____

comic book

Before you read:

1. Do you live in a house, an apartment, or a residence? Do you live alone?
2. Are you happy with the place where you live? Why or why not?

Read the following article. Pay special attention to *there* + *be* followed by singular and plural nouns.

FINDING AN APARTMENT

There are several ways to find an apartment. One way is to look in the newspaper. **There is** an "Apartments for Rent" section in the back of the newspaper. **There are** many ads for apartments. **There are** also ads for houses for rent and houses for sale.

Another way to find an apartment is by looking at the buildings in the neighbourhood where you want to live. **There are** often "For Rent" signs at the front of buildings. **There is** usually a phone number on the sign. You can call and ask for information about the apartment that you are interested in. You can ask:

How much is the rent?
Is heat included?
What floor is the apartment on?
Is there an elevator?
How many bedrooms **are there** in the apartment?
How many closets **are there** in the apartment?
Is the apartment available[2] now?

---

[2]*Available* means ready to use.

If an apartment interests you, you can make an appointment to see it. When you go to see the apartment, you should ask some more questions, such as the following:

> **Is there** a lease?[3] How long is the lease?
> **Is there** a janitor or manager?
> **Is there** a parking space for each tenant? Is it free, or do I have to pay extra?
> **Are there** smoke detectors? (In most places, the law says that the proprietor
>   must put a smoke detector in each apartment and in the halls.)
> **Is there** a laundry room in the building? Where is it?

The landlord may ask you a few questions, such as:

> How many people **are there** in your family?
> Do you have any pets?

You should check over the apartment carefully before you sign the lease. If **there are** some problems, you should talk to the proprietor to see if he or she will take care of them before you move in.

4.4   Using *There* + *Be*

We use *there* + *is* to introduce a singular subject into the conversation. We use *there* + *are* to introduce a plural subject. Observe the types of articles and quantity words that we can use in a statement with *there*.

SINGULAR

There + *Is*	Singular Word	Singular Noun	Prepositional Phrase
There's	a	janitor	in my building.
There's	one	dryer	in the basement.
There isn't	a	back door	in my apartment.
There's	no	back door	in my apartment.

---

[3]A *lease* is a contract between the owner (proprietor, sometimes called the landlord or landlady) and the renter (tenant). It tells how much the rent is, how long the tenant can stay in the apartment, and other rules.

PLURAL

There + Are	Plural Word	Plural Noun	Prepositional Phrase
There are	—	numbers	on the doors of the apartments.
There are	several	windows	in the bedroom.
There are	many	Canadians	in my building.
There are	some	children	in my building.
There are	few	pets	in my building.
There are	two	closets	in the hall.
There aren't	any	shades	on the windows.
There are	no	shades	on the windows.

1. A sentence that begins with *there* often shows a place or a time.

There is a smoke detector *in the hall.*
There are apartments available *in May.*

2. If two nouns follow *there*, use a singular verb (*is*) if the first noun is singular. Use a plural verb (*are*) if the first noun is plural.

There's *a* closet in the bedroom and two closets in the hall.
There *are two* closets in the hall and one closet in the bedroom.
There *is a* washer and a dryer in the basement.

3. In conversation, you will sometimes hear *there's* with plural nouns.

INFORMAL: There's a lot of empty apartments in my building.
FORMAL: There are a lot of empty apartments in my building.

EXERCISE 10   Use the words given with the patterns in the Language Notes box above to make a statement about the place where you live (house or apartment). If you live in a residence, use Exercise 11 instead.

EXAMPLES: **carpet/in the living room.**
There's a carpet in the living room.
OR
There isn't a carpet in the living room.

trees/in front of the building
There are two trees in front of the building.
OR
There are no trees in front of the building.

1. closet/in the living room
2. blinds/on the windows
3. door/on every room
4. window/in every room
5. lease
6. porch
7. number/on the door of the apartment
8. cockroaches/in the kitchen
9. microwave oven/in the kitchen
10. back door
11. fireplace
12. smoke detector

blinds

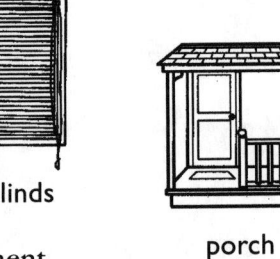

porch

cockroach

fireplace

EXERCISE 11   Make a statement about your residence and residence room with the words given. (If you live in an apartment or house, skip this exercise.)

> **EXAMPLES: window/in the room**
> **There's a window in the room.**
>
> **curtains/on the window**
> **There are no curtains on the window.**
> **There are shades.**

shade

1. closet/in the room
2. two beds/in the room
3. private bath/for every room
4. men and women/in the residence
5. cafeteria/in the residence

6. snack machines/in the residence
7. noisy students/in the residence
8. numbers/on the doors of the rooms
9. elevator(s)/in the residence
10. laundry room/in the residence

4.5   Questions with *There*

Questions and Answers with *There*

Is/Are + There	Noun Phrase	Prepositional Phrase	Short Answer
Is there	a laundry room	in your building?	No, there isn't.
Are there	any cabinets	in the kitchen?	Yes, there are.

Questions with *How Many*

How Many + Noun	*Are There*	Prepositional Phrase	Answer
How many closets	are there	in your apartment?	There are 3.
How many apartments	are there	in your building?	There are 10.

1. We usually use *any* to introduce a plural noun in a *yes/no* question.

    Are there any elevators in your building?

2. Do not make a contraction for a short *yes* answer.

    Is there an elevator in your building?
    Yes, there is. NOT: Yes, there's.

EXERCISE 12   Ask and answer questions with *there* and the words given to find out about another student's apartment and building. (If you live in a residence, use Exercise 13 instead.)

    EXAMPLES: a microwave oven/in your apartment

        A. Is there a microwave oven in your apartment?

        B. No, there isn't.

        closets/ in the bedroom

        A. Are there any closets in the bedroom?

        B. Yes. There's one closet in the bedroom.

1. children/in your building
2. a dishwasher/in the kitchen
3. a yard/in front of your building
4. trees/around your building
5. a basement/in the building
6. a laundry room/in the basement
7. a janitor/in the building
8. noisy neighbours/in the building
9. nosy[4] neighbours/in the building
10. an elevator/in the building
11. parking spaces/for the tenants
12. a lot of closets/in the apartment
13. how many apartments/in your building
14. how many parking spaces/behind your building

---

[4]A *nosy* person is a person who wants to know everyone's business.

EXERCISE 13   Ask and answer questions with *there* and the words given to find out about another student's residence. (If you live in an apartment or house, skip this exercise.)

>   EXAMPLE: **an exercise room/in your residence**
>   **A. Is there an exercise room in your residence?**
>   **B. No, there isn't.**

1. married students
2. private rooms
3. an exercise room
4. a computer room
5. an elevator
6. a bulletin board

7. graduate students
8. a quiet place to study
9. an air conditioner/in your room
10. a parking lot/for your residence
11. how many rooms/in your residence
12. how many floors/in your residence

EXERCISE 14   Use the words given to ask the teacher a question about his or her office. Your teacher will answer.

>   EXAMPLES: **pencil sharpener**
>   **A. Is there a pencil sharpener in your office?**
>   **B. No, there isn't.**
>
>   **books**
>   **A. Are there any books in your office?**
>   **B. Yes. There are a lot of books in my office.**

1. phone
2. answering machine
3. photos of your family
4. radio
5. computer

6. windows
7. calendar
8. bookshelves
9. plants
10. file cabinet

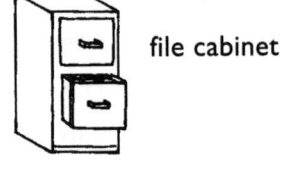 file cabinet

EXERCISE 15   A student is calling about an apartment for rent. Fill in the blanks with *there is, there are, is there, are there,* and other related words to complete this phone conversation between the student (S) and the landlady (L).

>   S.   I'm calling about an apartment for rent on Hudson Street.
>
>   L.   We have two apartments available. _____*There's*_____ a four-room apartment
>   (Example)
>
>   on the first floor and a three-room apartment on the fourth floor. Which one
>   are you interested in?

S. I prefer the smaller apartment. _____ an elevator in the
                                              (1)
    building?

L. Yes, there is. How many people _____ in your family?
                                              (2)

S. It's just for me. I live alone. I'm a student. I need a quiet apartment. Is this a
    quiet building?

L. Oh, yes. _____ no kids in the building.
                      (3)

S. I have a car. _____ parking spaces?
                         (4)

L. Yes. _____ 20 spaces behind the building.
                (5)

S. How _____ apartments _____ in the building?
                  (6)   (7)

L. _____ 30 apartments.
            (8)

S. Then _____ enough parking spaces for all the tenants.
                  (9)

L. Don't worry. Not everyone has a car. Parking is on a first-come, first-served
    basis.[5] And _____ plenty of[6] spaces on the street.
                          (10)

S. _____ in the building?
            (11)

L. Yes. There are washers and dryers in the basement.

S. How much is the rent?

L. It's $670 a month.

S. When can I see the apartment?

L. How about tomorrow at six o'clock?

S. That'll be fine. Thanks.

---

[5]A *first-come, first-served basis* means that people who arrive first will get something first (parking
spaces, theatre tickets, classes at registration).

[6]*Plenty of* means a lot of.

Language Notes

1. We use *there* only for the first mention of a noun in a conversation. After we introduce a new noun, we can refer to the noun again with *it, they,* or other pronouns.

   There's *an empty apartment* on the first floor. *It's* available now.
   There's *a janitor* in the building. *He's* in the basement now.
   There are a lot of *parking spaces. They're* for the tenants.
   There are two *washing machines. They're* in the basement.

2. We pronounce *there* and *they're* exactly the same. Listen to your teacher pronounce these examples.

   There are a lot of parking spaces. *They're* for the tenants.

EXERCISE 16   Fill in each blank with *there's, there are, it's,* or *they're.*

> EXAMPLE: *There's*_____ a small apartment for rent in my building.
>
> *It's*_____ on the fourth floor.

1. _____ two apartments for rent. _____ not on the same floor.

2. _____ a laundry room in the building. _____ in the basement.

3. The parking spaces are behind the building. _____ for the tenants with cars.

4. The parking spaces don't cost extra. _____ free for the tenants.

5. The apartment is small. _____ on the fourth floor.

6. The building has 30 apartments. _____ a big building.

7. The student wants to see the apartment. _____ on Hudson Street.

8. The building is quiet because _____ no kids in the building.

9. How much is the rent? _____ $670 a month.

10. Is the rent high? No, _____ not high.

EXERCISE 17   Ask a question about this school using *there* and the words given. Another student will answer. If the answer is "yes," ask a question with *where*.

> **EXAMPLES: a cafeteria**
>
> **A. Is there a cafeteria at this school?**
>
> **B. Yes, there is.**
>
> **A. Where is it?**
>
> **B. It's on the first floor.**
>
> **lockers**
>
> **A. Are there any lockers at this school?**
>
> **B. Yes, there are.**
>
> **A. Where are they?**
>
> **B. They're near the gym.**

1. a library
2. vending machines
3. public telephones
4. a computer room
5. a cafeteria
6. a gym
7. a swimming pool

8. tennis courts
9. residences
10. a parking lot
11. a bookstore
12. copy machines
13. a student lounge
14. a fax machine

Avoid these common mistakes in sentences that require *there*.

1. Don't confuse *there, they're,* and *their*.

Wrong:	Their are two chairs in the living room.
Wrong:	They're are two chairs in the living room.
Right:	*There are* two chairs in the living room.

2. Don't forget to use *there + is/are* to introduce a subject.

Wrong:	Are three students from Haiti in my class.
Wrong:	In my class three students from Haiti.
Right:	*There are* three students from Haiti in my class.

3. Don't confuse *it* and *there*.

Wrong:	It's a closet in my bedroom.
Right:	*There's* a closet in my bedroom. It's not very big.

4. Don't confuse *have* and *there*.

Wrong:	Have a closet in my bedroom.
Right:	*There's* a closet in my bedroom.
Right:	My bedroom *has* a closet.

EXERCISE 18   A woman is showing her new apartment to her friend. Find the mistakes in this conversation and correct them.

A   Let me show you around my new apartment.

B.   It's a big apartment.

A.   It's big enough for my family. ~~They're~~ *There* are four bedrooms and two bathrooms. Has each bedroom a large closet. Let me show you my kitchen too.

B.   Oh. It's a new dishwasher in your kitchen.

A.   It's wonderful. You know how I hate to wash dishes.

B.   Is there a microwave oven?

A.   No, there isn't, unfortunately.

B.   Are any washers and dryers for clothes?

A.   Oh, yes. They're in the basement. In the laundry room are five washers and five dryers. I never have to wait.

B.   There are a lot of people in your building?

A.   In my building 30 apartments.

B.   Is a janitor in your building?

A.   Yes. There's a very good janitor. He keeps the building very clean.

B.   I suppose this apartment costs a lot.

A.   Well, yes. The rent is high. But I share the apartment with my cousins.

EXERCISE 19   Find a partner and pretend that one of you is looking for an apartment and the other person is the landlady, landlord, or manager. Ask and answer questions about the apartment, the building, parking, laundry, and rent. Write your conversation. Then read it to the class.

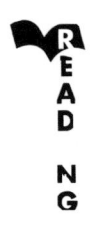

Before you read:

1.   Do most people in your country live in apartments or houses? What about your family?
2.   Do you prefer to live alone, with a roommate, or with your family? Why?

Read the following phone conversation between a student (S) and the manager (M) of a building. Pay special attention to the definite article (*the*), the indefinite articles (*a, an*), and indefinite quantity words *some* and *any*.

CALLING ABOUT AN APARTMENT

S.   Hello? I want to speak with **the** landlord. Is he home?

M.   I'm **the** manager of **the** building. Can I help you?

S.   I need to find **a** new apartment.

M.   Where do you live now?

S.   I live in **a** big apartment on Victoria Avenue. I have **a** roommate, but he's graduating, and I need **a** smaller apartment. Are there **any** small apartments for rent in your building?

M.   There's one.

S.   What floor is it on?

M.   It's on **the** third floor.

S.   Does it have **a** bedroom?

M.   No. It's **a** studio apartment. It has **a** living room and **a** kitchen.

S.   Is **the** living room big?

M.   So-so.

S.   Does **the** kitchen have **a** stove and **a** refrigerator?

M.   Yes. **The** refrigerator is old, but it works well. **The** stove is pretty new.

S.   When can I see **the** apartment?

M.   **The** janitor can show it to you tomorrow at 9 a.m.

4.6   Articles and Quantity Words

We use articles and quantity words to introduce nouns in conversations.

	Indefinite	Definite
Singular	*a, an*	*the*
Plural	*some, any*	*the*

1. We use the indefinite article (*a* or *an*) to bring a singular noun into the conversation for the first time. After this noun becomes part of the conversation, we refer to it with *the* or a pronoun (*it, he, she*).

> My apartment has *a living room*, but *the living room* isn't very big.
> There's *a refrigerator* in the kitchen. *The refrigerator* is old, but *it* works well.
> There's *a manager* in the building. He shows apartments.

2. We introduce a plural noun with *some, any*, a number, or no article. After a plural noun becomes part of the conversation, we refer to it with *the* or the pronoun *they*.

> There are *three closets* in my apartment. *They're* not very big.
> There aren't *any three-bedroom apartments* in the building. There are *some studio apartments*. *They* don't have a bedroom.
> There are *washers and dryers* in my building. *They're* in the basement.

3. We use *the* before a noun if it is the only one.

> May I speak to *the landlord* of the building?
> There is a studio apartment on *the third floor*. (There is only one third floor.)

4. We use *the* before a singular or plural noun to refer to specific people or things in our experience. Two tenants who share the experience of living in the same building might have the following conversation:

> A. I need to talk to *the landlord*. Do you know where he is?
> B. He's in *the basement* with *the janitor*.
> A. I need to talk to him about *the washing machines*. They don't work.
> B. I know. *The tenants* are angry.

EXERCISE 20   These are conversations between two students. Fill in each blank with *the, a, an, some,* or *any.*

Conversation 1

A. Is there _____*a*_____ copy machine in our library?
      <u>Example</u>

B. Yes. There are several copy machines in _____ library.
                                                                          (1)

A. Are _____ copy machines free?
            (2)

B. No. You need to use _____ dime[7] for _____ copy machines.
                                        (3)   (4)

---
[7]A *dime* is a 10-cent coin.

Conversation 2

A. Is there _____ cafeteria at this school?
                    (1)

B. Yes, there is.

A. Where's _____ cafeteria?
                  (2)

B. It's on _____ first floor.
                 (3)

A. Are there _____ snack machines in _____ cafeteria?
                     (4)   (5)

B. Yes, there are.

A. I want to buy _____ soft drink.
                       (6)

B. _____ machine is out of order today.
        (7)

Conversation 3

A. Is there _____ bookstore for this college?
                    (1)

B. Yes, there is.

A. Where is _____ bookstore?
                   (2)

B. It's on Green Street.

A. I need to buy _____ dictionary.
                        (3)

B. Today is _____ holiday. _____ bookstore is closed today.
                   (4)   (5)

EXPANSION ACTIVITIES

DISCUSSIONS   In a small group or with the entire class, discuss the following:

1. How do people rent apartments in your hometown? Is rent high? Is heat usually included in the rent? Does the proprietor usually live in the building?

2. What are some differences between a typical apartment in this city and a typical apartment in your hometown?

SAYINGS

1. The following sayings use the plural form. Discuss the meaning of each saying. Do you have a similar saying in your language?

    A cat has nine lives.
    A picture is worth a thousand words.

2. The following sayings use *there*. Discuss the meaning of each saying. Do you have a similar saying in your language?

    Where there's a will, there's a way.
    Where there's smoke, there's fire.

WRITING

1. Write a description of a room or place that you like very much. (Review prepositions in Lesson One.)

    ### Example

    My favourite place is my living room. There are many pictures on the walls. There's a picture of my grandparents behind the sofa. There are a lot of pictures of my children on the wall next to the sofa.

    There's a TV set in the corner. Under the TV there is a VCR. There's a box of videocassettes next to the VCR....

2. Write a comparison of your apartment in this city and your apartment or house in your hometown.

    ### Example

    There are many differences between my apartment in Vancouver and my apartment in Kiev, Ukraine. In my Kiev apartment, there is a door to every room. In my Vancouver apartment, only the bedrooms have doors. In my Kiev apartment, there is a small window inside each large window. In the winter I can open this small window to get some fresh air. My apartment in Vancouver doesn't have this small window. I have to open the whole window to get air. Sometimes the room becomes too cold....

OUTSIDE ACTIVITIES

1. Bring the section of the newspaper that has apartments for rent. Ask your teacher to help you understand the abbreviations.

2. Do you have a picture of your house, apartment, or apartment building in your country? Bring it to class and tell about it.

SUMMARY OF LESSON FOUR

1. Singular and Plural
   Singular means one. *Plural* means more than one. The plural noun form usually ends with *-s* or *-es*.

   > boy—boys
   > box—boxes
   > story—stories

   (Exceptions: *men, women, people, children, feet, teeth*)

2. There
   Use *there* to introduce a new noun into the conversation. Do not continue to use *there* for another mention of this noun. Use the definite article or a definite pronoun.

   > *There's* an empty apartment in my building. *It's* big. Are you interested in renting *the* empty apartment?
   > *There are* two washing machines in the basement. *They're* out of order now.
   > *There's* a Chinese man on the first floor. *He* doesn't speak much English.
   > *Are there* any parking spaces? Where are *they*? Are *the* parking spaces for students?

3. Articles
   - To make a generalization:
     Singular   *A dog* has good hearing.
     Plural   *Dogs* have good hearing.
                 I like *dogs.*

   - To introduce a new noun into the conversation:
     Singular   I have *a dog.*
     Plural   I have (*some*) *turtles.*
               I don't have (*any*) *birds.*

   - To talk about a previously mentioned noun:
     Singular   I have a dog. *The dog* barks when the mail carrier arrives.
     Plural   I have some turtles. I keep *the turtles* in the bathroom.

   - To talk about specific items or people from our experience:
     Singular   *The janitor* cleans the basement once a week.
     Plural   *The tenants* have to take out their own garbage.

   - To talk about the only one:
     The prime minister lives in Ottawa.

LESSON FOUR TEST/REVIEW

Part 1   Write the plural form for each noun.

box _boxes_   month _____   child _____

card _____   match _____   desk _____

foot _____   shelf _____   key _____

potato _____   radio _____   story _____

woman _____   mouse _____   bus _____

Part 2   Fill in each blank with *there, is, are, it,* or *they* or a combination of more than one of these words.

A. ___*Are there*___ any museums in Toronto?
       Example

B. Yes, _____ a lot of museums in Toronto.
          (1)

A. _____ a natural history museum in Toronto?
    (2)

B. Yes, _____ is.
         (3)

A. Where _____ the natural history museum?
        (4)

B. _____ near downtown.
     (5)

A. _____ any mummies in this museum?
     (6)

mummy

B. Yes, there are. _____ from Egypt.
          (7)

A. _____ a dinosaur in this museum?
    (8)

B. Yes, there is. _____ on the second floor.
         (9)

dinosaur

A. How many floors _____ in this museum?
          (10)

B. _____ four floors and a basement.
     (11)

A. _____ a parking lot near this museum?
     (12)

B. Yes, _____, but _____ not very big.
                (13)   (14)

Part 3   Fill in each blank with *the, a, an, some, any,* or *X* for no article.

A. Do you like your apartment?

B. No, I don't.

A. Why not?

B. There are many reasons. First, I don't like _____*the*_____ janitor. He's impolite.

A. Anything else?

B. I want to get _____ dog.
                      (1)

A. So?

B. It's not permitted. _____ landlord says that _____
                              (2)   (3)
   dogs make a lot of noise.

A. Can you get _____ cat?
                      (4)

B. Yes, but I don't like _____ cats.
                               (5)

A. Is your building quiet?

B. No. There are _____ children in _____ building.
                        (6)   (7)

   When I try to study, I can hear _____ children in the next apartment.
                                          (8)

   They watch TV all the time.

A. You need to find _____ new apartment.
                           (9)

B. I think you're right.

LESSON FIVE

GRAMMAR

Frequency Words with the
  Simple Present Tense
Prepositions of Time

CONTEXT

Three Special Days

Lesson Focus Frequency Words and Prepositions of Time

We use frequency words and prepositions of time with the simple present tense to talk about habits and regular activities or customs. Frequency words, such as *always, usually,* and *never,* tell how often we repeat an activity. Prepositions of time, such as *in, on,* and *at,* tell when the activity takes place.

I *usually* work *on* Saturday.

Before you read:

1. What is your favourite holiday? When is it?
2. Do you celebrate Mother's Day in your country? When?
3. Do people send cards for special occasions?

Read the following article. Pay special attention to the frequency words.

THREE SPECIAL DAYS

Valentine's Day is **always** on February 14. On this day, men **often** give flowers or candy to their wives, partners, or girlfriends. People **sometimes** send cards, called valentines, to friends and relatives. A valentine **usually** has a red heart and a message of love. Young children **usually** have a party at school and exchange cards.

Another special day is St. Patrick's Day. It is **always** on March 17. It is really an Irish holiday, but many Canadians like St. Patrick's Day even if they are not Irish. In Montreal, there is **always** a parade on St. Patrick's Day. People **often** wear green clothes on this day, and **sometimes** bars serve green beer.

Businesses are **never** closed for Valentine's Day or St. Patrick's Day. People **never** take a day off from work for these days. Schools and government offices are **always** open (except if these days fall on a Sunday).

Another special day is Mother's Day. It is **always** in May, but it isn't **always** on the same date. It is **always** on the second Sunday in May. People **usually** buy presents for their mothers or send special cards. Husbands **often** take their wives out to dinner.

5.1 Frequency Words with the Simple Present Tense

The frequency words are listed in order from the most frequent to the least frequent:

Frequency Word	Frequency	Example
Always	100%	Mother's Day is always in May.
Usually		I usually take my mother out to dinner.
Often		People often wear green on St. Patrick's Day.
Sometimes		Bars sometimes serve green beer.
Rarely/Seldom		We rarely give flowers to children.
Never	0%	Businesses are never closed for Valentine's Day.

Language Notes

1. Frequency words come after the verb *be* but before other main verbs.

Businesses are *never* closed for St. Patrick's Day.

People *never* take the day off from work for St. Patrick's Day.

2. The following words can also come at the beginning of a sentence: *usually, often,* and *sometimes.*

Children *usually* send their mothers special cards.
Usually children send their mothers special cards on Mother's Day.

A valentine *often* has a red heart.
Often a valentine has a red heart.

Bars *sometimes* serve green beer on St. Patrick's Day.
Sometimes bars serve green beer on St. Patrick's Day.

EXERCISE I   Fill in each blank with an appropriate frequency word.

EXAMPLE: Husbands _____*often*_____ give flowers or candy to their wives.

1. Valentine's Day is _____ on February 14.

2. People _____ send valentine cards to their friends.

3. A valentine card _____ has a red heart and a message of love.

4. Young children _____ have a Valentine's Day party at school.

5. St. Patrick's Day is _____ on March 17.

6. In Montreal there is _____ a parade on St. Patrick's Day.

7. Businesses are _____ closed for St. Patrick's Day and Valentine's Day.

8. Mother's Day is _____ in May.

9. Mother's Day is _____ on a Saturday in Canada.

10. Husbands _____ take their wives out to dinner for Mother's Day.

EXERCISE 2   Add a verb (phrase) to make a **true** statement about people from your country.

EXAMPLE: **people from my country/often**

People from my country often go to the forest on the weekends to pick mushrooms.

1. people from my country/often

_____

2. people from my country/seldom

_____

3. women from my country/usually

_____

4. women from my country/rarely

_____

5. men from my country/usually

_____

6. men from my country/rarely

_____

EXERCISE 3   Add a frequency word to each sentence to make a **true** statement about yourself. Find a partner, and tell your partner about your habits.

EXAMPLE: **I eat fish.**

I usually eat fish on Fridays.

OR

I rarely eat fish.

OR

Usually I eat fish on Fridays.

1. I cook the meals in my house.
2. I stay home on Sundays.
3. I smoke.
4. I read the newspaper in English.
5. I buy a lottery ticket.
6. I'm tired in class.
7. I use my dictionary to check my spelling.

EXERCISE 4   Add a verb phrase to make a **true** statement about yourself.

> **EXAMPLE: I/never**
>
> *I never go to bed after 11 o'clock.*
> _____
>
> **OR**
>
> *I'm never in a good mood in the morning.*
> _____

1. I/never

   _____

2. I/always/in the morning

   _____

3. I/usually/on Sunday

   _____

4. I/often/on the weekend

   _____

5. I/seldom

   _____

6. I/sometimes/in class

   _____

EXERCISE 5   Use the words given below to write a sentence about your impressions of Canadians. Discuss your answers in a small group or with the entire class.

1. Canadians/rarely

_____

2. Canadians/often

_____

5.2 *Yes/No* Questions with *Ever*

We use *ever* in a *yes/no* question when we want an answer that has a frequency word.

Do/Does	Subject	*Ever*	Main Verb	Complement	Short Answer
Do	you	ever	celebrate	Mother's Day?	Yes, I always do.
Does	your teacher	ever	speak	Chinese in class?	No, he never does.

Be	Subject	*Ever*		Complement	Short Answer
Is	Mother's Day	ever		on a Sunday?	Yes, it always is.
Are	you	ever		bored in class?	No, I never am.

Language Notes

1. In a short answer the frequency word comes between the subject and the verb.

2. The verb after *never* is affirmative. We do not put two negatives together.

   Is Mother's Day ever on a Saturday?
   No, it never *is*.

3. We can also give a short *yes* or *no* answer with just the frequency word.

   Do you *ever* buy your mother a present for
      Mother's Day?
   Yes, *always*.

   Is St. Patrick's Day *ever* on a Sunday?
   Yes, *sometimes*.

EXERCISE 6   Add *ever* to ask these questions. Another student will answer.

> **EXAMPLES: Do you eat in a restaurant?**
>> **A. Do you ever eat in a restaurant?**
>> **B. Yes, I often do.**   OR   **Yes, often.**
>
> **Are you bored in class?**
>> **A. Are you ever bored in class?**
>> **B. No, I never am.**   OR   **No, never.**

1. Do you use public transportation?
2. Do you drink coffee at night?
3. Do you drink tea in the morning?
4. Do you speak English at home?
5. Do you watch TV at night?
6. Do you rent videos?
7. Are you late to class?
8. Do you ask for directions on the street?
9. Are you homesick?
10. Are you lazy on Saturdays?
11. Does it snow in March?

EXERCISE 7   Add *ever* to these questions to ask about Canadians. Another student will answer.

> **EXAMPLES: Do Canadians eat fast food?**
>> **A. Do Canadians ever eat fast food?**
>> **B. Yes, they sometimes do.**
>
> **Are Canadians friendly to you?**
>> **A. Are Canadians ever friendly to you?**
>> **B. Yes, they usually are.**

1. Do Canadians eat with chopsticks?
2. Do Canadians carry cellular phones?
3. Do Canadians say "Have a nice day"?
4. Do Canadians kiss when they meet?
5. Do Canadians shake hands when they meet?
6. Are Canadians impolite to you?
7. Do Canadians pronounce your name incorrectly?
8. Do Canadians ask you what country you're from?
9. Are Canadians curious about your country?

chopsticks

EXERCISE 8   Check (✔) the activities that you usually, often, or always do. Find a partner. Ask "Do you ever … ?" with the words given. Write a sentence about your partner. Tell the class something interesting you learned about your partner.

EXAMPLE: ____✔____ **jog in the morning**

Ana always jogs in the morning in a park near her house. _____

1. _____ ride a bike in the summer

_____

2. _____ visit relatives on Sunday

_____

3. _____ go to sleep before 9 p.m.

_____

4. _____ (women) wear high heels

_____

_____ (men) wear a suit and tie

_____

5. _____ do exercises

_____

6. _____ eat meat

_____

7. _____ drink beer

_____

8. _____ buy the Sunday newspaper

_____

9. _____ put sugar in your coffee

_____

10. _____ take a nap in the afternoon

_____

11. _____ eat in a restaurant

_____

12. _____ use a fax machine

_____

13. _____ bake bread

_____

14. _____ use cologne or perfume

_____

15. _____ take a bubble bath

_____

bubble bath

16. _____   _____

5.3 Frequency Expressions and Questions with *How Often*

We ask a question with *how often* when we want to know the frequency of an activity.

How Often	Do/Does	Subject	Verb	Complement	Answer
How often	do	you	visit	your mother?	Once a week.
How often	does	the mail	come?		Every day.

Language Notes

1. Expressions that show frequency are these:
   every day (week, month, year)
   every other day (week, month, year)
   from time to time
   once in a while

2. Frequency expressions can come at the beginning of a sentence or at the end of a sentence.

   I learn more about Canadians *every day.*
   Every day I learn more about Canadians.

   From time to time, I look up words in my dictionary.
   I look up words in my dictionary *from time to time.*

EXERCISE 9   Ask a question with "How often do you ... ?" and the words given. Another student will answer.

EXAMPLE: **get a haircut**
A. How often do you get a haircut?
B. I get a haircut every other month.

1. come to class
2. shop for groceries
3. visit the dentist
4. call long distance to your country
5. go out to dinner
6. use public transportation.
7. renew your driver's licence
8. buy the newspaper
9. buy a lottery ticket

EXERCISE 10   Find a partner. Interview your partner about one of his or her teachers, friends, or relatives. Ask about this person's usual activities.

EXAMPLE   **A. What's your math teacher's name?**
B. Her name is Kathy Carlson.
A. Does she give a lot of homework?
B. No, she doesn't.
A. What does she usually wear to class?
B. She usually wears a skirt and blouse.
A. Does she ever wear jeans to class?
B. No, she never does.

EXERCISE 11   In a small group or with the entire class, use frequency words to talk about the activities of a famous person (the prime minister, a singer, an actor, etc.).

EXAMPLE: **The prime minister of Canada often meets with leaders of other countries.**

EXERCISE 12   Write a few sentences to complain about a member of your family or another person you know. Use frequency words.

Example: *My sister never helps with the housework.*

She always talks on the phone.

She always leaves dirty dishes in the sink.

EXERCISE 13 Find a partner from another country, if possible. Talk about a special holiday in your country. Ask your partner questions about the date of the holiday, food, clothing, preparations, activities, and so on.

> **Example: A. We celebrate the Lunar New Year.**
> **B. Do you wear special clothes?**
> **A. Yes, we do.**
> **B. What kind of clothes do you wear?**

EXERCISE 14 Editing Practice. Read a student's composition about his or her teacher. Find the mistakes with present tense verbs (including spelling) and frequency words. Add the verb *be* where necessary.

My English teacher is Barbara Nowak. She ~~teachs~~ *teaches* grammar and composition at Mohawk College. She very nice, but she's very strict. She give a lot of homework, and we take a lot of tests. If I pass the test, I very happy. English's hard for me.

Every day, at the beginning of the class, she takes attendance and we hand in our homework. Then she's explains the grammar. We do exercises in the book. The book have a lot of exercises. Most exercises is easy, but some hard. Sometimes we says the answers out loud, but sometimes we write the answers. Sometimes the teacher askes a student to write the answers on the chalkboard.

Everybody like Barbara because she make the class interesting. She brings often songs to class, and we learn the words. Sometimes we watch a movie in class. Always I enjoy her lessons.

After class I sometimes going to her office if I want more help. She very kind and always trys to help me.

Barbara dresses very informally. Sometimes she wear a skirt, but usually she wears jeans. She about 35 years old, but she's looks like a teenager. (In my country, never a teacher wear jeans.)

I very happy with my teacher. She understand the problems of a newcomer because she's also a newcomer. She's comes from Poland, but she speakes English very well. She know it's hard to learn another language.

5.4   Prepositions of Time

We can use prepositions to talk about time.

Preposition	Example

On: days and dates	When do you shop for groceries?
	    On Saturdays.
	When do Canadians celebrate Canada Day?
	    On July 1.

In: months	When do Canadians celebrate Mother's Day? *In* May.
In: years	When will February have 29 days? *In* 2000, 2004, 2008, and so on.

At: specific time of day	What time do you eat lunch?
	    At noon.
	What time does the class start?
	    At eight o'clock.

In the morning
In the afternoon
In the evening
	When do you work?
	    In the morning.
	When do you go to school?
	    In the evening.

At night	When do you call your family? *At* night.
In: seasons	When do we have vacation? *In* the summer.
From ... to: a beginning and ending time	What hours do they work? *From* nine *to* five.

EXERCISE 15   Answer these questions. Use the correct preposition.

1. When do you get up in the morning?
2. What time does your English class begin?
3. What days does your English class meet?
4. When is your birthday?
5. What time do you go to bed?
6. When do Canadians celebrate Labour Day?
7. When do students in your country have vacation?
8. What is the cheapest time to call long distance?
9. What is the most expensive time to call long distance?
10. When is Valentine's Day?
11. When is Mother's Day in Canada?

EXPANSION ACTIVITIES

PROVERB

The following proverb contains a frequency word. Discuss the meaning of this proverb. Do you have a similar proverb in your language?

A watched pot never boils.

WRITING

1. Write about one of your teachers. Describe your teacher and tell about his or her classroom behaviour and activities.

2. Write about a holiday in your country. Tell how people celebrate this holiday, or write about how you celebrate your birthday or another special day.

OUTSIDE ACTIVITY

Ask a Canadian to do Exercise 5. See how your answers compare with a Canadian's answers. Report the Canadian's answers to the class.

SUMMARY OF LESSON FIVE

1. Frequency Words

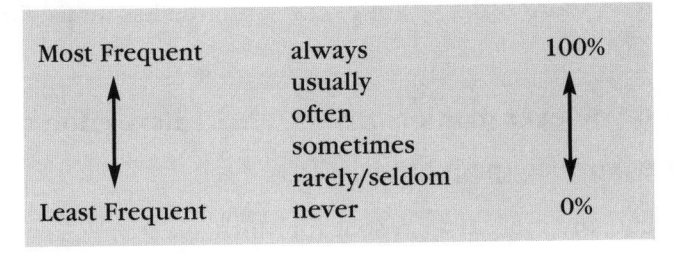

Most Frequent	always	100%
	usually	
	often	
	sometimes	
	rarely/seldom	
Least Frequent	never	0%

2. Frequency Questions

Do you *ever* wear a suit and tie? I seldom do.
Are you *ever* bored in class? Yes, sometimes.
How often do you go to the library? About once a month.

3. Frequency Words with the Simple Present Tense Showing Regular Activities, Habits, and Customs

We *always* have a test at the end of a lesson.
The teacher *usually* arrives on time.
People *often* take their mothers out to dinner on Mother's Day.

4. The Position of Frequency Words

Subject	Frequency Word	Verb
I	usually	walk.
I	sometimes	drive.

Subject	*Be*	Frequency Word	Complement
We	are	usually	late.
She	is	sometimes	early.

Frequency Expression	Subject	Verb	Complement	Frequency Expression
Every day	I	watch	TV.	
	I	watch	TV	every day.
Once in a while,	she	eats	fish.	
	She	eats	fish	once in a while.

5. Review prepositions of time on page 119. Review the simple present tense in Lessons One, Two, and Three.

LESSON FIVE TEST/REVIEW

Part 1   Find the mistakes with frequency words and expressions, and correct them (including mistakes with word order). Not every sentence has a mistake. If the sentence is correct, write **C**.

> **EXAMPLES: Do you ever drink coffee?   No, I never ~~don't~~. ** *do*
>
> **I never eat spaghetti.**   *C*

1. Always I give my mother a present for Mother's Day.

2. I rarely go downtown.

3. They never are on time.

4. It snows seldom in April.

5. Do you ever take the bus? Yes, rarely.

6. Are you ever late to class? Yes, always I am.

7. Do you ever use chopsticks? Yes, I ever do.

8. What often do you go to the library? I go to the library twice a month.

9. I once in a while eat in a restaurant.

10. Every other day she cooks chicken.

Part 2   This is a conversation between two students. Fill in each blank to complete the conversation.

A. Who _____*is*_____ your English teacher?

B. His name _____ David.
                              (1)

A. _____ David?
             (2)

B. Yes. I like him very much.

    A. _____ he wear a suit to class?
                    (3)

B. No, he _____. He always _____ jeans and
                    (4)   (5)

running shoes.

A. _____?
                  (6)

B. He _____ about 60 years old, but he _____ like a young man.
              (7)   (8)

A. _____ your language?
                    (9)

B. No, he doesn't speak German, but he _____ Polish and Russian.
                                              (10)

And English, of course.

A. _____ does your class meet?
              (11)

B. It meets three days a week: Monday, Wednesday, and Friday.

A. My class _____ two days a week: Tuesday and Thursday.
                  (12)

B. Tell me about your English teacher.

A. Her name _____ Dr. Misko. She never _____ jeans to
                    (13)   (14)

class. She _____ wears a dress or suit. She (not) _____
                  (15)   (16)

my language. She only _____ English.
                            (17)

B. Do you like her?

A. Yes, but she _____ a lot of homework and tests.
                      (18)

B. _____ does she give a test?
          (19)

A. Once a week. She gives a test every Friday. I (not) _____ like tests.
                                                              (20)

B. My teacher sometimes teaches us Canadian songs. _____ your
                                                                    (21)

teacher _____ _____ you Canadian songs?
                (22)   (23)

A. No, she never _____ .
                        (24)

B. What book_____ ?
                            (25)

A. My class uses *Grammar in Context.*

B. What _____ ?
                        (26)

A. *Context* means the words that help you understand a new word or idea.

B. How _____ ?
                    (27)

A. C-O-N-T-E-X-T.

Part 3   Fill in the blanks with the correct preposition.

   EXAMPLE: Some people go to church _____*on*_____ Sundays.

   1. We have classes _____ the evening.

   2. Valentine's Day is _____ February.

   3. Valentine's Day is _____ February 14.

   4. A news program begins _____ 6 o'clock.

   5. I watch TV _____ night.

   6. We have vacation _____ the summer.

   7. Many Canadians work _____ nine _____ five o'clock.

   8. I drink coffee _____ the morning.

   9. I study _____ the afternoon.

LESSON SIX

GRAMMAR

Possession
Object Pronouns

CONTEXT

Names
More About Names

Lesson Focus   Possession; Object Pronouns

- Nouns have a possessive form. We add an apostrophe + _s_ to most singular nouns. We add an apostrophe to most plural nouns. Compare the possessive nouns in these sentences.

    Marilyn's house is beautiful.   _My parents'_ car is new.

- We can also use possessive adjectives to show possession. Compare these sentences to the ones above.

    Her house is beautiful.   _Their_ car is new.

- We can use object pronouns to substitute for object nouns.

    Do you live near your _parents_?   Yes, I live near _them_.

Before you read:

1. What is your complete name? What do your friends call you?
2. Do you like your name?

Read the following article. Pay special attention to possessive forms.

NAMES

Canadians usually have three names: a first name, a middle name, and a last name (or sur-name). For example: Barbara Ann Ellis or Edward David Orleans. Some people use an initial when they sign **their** names: Barbara A. Ellis, Edward D. Orleans. Not everyone has a mid-dle name.

Canadian women often change **their** last names when they get married. For example, if Barbara Ellis marries Edward Orleans, her name becomes Barbara Orleans. Not all women follow this custom. Sometimes a woman keeps **her** maiden name[1] and adds **her husband's** name, with or without a hyphen (-): For example, Barbara Ellis-Orleans or Barbara Ellis Orleans. Sometimes a woman does not use her **husband's** name at all. In this case, if the couple has children, they have to decide if **their** children will use their **father's** name, **their mother's** name, or both. A man does not usually change **his** name when he gets married.

In the province of Quebec, a woman's maiden name is **her** legal name whether she gets married or not.

Some people use **their mother's** last name as a middle name: For example, Pierre Elliott Trudeau, Lester Bowles Pearson.[2]

---

[1] A _maiden name_ is a woman's family name before she gets married.

[2] These are the names of two Canadian prime ministers.

6.1   Possessive Form of Nouns

Singular	-_S_ Plural	Irregular Plural
Nouns + '_s_	Nouns + _s_'	Nouns + '_s_
Barbara's husband father's name	parents' house students' desks	children's toys women's dresses

EXAMPLES: I use my *father's* last name.

I don't use my *mother's* last name.

Ted and Mike are *boys'* names.

My *parents'* names are Kathleen and Arthur.

Elizabeth and Sandra are *women's* names.

What are your *children's* names?

Language Notes

1. These irregular plural nouns do not end in -_s_:

men   women   children   people

We use '_s_ to make the possessive form of these plural nouns.

Mary and Susan are *women's* names.

2. We can add '_s_ or just an apostrophe (') to names that end in _s_. Both forms are correct.

What is *Charles's* last name?
or
What is *Charles'* last name?

3. We use the possessive form for people and other living things.

My *brother's* name is Joe.
My *dog's* name is Lucky.

4. For inanimate (non-living) objects, we usually use "the _____ of _____."

The door of the classroom is closed.
Terry Fox College is *the name of my school.*

5. We don't use an article with a possessive noun.

Wrong: Maria's the school has good ESL classes.
Right: Maria's school has good ESL classes.

EXERCISE 1   Fill in each blank with the possessive form of a noun to make a true statement.

EXAMPLE: I use my _____*father's*_____ last name.

1. I use my _____ last name.

2. I don't use my _____ last name.

3. A Canadian married woman often uses her _____ last name.

4. A married woman in my country uses her _____ last name.

5. A Canadian single woman usually uses her _____ last name.

6. A Canadian man rarely uses his _____ last name.

7. Pierre Trudeau uses his _____ maiden name as a middle name.

EXERCISE 2   Some of the following sentences can show possession with *'s* or *'*. Rewrite these sentences. Write "no change" for the others.

> EXAMPLES: **The teacher knows the names of the students.**
>
> *The teacher knows the students' names.*
>
> **The door of the classroom is usually closed.**
>
> *No change.*

1. The teacher always corrects the homework of the students.

_____

2. The name of the textbook is *Grammar in Context*.

_____

3. The job of the teacher is to explain the grammar.

_____

4. What are the names of your parents?

_____

5. The colour of the book is blue.

_____

6. Do you use the last name of your father?

_____

7. What is the name of your dog?

_____

8. The names of my children are Jason and Jessica.

_____

6.2   Possessive Adjectives

We can use possessive adjectives to show possession. Compare the subject
pronouns and the possessive adjectives in the chart.

Subject Pronouns	Possessive Adjectives	Examples
I	my	*I* like *my* name.
you	your	*You*'re a new student. What's *your* name?
he	his	*He* likes *his* name.
she	her	*She* doesn't like *her* name.
it	its	Is *it* your dog? What's *its* name?
we	our	*We* use *our* nicknames.
they	their	*They* are my friends. *Their* last name is Jackson.

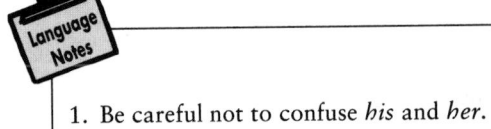
Language
Notes

1. Be careful not to confuse *his* and *her*.

My mother lives in Calgary. *Her* brother lives
  in Edmonton.

My uncle speaks English well. *His* wife is
  Canadian.

2. Be careful not to confuse *his* and *he's*. They
sound similar.

   He's a doctor. *His* wife is a lawyer.

3. Be careful with *your* and *you're*. They sound
the same.

   You're a good teacher. *Your* pronunciation
      is clear.

4. Don't use an article with a possessive
adjective.

   My ~~the~~ brother lives in Fredericton.

   ~~The~~ *M*y brother lives in Hamilton.

5. We can use a possessive adjective and a possessive noun together. We can use two (or more)
possessive nouns together.

   My sister's name is Barbara.
   My sister's husband's name is Edward.

EXERCISE 3   Fill in the blank with the possessive adjective that relates to the subject.

EXAMPLE: I like _____*my*_____ teacher.

1. He loves _____ mother.

2. She loves _____ father.

3. A dog loves _____ master.

4. Many Canadian women change _____ names when they get married.

5. Often a woman keeps _____ maiden name and adds _____ husband's name.

6. Canadian men don't usually change _____ names when they get married.

7. Do you use _____ father's last name?

8. I bring _____ book to class.

9. We use _____ books in class.

10. The teacher brings _____ book to class.

11. Some students do _____ homework in the library.

6.3   Questions with *Whose*

Whose + a noun in a question asks about possession.

Whose Noun	*Do/Does*	Subject	Verb?	Answer
Whose name	do	you	use?	I use my father's last name.
Whose pen	does	she	need?	She needs your pen.

We often use *whose* + a noun in a question with *be* to ask about the owner of an object.

Whose Noun	*Be*	*This/That* *These/Those*	Answer
Whose book	is	that?	It's Bob's book.
Whose glasses	are	those?	They're my glasses.

Language Notes

Don't confuse *whose* with *who's*. They are pronounced the same way.

Whose name do you use? I use my father's last name.
Who's that man over there? He's my brother.

EXERCISE 4 Write a question with *whose* and the words given. Answer with the words in parentheses ( ).

Examples: sister/that (Robert)

Whose sister is that? That's Robert's sister.

children/these (Robert)

Whose children are these? These are Robert's children.

1. office/this (the dean)

   _____

2. offices/those (the teachers)

   _____

3. dictionary/that (the teacher)

   _____

4. books/those (the students)

   _____

5. car/that (my parents)

   _____

6. house/this (my cousins)

_____

7. papers/those (Mr. Ross)

_____

8. diskettes/these (the programmer)

_____

6.4 Possessive Pronouns

Compare the three forms in this table.

Subject Pronouns	Possessive Adjectives	Possessive Pronouns
I	my	mine
you	you	yours
he	his	his
she	her	hers
it	its	—
we	our	ours
they	their	theirs
who	whose	whose

1. A noun never follows a possessive pronoun. Compare the possessive adjective and the possessive pronoun in these sentences.

You don't use your middle initial.   I use *my middle initial.*
You don't use your middle initial.   I use *mine.*

His name is Robert.   *Her name* is Sophie.
His name is Robert.   *Hers* is Sophie.

This is my book.   *Whose book* is that?
This is my book.   *Whose* is that?

2. After a possessive noun, we can omit the noun.

Robert's wife speaks English.   *Roger's wife* doesn't speak English.
Robert's wife speaks English.   *Roger's* doesn't.

EXERCISE 5   In each sentence below, replace the underlined words with a possessive pronoun.

> EXAMPLE: **Your book is new. <u>My book</u> is old.**
>
> **Your book is new. Mine is old.**

1. His name is Charles. <u>Her name</u> is Paula.
2. My car is old. <u>Your car</u> is new.
3. I like my English teacher. Does your brother like <u>his English teacher</u>?
4. I have my dictionary today. Do you have <u>your dictionary</u>?
5. Please let me use your book. I don't have <u>my book</u> today.
6. Whose sweater is this? <u>Whose sweater</u> is that?
7. My parents' apartment is big. <u>Our apartment</u> is small.
8. My teacher comes from Toronto. <u>Paula's teacher</u> comes from Windsor.

EXERCISE 6   Find a partner. Compare yourself to your partner. Compare physical characteristics, clothes, family, home, job, car, etc. Report some interesting facts to the class.

> Example: *My hair is straight. Mark's is curly.*
>
> *His eyes are blue. Mine are brown.*
>
> *My family lives in this city. Mark's family lives in Romania.*

6.5   The Subject and the Object

In a sentence, the subject (S) comes before the verb (V). An object (O) comes after the verb.

```
    S    V    O
   Bob likes Mary.
```

We can use pronouns to take the place of subject and object nouns in a sentence.

```
    S    V    O           S    V    O
   Bob likes Mary because she helps him.
```

R
E   ## Before you read
A
D   1. What are common names in English?
          2. What is a very common first name in your country? What is a very common
N   last name in your country?
G
          Read the following conversation. Pay special attention to object pronouns.

MORE ABOUT NAMES

A. I have many questions about names in English. Can you answer **them** for me?

B. Of course.

A. Tell **me** about your name.

B. My name is William, but my friends call **me** Bill.

A. Why do they call **you** Bill?

B. Bill is a common nickname for William.

A. Is William your first name?

B. Yes, of course.

A. What's your full name?

B. William Michael Henderson.

A. Do you ever use your middle name?

B. I use **it** only for very formal occasions. I sign my name William M. Henderson, Jr. (junior).

A. What does "junior" mean?

B. It means that I have the same name as my father. His name is William Michael Henderson, Sr. (senior).

A. What's your wife's name?

B. Anna Marie Simms-Henderson. I call **her** Annie.

A. Why does she have two last names?

B. Simms is her father's last name, and Henderson is mine. She uses both names with a hyphen (-) between **them**.

A. Do you have any children?

B. Yes. We have a son and a daughter. Our son's name is Richard, but we call **him** Dick. Our daughter's name is Elizabeth, but everybody calls **her** Lizzy.

A. What do your children call **you**?

B. They call **us** Mommy and Daddy, of course.

6.6   Object Pronouns

Compare the subject and object forms of the pronouns.

Subject	Object
I	me
you	you
he	him
she	her
it	it
we	us
you	you
they	them*

*NOTE: We use *them* for plural people and things.

Language Notes

1. We can use an object pronoun to substitute for the object noun.

I have a *middle initial*. I use *it* when I sign my name.
Richard is my son's name. We call *him* Dick.
I have *some questions*. Can you answer *them* for me?

2. An object pronoun can follow a preposition.

I have two last names. I use both *of them*.
My sister has a son. She always talks *about him*.

EXERCISE 7   Fill in each blank. Substitute the underlined words with an object pronoun.

EXAMPLE: I look like <u>my father</u>, but my brother doesn't look like ___*him.*___

1. <u>My brother's</u> name is Stanislaw, but we call _____ Stan.

2. <u>I</u> understand the teacher, and the teacher understands _____.

3. I use <u>my dictionary</u> when I write, but I don't use _____ when I speak.

4. I like <u>this city</u>. Do you like _____?

5. I talk to <u>Canadians</u>, but I don't always understand _____.

6. We listen to <u>the teacher</u>, and we talk to _____.

7. When <u>we</u> make a mistake, the teacher corrects _____.

8. <u>The prime minister</u> has advisors. They help _____ make decisions.

9. <u>You</u> understand me, and I understand _____.

10. <u>My friends</u> sometimes visit me, and I sometimes visit _____.

EXERCISE 8   Two students are talking. Fill in each blank with an appropriate object pronoun.

A. How do you like Ms. Miller, your new English teacher?

B. I like _____*her*_____, but she gives a lot of homework. This week we have

to write a composition, and she says we have to type _____.
                                                                              (1)

May I borrow your typewriter?

A. I never use _____ any more. I have a word processor. You can
                        (2)

come to my house and use _____ , if you like.
                                         (3)

B. But I don't know how.

A. I'll teach _____.
                        (4)

B. It's going to be hard. I don't know anything about computers.

A. Don't worry. You just need to know a few commands. You can learn

_____ in less than an hour.
        (5)

B. I don't want to bother _____.
                                     (6)

A. You're not bothering _____. I'm glad to help _____.
                                  (7)   (8)

Come to my house tomorrow.

B. Can I bring my brother too? You can teach both of _____ at the
                                                                        (9)

same time.

A. Do I know your brother?

B. You sit next to _____ in math class.
                               (10)

A. Do you mean Roberto?

B. Yes. He's my brother.

A. Of course! He looks just like _____ . Sure. Bring _____ .
                                                    (11)   (12)

    I'll be happy to teach both of _____ at the same time.
                                                    (13)

B. Thanks a lot. I'll see _____ tomorrow.
                                    (14)

EXERCISE 9   Fill in each blank with *I, I'm, my, mine,* or *me.*

   EXAMPLE: ___*I'm*___ a foreign student. ___*I*___ come from Japan.

                  ___*My*___ roommate's parents live in Canada, but ___*mine*___

              live in Japan. ___*My*___ parents write to ___*me*___ twice a month.

   1. _____ 20 years old.

   2. _____ parents don't live in Canada.

   3. _____ study at the University of Alberta.

   4. _____ major is engineering.

   5. _____ have a roommate.

   6. _____ roommate's name is Kelly. _____ is Yuki.

   7. _____ roommate helps _____ with my English.

EXERCISE 10   Fill in each blank with *he, he's, his,* or *him.*

   EXAMPLE: I have a good friend. ___*His*___ name is Kim. ___*He's*___ Korean.

                  ___*He*___ lives in Toronto. I like ___*him*___ .

   1. _____ married.

   2. _____ works in an office.

   3. _____ an accountant.

4. _____ cousin helps _____ in _____ business.

5. _____ 37 years old. _____ wife is 35.

6. My wife and _____ wife are friends.

7. My wife is a doctor. _____ is a computer programmer.

EXERCISE 11   Fill in each blank with *she, she's, her,* or *hers.*

> **EXAMPLE: I have a friend. ___Her___ name's Diane. ___She's___ Canadian.**
>
> ___She___ **lives in Halifax. My native language is Vietnamese.**
>
> ___Hers___ **is English.**

1. _____ an interesting person.

2. I like _____ very much.

3. _____ married.

4. _____ has two children.

5. My children go to Richard Bennett School. _____ go to King Academy.

6. _____ a nurse. _____ likes _____ job.

7. _____ husband is a teacher.

EXERCISE 12   Fill in each blank with *they, they're, their, theirs,* or *them.*

> **EXAMPLE: Diane and Richard are my friends. ___They___ live in Halifax.**
>
> ___Their___ **house is beautiful. ___They're___ happy. I see ___them___ on the weekends.**

1. _____ Canadians.

2. _____ both work.

3. _____ have two children.

4. _____ children go to public school.

5. My apartment is small. _____ is big.

6. _____ interested in art.

7. I talk to _____ once a week.

EXERCISE 13 Fill in each blank about a cat. Use *it*, *it's*, or *its*.

> EXAMPLE: ___*It's*___ an independent animal. ___*It*___ always lands on
>
> ___*its*___ feet.

1. _____ likes to eat fish.

2. _____ a small animal.

3. _____ fur is soft.

4. _____ catches mice.

5. _____ claws are sharp.

6. _____ a clean animal.

7. Do you see that cat? Yes, I see _____ .

EXERCISE 14 Fill in each blank with *we*, *we're*, *our*, *ours*, or *us*.

> EXAMPLE: ___*We*___ study English. ___*We're*___ overseas students.
>
> ___*Our*___ teacher is Canadian. He helps ___*us*___ .

1. _____ come from different countries.

2. _____ in class now.

3. _____ classroom is comfortable.

4. The teacher asks _____ a lot of questions.

5. The teacher's textbook has the answers. _____ don't have the answers.

6. _____ interested in English.

EXERCISE 15 Fill in each blank with *you*, *you're*, *your*, or *yours*.

> EXAMPLE: ___*You're*___ a good teacher. Students like ___*you*___ . My other
>
> teacher's name is hard to pronounce. ___*Yours*___ is easy to
>
> pronounce.

1. _____ explain the grammar well.

2. We all understand _____ .

3. Our pronunciation is sometimes hard to understand. _____ is clear.

4. _____ a kind teacher.

5. _____ class is very interesting.

6. _____ have a lot of experience with ESL students.

6.7 Questions About the Subject

Compare these statements and related questions.

Wh- Word	Do/Does	Subject	Verb	Complement
When	does	Sarah she	watches watch	TV. TV?
Where	do	My parents your parents	live live?	in Iran.
Who(m)	does	Your sister she	likes like?	someone.
		Someone Who Someone Who	has has needs needs	my book. my book? help. help?

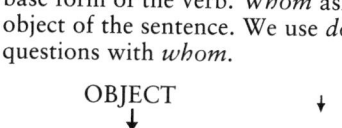

1. Most *wh-* questions use *do* or *does* and the base form of the verb. *Whom* asks about the object of the sentence. We use *do* or *does* in questions with *whom*.

> OBJECT
> ↓   ↓
> I see someone.   *Whom* do you see?

Informally, Canadians often say *who* instead of *whom*.

> *Who* do you see?

2. *Who* asks about the subject of the sentence. We don't use *do* or *does* with questions about the subject.

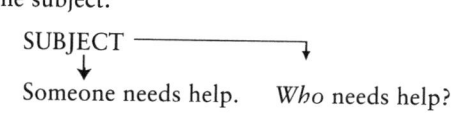

> SUBJECT ──────────┐
> ↓   ↓
> Someone needs help.   *Who* needs help?

3. Notice that we use the *-s* form of the verb to ask a present tense question about the subject. The answer can be singular or plural.

> Who *has* a new car?
> Jake *has* a new car.
> Denis and Marika *have* a new car.

4. We can answer a *who* question with a short answer.

> Who needs help?   I *do*.
> Who knows the answer?   Marta *does*.
> Who is from Egypt?   Soubhi *is*.

EXERCISE 16   Talk about some jobs in your house. Ask another student, "Who _____s in your house?" The other student will answer.

> **EXAMPLES: take out the garbage**
> **A. Who takes out the garbage in your house?**
> **B. My brother does.**
>
> **vacuum the carpet**
> **A. Who vacuums the carpets in your house?**
> **B. Nobody does. We don't have carpets.**

1. cook the meals
2. make your bed
3. pay the bills
4. wash the dishes
5. shop for groceries
6. wash the clothes
7. vacuum the carpet
8. dust the furniture
9. sweep the floor

EXERCISE 17   Fill in each blank with *who, whom, who's,* or *whose.*

> **EXAMPLE:**   ___*Who*___ speaks Japanese? Yoko does.

1. _____ has the textbook? The teacher does.

2. _____ your English teacher? Bob Marks is.

3. There's a dictionary on the floor. _____ dictionary is it?

4. _____ do you see on the weekends? I see my friends.

EXERCISE 18   Circle the correct word to complete this conversation between two students.

> **EXAMPLE:**   (Whose, Who's, Who, Whom) book do you have?

A. (Whose, Who's, Who, Whom) your English teacher?

B. (My, Mine, Me) teacher's name is Charles Flynn.

A. (My, Mine, Me) is Marianne Peters. She's Mr. Flynn's wife.

B. Oh, really? His last name is different from (she, her, hers).

A. Yes. She uses (her, hers, his, he's) father's last name, not her (husband's, husbands', husbands, husband).

B. Do they have children?

A. Yes.

B. (Whose, Who's, Who, Whom) name do they use?

A. (They, They're, Their, Theirs) children use both last names.

B. How do you know so much about (you, you're, your, yours) teacher and (she, she's, her, hers) children?

A. We talk about (we, us, our, ours) names in class. We also talk about Canadian customs. She explains her customs, and we explain (our, ours, us).

B. Mr. Flynn doesn't talk about (her, his, he's, hers) family in class.

A. Do you call (her, his, him, he) "mister"?

B. Of course. (He, He's, His) the teacher. We show respect.

A. But we call Marianne by (her, hers, she) first name. (She, She's, Her) prefers that.

B. I prefer to call (our, us, ours) teachers by (they, they're, their, theirs) last names. That's the way we do it in my country.

A. And in (me, my, mine) too. But (we, we're, us) in Canada now. There's an expression: When in Rome, do as the Romans do.

EXPANSION ACTIVITIES

PROVERBS   The following proverbs use possessive forms. Discuss the meaning of each proverb. Do you have a similar proverb in your language?

The dog's bark is not might, but fright.
A fool and his money are soon parted.

DISCUSSION   Discuss naming customs in your country. Do people have a middle name? Do fathers and sons ever have the same name? Tell about your name. Does it mean something?

OUTSIDE ACTIVITY   Ask a Canadian to tell you about his or her name. Tell the class something interesting you learned from this Canadian.

SUMMARY OF LESSON SIX

1. Pronouns and Possessive Forms

Subject Pronoun	Object Pronoun	Possessive Adjective	Possessive Pronoun
I	me	my	mine
you	you	your	yours
he	him	his	his
she	her	her	hers
it	it	its	—
we	us	our	ours
they	them	their	theirs
who	whom	whose	whose

My name is Rosa.
I come from Argentina.
The teacher helps *me.*
Your country is small. *Mine* is big.

Their names are Ly and Tran.
They come from Vietnam.
The teacher helps *them.*
Your country is big. *Theirs* is small.

Who has a new car?
With *whom* do you live? (Informal: *Who* do you live with?)
Whose book is that?
This is my dictionary. *Whose* is that?

2. Possessive Nouns
   Jack*'s* car is old.
   His parents*'* car is new

   The children*'s* toys are on the floor.
   What's the name *of our textbook*?

3. Words That Sound Alike
   A. *There, their,* and *they're*
      There are three closets in my apartment.
      Where's the dictionary? It's over *there.*
      My sisters live in Poland. *They're* both married.
      My parents have a car, but I never use *their* car.

   B. *He's* and *his* (The pronunciation is similar but not the same.)
      He's my brother. *His* name is Charles.

   C. *Who's* and *whose*
      Who's that man? He's my brother.   *Whose* coat is this? It's my coat.

   D. *It's* and *its*
      I have a turtle. *It's* very old. *Its* name is Shelly.

   E. *Your* and *you're*
      You're a very intelligent person.   I like *your* ideas.

LESSON SIX TEST/REVIEW

Part 1   Choose the correct word to complete these sentences.

> **EXAMPLE:** Most Canadian women change _____*c*_____ names when they get
> married, but not all do.
>
> **a. her   b. hers   c. their   d. theirs**

1. I have two _____ .

    a. sisters   b. sister's   c. sisters'   d. sister

2. _____ names are Lynne and Suzanne.

    a. Their   b. Theirs   c. They're   d. They   e. Hers

3. _____ both married.

    a. Their   b. They're   c. They   d. Them   e. There

4. Lynne uses _____ .

    a. the last name her husband
    b. the last name of his husband
    c. her husband's last name
    d. his husband's last name

5. Suzanne uses _____ father's last name.

    a. we   b. our   c. ours   d. us

6. I have one brother. _____ married.

    a. He's   b. His   c. He   d. Him

7. _____ wife is very nice.

    a. Him   b. Her   c. His   d. He's

8. _____ first name is Sandra.

    a. My   b. mine   c. I'm   d. Me

9. My friends call _____ "Sandy."

    a. me   b. my   c. mine

10. My sister often uses her middle name, but I rarely use _____ .

    a. my   b. mine   c. me   d. I'm

11. You have a dog, but I don't know _____ name.

      a. it   b. it's   c. its

12. _____ your teacher?

      a. Whom   b. Who   c. Whose   d. Who's

13. The teacher's name is on _____.

      a. the door of her office
      b. her office's door
      c. the door her office
      d. her the office's door

14. _____

      a. Who's is that office?
      b. Whose is that office?
      c. Who's office is that?
      d. Whose office is that?

15. Her _____ names are Kevin and Jenny.

      a. childs'   b. children's   c. childrens   d. childrens'

16. _____ has the newspaper?

      a. Whom   b. Whose   c. Who   d. Who's

17. Who _____ more time with the test?

      a. need   b. does need c. needs   d. does needs

Part 2   Two women are talking about names. Fill in each blank with possessive forms and subject and object pronouns. Add apostrophes where necessary.

A. What's your last name?

B. It's Woods.

A. Woods sounds like an English name. But _____*you're*_____ Polish, aren't you?

B. Yes, but Canadians have trouble pronouncing _____ name, so I use
                                                  (1)

    the name "Woods."

A. What's _____ real last name?
                (2)

B. Wodzianicki.

A. My name is hard for Canadians too, but _____ like my name, and I
                                                    (3)
    don't want to change _____ . I'm proud of it.
                              (4)

B. What's _____ last name?
                (5)

A. Lopez Hernandez.

B. Why do _____ have two last names?
                  (6)

A. I come from Argentina. Argentinians have two last names. Argentinians

    use both parents _____ names.
                          (7)

B. What happens when a woman gets married? Does she use _____
                                                                    (8)
    parent _____ names and _____ husband _____
                (9)   (10)   (11)
    name too?

A. No. When a woman gets married, she usually drops _____
                                                            (12)
    mother _____ name. She adds "of" (in Spanish, "de") and _____
                (13)   (14)
    husband _____ name. My sister is married. _____ name is
                (15)   (16)
    Maria Lopez de Castillo. Lopez is _____ father _____ name
                                            (17)   (18)
    and Castillo is her husband _____ name. _____ kids _____
                                      (19)   (20)   (21)
    last name is Castillo Lopez.

B. That's confusing. Everybody in the family has a different last name.

A. It's not confusing for us. You understand your customs, and we understand

    _____ .
        (22)

B. Do your sister _____ kids have English first names?
                        (23)

A. My sister gave _____ Spanish names, but _____ friends gave
    (24)   (25)

    them English names. Her daughter _____ name is Rosa, but _____
                                       (26)   (27)

    friends call her Rose. _____ son _____ name is Eduardo, but
                           (28)   (29)

    _____ friends call _____ Eddie. Ricardo is the youngest one.
    (30)   (31)

    _____ still a baby, but when he goes to school, _____ friends will
    (32)   (33)

    probably call _____ Rick.
                  (34)

LESSON SEVEN

GRAMMAR

Present Continuous Tense

CONTEXT

Student Life
Observations About Canadians

Lesson Focus   Present Continuous Tense

We use the present tense of *be* + verb + *-ing* to form the present continuous tense. We use the present continuous tense to talk about an action in progress now.

We*'re studying* Lesson Seven now.
The teacher *is explaining* the grammar now.

Before you read:

1. What are you studying this term?
2. How many courses are you taking?
3. Besides English, are you learning something new?

Read the following letter. Pay special attention to the present continuous verbs.

STUDENT LIFE

Dear Family,

I'**m writing** you this letter to tell you about my life as a student in Canada. Many new things **are happening**, and I want to tell you all about my life here.

First of all, I'**m living** in a residence with a Canadian roommate, Her name is Carole Kaplan, and she's from Alberta. She'**s majoring** in chemistry. You know, of course, I'**m majoring** in music. Carole and I are very different, but we get along[1] very well. We speak English all the time, and because of her, my English **is improving**. She's not here right now because she'**s studying** for a big test with some friends.

This term I'**m taking** seven courses (22 course hours). It's hard, but I'**m getting** good grades. I'**m learning** a new instrument—the guitar. It's a lot of fun for me and not very difficult. I'**m meeting** a lot of new people in my classes, students from all over the world.

There's one thing I'm not happy about. The food here in the residence cafeteria is not very good. It's greasy, and I'**m gaining** weight. Carole and I **are thinking** about getting an apartment for next term. We want to cook for ourselves and have more freedom.

Thank you for the sweater you sent me. **I'm wearing** it now. It's so cold this week. In fact, it'**s snowing** now. It's so strange to see snow. I'**m looking** out of my window. Children **are playing** in the snow. They'**re making** a snowman and **throwing** snowballs.

---

[1]When people *get along well*, they have a good relationship.

I have to finish this letter now. I**'m writing** a term paper[2] for my music theory class. Please write soon and tell me what **is happening** with all of you.

I hope you are well.

Love,
Reiko

7.1   Present Continuous Tense—Forms

The present continuous tense is: Subject + *be* + verb + *-ing*.

Subject	*Be*	Verb + *-ing*
I	am	studying.
You We They Reiko and Zara	are	reading. learning. practising. writing.
He She It Kim	is	eating. sitting. sleeping. standing.

1. We can make a contraction with subject pronoun and a form of *be*. Most nouns can also contract with *is*.[3]

I'm	working.	*He's*	eating.
You're	reading.	*She's*	sitting.
We're	learning.	*It's*	snowing.
They're	practising.	*Reiko's*	writing.

2. To form the negative, we put *not* after the verb *be*. Compare these sentences.

Reiko *is writing* a letter. She *isn't writing* a composition.

Children *are playing* in the park. They *aren't playing* inside.

---

[2]A term paper is a paper that students write for class. The student researches a topic. It often takes a student a full term (or semester) to produce this paper.

[3]See Lesson One, page 10, for exceptions.

EXERCISE 1   Fill in the missing part of each sentence.

EXAMPLES: I '*m*_____ writing a letter.

I'm look _ing_____ out of my window.

1. My roommate and his friend _____ studying.

2. I'm learn _____ to play the guitar.

3. New things _____ happening.

4. I'm meet _____ a lot of new people.

5. I_____ major_____ in music.

6. My roommate is _____ing in chemistry.

7. I'm_____ a sweater now.

8. Children are _____ing snowballs.

Language Notes

1. We can use the present continuous tense to talk about an action that is in progress now, at this moment.

   Reiko *is writing* a letter to her family now.
   It's *snowing* now.
   Children *are making* a snowman and *throwing** snowballs.

   *NOTE: When the subject is doing two or more things in the present continuous tense, we don't repeat the *be* verb.

2. We can use the present continuous tense to talk about a long-term action that is in progress. (It may not be happening at this exact moment.)

   Reiko and her roommate *are gaining* weight.
   Reiko *is writing* a term paper this term.
   She's *majoring* in chemistry.

3. We can use the present continuous tense to describe a state or condition, using the following verbs: *sit, stand, wear, sleep*.

   She's *wearing* a sweater now.
   She's *sitting* near the window.

EXERCISE 2   Answer the following questions with a complete sentence.

EXAMPLE: **What's Reiko majoring in?**
She's majoring in music.

1. Why's Reiko's English improving?
2. What instrument is she learning to play?
3. How many courses is she taking this term?
4. Why's Reiko unhappy about the food?
5. What are Reiko and her roommate thinking about doing?
6. What's Reiko wearing now?

7.2   Spelling of the *-ing* Form

The chart below shows the spelling of the *-ing* form. Fill in the last examples.

Rule	Verbs	*-ing* Form
Add *-ing* to most verbs.	eat	eat*ing*
	go	go*ing*
	study	study*ing*
	work	*working*
	worry	
For a one-syllable verb that ends in a consonant + vowel + consonant (CVC), double the final consonant and add *-ing*.	p l a n ↓↓↓ CVC	plan*ning*
	s t o p ↓↓↓ CVC	stop*ping*
	s i t ↓↓↓ CVC	sit*ting*
	r u n ↓↓↓ CVC	
	d r a g ↓↓↓ CVC	
Do not double a final *w, x,* or *y*.	show	show*ing*
	mix	mix*ing*
	stay	stay*ing*
	fix	
	pay	
For a two-syllable word that ends in CVC, double the final consonant only if the last syllable is stressed.	refér	refer*ring*
	admít	admit*ting*
	begín	begin*ning*
	occúr	
	prefér	

Rule	Verbs	*-ing* Form
When the last syllable of a two-syllable word is not stressed, do not double the final consonant.[4]	lísten	listen*ing*
	ópen	open*ing*
	óffer	offer*ing*
	vísit	_____
	májor	_____
If the word ends in a consonant + *e*, drop the *e* before adding *-ing*.	live	liv*ing*
	take	tak*ing*
	write	writ*ing*
	drive	_____
	make	_____

EXERCISE 3   Write the *-ing* form of the verb. (Two-syllable words that end in CVC have accent marks to show which syllable is stressed.)

EXAMPLES: **play** ____*playing*____

                 make ____*making*____

1. plan _____

2. ópen _____

3. sit _____

4. begín _____

5. hurry _____

6. háppen _____

7. stay _____

8. grow _____

9. marry _____

10. grab _____

11. write _____

12. fix _____

13. wipe _____

14. carry _____

15. drink _____

16. smoke _____

17. wait _____

18. serve _____

---

[4] There are some exceptions to this rule in Canadian spelling. For example, trável/travelling; cóunsel/counselling; prógram/programming. American spelling follows the rule: traveling, counseling, programing.

EXERCISE 4   Fill in each blank with the present continuous tense of the verb in parentheses ( ). Use correct spelling.

> **EXAMPLE: Reiko** _____*is writing*_____ **a letter.**
>   (write)

1. She's _____ in a residence.
                (live)

2. Reiko and her roommate _____ weight.
                                    (gain)

3. Reiko _____ in chemistry.
            (not/major)

4. Children outside _____ a snowman and _____
                            (make)   (throw)

   snowballs.

5. Reiko _____ a term paper on music history.
            (write)

6. I _____ in the blanks with the correct verb form.
        (fill)

7. My teacher _____ corrections.
                    (make)

8. We _____ the textbook.
            (use)

9. We _____ reading now.
        (not/study)

10. We _____ Exercise 4.
            (finish)

EXERCISE 5   Make a **true** affirmative statement or negative statement about your activities now with the words given.

> **EXAMPLES: wear a watch**
>   **I'm wearing a watch (now).**
>
>   **drink coffee**
>   **I'm not drinking coffee (now).**

1. sit at the back of the room
2. speak my native language
3. pay attention
4. ask questions
5. learn the present continuous tense
6. look out the window
7. look at the chalkboard
8. write a composition
9. use my textbook
10. wear jeans
11. _____
12. _____

EXERCISE 6   Make a **true** affirmative statement or negative statement about yourself with the words given. Talk about a long-term action.

EXAMPLES: **look for a job**
I'm looking for a job.

live in a hotel
I'm not living in a hotel.

1. look for a new apartment
2. learn a lot of English
3. gain weight
4. lose weight
5. spend a lot of money
6. save my money
7. write a term paper
8. try to understand Canadian customs
9. meet Canadians
10. learn how to drive
11. live in a residence
12. _____

7.3   Questions with the Present Continuous Tense

Compare statements and questions with the present continuous tense:

Wh-Word	*Be*	Subject	*Be*	Verb-*ing*	Complement	Short Answer
		Reiko	is	wearing	a sweater.	
	Is	Reiko		wearing	a hat?	No, she isn't.
What	is	Reiko		wearing?		
Why	isn't	Reiko		wearing	a hat?	
		Who	is	wearing	a hat?	
		Children	are	playing.		
	Are	they		playing	inside?	No, they aren't.
Where	are	they		playing?		
Why	aren't	they		playing	inside?	

Language Notes

When the question is "What ... doing?" we usually answer with a different verb. Compare these questions and answers.

What's she *doing*?
What *are* the children *doing*?
What *are* you *doing*?

She's *writing* a letter.
They're *playing* in the snow.
I'm *studying* verbs.

EXERCISE 7   Use the words given to ask a question about what this class is doing now. Another student will answer.

> EXAMPLE: **we/use the textbook now**
> **A. Are we using the textbook now?**
> **B. Yes, we are.**

1. the teacher/wear a sweater
2. the teacher/write on the chalkboard
3. the teacher/erase the chalkboard
4. the teacher/sit at the desk
5. the teacher/take attendance
6. the teacher/explain the grammar
7. the teacher/help the students
8. we/practise the present continuous tense
9. we/practise the past tense
10. we/review Lesson Six
11. we/make mistakes
12. what/the teacher/wear
13. where/the teacher/stand or sit
14. what exercise/we/do
15. what/you/think about
16. what/the teacher/do
17. who/wear/jeans

EXERCISE 8   Ask a question about long-term action with the words given. Another student will answer.

> EXAMPLE: **you/study math this term**
> **A. Are you studying math this term?**
> **B. Yes, I am.**

1. you/plan to buy a car
2. you/study biology this term
3. you/take other courses this term
4. you/look for a new apartment
5. you/look for a job
6. you/learn about Canadian customs
7. your English/improve
8. your vocabulary/grow
9. the teacher/help you
10. the students/make progress
11. you/learn about other students' countries

EXERCISE 9   Ask and answer questions about Reiko's letter.

> EXAMPLE: **Reiko/lose weight**
> **A. Is Reiko losing weight?**
> **B. No, she isn't. She's gaining weight.**

1. Reiko/live in an apartment
2. she/major in art
3. she/study the guitar
4. her roommate/major in chemistry
5. Reiko/wear a new sweater
6. what/Reiko/major in
7. how many courses/Reiko/take
8. _____

EXERCISE 10   Read each sentence. Then ask a *wh-* question about the words in parentheses ( ). Another student will answer.

> **EXAMPLE: We're doing an exercise. (What exercise)**
>   **A. What exercise are we doing?**
>   **B. We're doing Exercise 10.**

1. We're practising a tense. (What tense)
2. We're using a textbook. (What kind of book)
3. You're listening to the teacher. (Why)
4. The teacher's helping the students. (Why)
5. I'm answering a question. (Which question)
6. We're practising questions. (What kind of questions)
7. Your English ability is improving. (Why)
8. Your life is changing. (How)

EXERCISE 11   Read each sentence. Then write a question about the words in parentheses ( ). Write an answer. Refer to Reiko's letter on pages 149 and 150.

> **EXAMPLE: Reiko is writing a letter. (to whom)** OR **(who ... to)**
>   **A. Who is she writing to?** OR **To whom is she writing?**
>   **B. She's writing to her family.**

1. She's learning a new instrument. (what instrument)

    A. _____

    B. _____

2. She's gaining weight. (why)

    A. _____

    B. _____

3. Her roommate is studying. (who ... with) OR (with whom)

    A. _____

    B. _____

4. She's wearing something new. (what)

    A. _____

    B. _____

5. Her English is improving. (why)

    A. _____

    B. _____

6. She's taking courses. (how many courses)

    A. _____

    B. _____

7. She's meeting new students. (what kind)

    A. _____

    B. _____

8. Reiko and Carole are planning to move. (why)

    A. _____

    B. _____

EXERCISE 12   Check (✔) the actions that you are doing right now or at this general point in time. Find a partner and ask if he or she is doing these things. Report some interesting information to the class.

    EXAMPLES: ___✔___ plan to buy a computer
                    Both Raul and I are planning to buy a computer.

               ___✔___ learn to drive a car
                    Maria is learning to drive a car. Her neighbour is teaching her.

1. _____ wear jeans   8. _____ plan to buy a computer

2. _____ hold a pencil   9. _____ take a computer class this term

3. _____ chew gum   10. _____ get tired

4. _____ think about the weekend   11. _____ gain weight

5. _____ live in a residence   12. _____ learn about the history of Canada

6. _____ look for a job   13. _____ learn how to drive

7. _____ plan to take a vacation   14. _____ _____

Before you read:

1. What Canadian behaviour and customs are strange to you?
2. Is your behaviour in Canada different from your behaviour in your country?

Read the following letter. Pay special attention to verbs—simple present and present continuous.

OBSERVATIONS ABOUT CANADIANS

Dear Family,

I**'m sitting** in the school cafeteria now. I**'m writing** this letter between classes. I **see** many examples of strange behaviour and customs around me. You always **ask** me about Canadian customs, so I **think** you probably **want** to know about life in Canada.

I**'m looking** at a young couple at the next table. The young man and women **are touching, holding** hands, and even **kissing**. It looks strange because people never **kiss** in public in our country. At another table, a young man and women **are sitting** with a baby. The man **is feeding** the baby. Men never **feed** the baby in our country. Why **isn't** the woman **feeding** the baby?

Two women **are putting** on makeup. I **think** this is bad public behaviour. They**'re** also **smoking**. In our country women never **smoke** in public. These women **are wearing** shorts. In our country women never **wear** shorts.

A group of students **is listening** to the radio. The music is very loud. Their music **is bothering** other people, but they **don't care**. **I'm sitting** far from them, but I **hear** their music.

A young man **is resting** his feet on another chair. His friend **is eating** a hamburger with his hands. Why **isn't** he **using** a fork and knife?

These kinds of behaviour **look** bad to me. **I'm trying** to understand Canadian customs, but **I'm having** a hard time. I still **think** many of these actions are rude.[5]

Your son,

Ali

 **7.4**   **Contrast of Present Continuous and Simple Present**

Compare the simple present and present continuous tenses.

Simple Present	Present Continuous
He sometimes wears a suit.	He's wearing jeans now.
He doesn't usually wear shorts.	He isn't wearing a belt.
Does he ever wear a hat?	Is he wearing a T-shirt?
Yes, he does.	No, he isn't.
When does he wear a hat?	What is he wearing?
Who wears a hat?	Who is wearing a T-shirt?

---

[5]*Rude* means impolite.

1. We use the simple present tense to talk about a general truth, a habitual activity, or a custom.

   The Queen *lives* in England. (general truth)
   We usually *learn* about Canadian life. (habitual activity)
   Canadians *eat* hamburgers with their hands. (custom)

2. We use the present continuous for an action that is in progress at this moment, or for a longer action that is in progress at this general time.

   Ali *is writing* a letter to his family now. (at this moment)
   He's *looking* at Canadians in the school cafeteria. (at this moment)
   He's *trying* to understand Canadian customs. (at this general time)
   He's *learning* more and more about Canadians all the time. (at this general time)

3. When we use *live* in the simple present, we mean that this is a person's home. In the present continuous, it shows a temporary, short-term residence.

   Ali *is living* in a residence this term.
   His family *lives* in Jordan.

4. "What do you do (for a living)?" asks about your job. "What are you doing?" asks about your activity at this moment.

   What *does* she *do* for a living? She's a nurse.
   What *is* she *doing*? She's *waiting* for the bus.

EXERCISE 13   Look at the pictures. Use the verb in parentheses ( ) to tell what is happening in the picture. Then fill in the blank with the simple present tense to tell about Canadian customs. Then tell about customs in your country.

> **EXAMPLE: These men (hug)** _____*are hugging.*_____
>
> **Canadian men seldom** _____*hug.*_____
>
> *Russian men sometimes hug.*

1. These people (shake) _____ hands.

   Canadians often _____ hands.

   _____

2. These women (walk) _____ arm-in-arm.

   Canadians of the same sex rarely _____ arm-in-arm.

   _____

3. These people (kiss) _____ .

   Canadians sometimes _____ in public.

   _____ in public.

4. This man (feed) _____ his baby.

   Canadian fathers sometimes _____ their babies.

   _____

5. This man (wear) _____ a turban.

   Canadian men never _____ a turban.

   _____

6. These people (bow) _____ .

   Canadians never _____ when they meet.

   _____

7. These people (eat) _____ with their hands.

   Canadians sometimes _____ with their hands.

   _____

8. These women (wear) _____ shorts.

   Canadian women often _____ shorts in the summer.

   _____

EXERCISE 14　Two students meet in the cafeteria and discuss Canadian customs and customs of their country. Fill in each blank with the correct form of the verb in parentheses ( ). Practise the simple or the present continuous.

A. Hi. What ___*are you doing*___ here?
　　　　　　　　(you/do)

B. I _____ lunch. I always _____ lunch at this time.
　　　(1 eat)　　　　　　　　　　　　　　(2 eat)

But I _____ Canadian behaviour and customs.
    (3 also/observe)

A. What do you mean?

B. Well, look at that man over there. He _____ an earring. It looks
                                              (4 wear)

so strange. Only women _____ earrings in my country.
                            (5 wear)

A. It *is* strange. And look at that women. She _____ three earrings
                                                    (6 wear)

in one ear!

B. And she _____ running shoes with a dress. In my country,
                (7 wear)

people only _____ running shoes for sports activities.
                (8 use)

A. Look at that student over there. He _____ a coloured pen to
                                          (9 use)

mark his textbook. In my country, we never _____ in our
                                                (10 write)

textbooks because they _____ to the institution, not to the
                          (11 belong)

students.

B. Many university activities are different here. For example, my English

teacher usually _____ at the desk in class. In my country,
                    (12 sit)

the teacher always _____ in class. And the students always
                        (13 stand)

_____ when the teacher _____ the room.
    (14 stand up)   (15 enter)

A. And university students always _____ English or another foreign
                                        (16 study)

language. Here, not everybody knows another language. My Canadian

roommate _____ seven courses this term, but no foreign language.
                (17 take)

B. By the way, how many classes _____ this term?
                                      (18 you/take)

A. Six. In my country, I usually _____ eight courses a term, but my
                                             (19 take)

advisor here says I can only take six.

B. I have to go now. My girlfriend _____ for me at the library.
                                                (20 wait)

7.5   Nonaction Verbs

We do not usually use the present continuous tense with certain verbs that are
called nonaction verbs. They describe a state or condition, not an action. We use
the simple present, even when we talk about now.

Nonaction Verbs	
believe	own
cost	prefer
have	remember
hear	see
know	seem
like	think
love	understand
need	want

1. Compare the action and nonaction verbs in these sentences.
   Some students *are listening* to the radio. Ali *hears* the music.
   Ali *is looking* at students in the cafeteria. He *sees* some strange behaviour.
   He's *learning* about Canadian customs. He *knows* Canadian customs are different.

2. Some verbs can be used both as action verbs (simple tense or continuous tense) or nonaction verbs
(simple tense only), depending on their meaning. Study *have* and *think*, and the group of sense-perception
verbs in the following tables.

Have

Action	Nonaction

In these idiomatic expressions:
  have difficulty
  have problems/trouble
  have a good/bad/hard time
  have a party
  have breakfast/lunch/dinner
    (have = eat)
  have coffee/a Coke/water
    (have = drink)
  have a baby
 	
Example: He's *having* problems now.
	For possession:
	Example: She *has* a bike.
	
	With an illness:
	  have a backache
	  have a cold
	  have a sore throat
	  have a fever
	  have a stomach ache
	  have a toothache
	  have the flu
	Example: He *has* a cold now.

Think

Action	Nonaction
To think about something. Example: Ali *is thinking* about his family now.	To believe, to have an opinion. Example: Ali *thinks* (that) many Canadian customs are strange. (This is his opinion.)

Sense Perception Verbs:
look, sound, taste, feel, smell

Action	Nonaction
When these verbs describe a state, they are action verbs. Examples: Ali *is looking* at a woman in shorts. She *is smelling* the milk.	When these verbs describe a taste, they are nonaction verbs. Example: Some kinds of Canadian behaviour *look* bad to Ali. The milk *smells* bad.

EXERCISE 15   Fill in each blank with the simple present or the present continuous of the verb in parentheses ( ). Use the simple present for regular activity and with nonaction verbs.

> **EXAMPLES:** Ali _____*wants*_____ to understand Canadian behaviour.
>   (want)
>
> He _____*is looking*_____ at some Canadians in the cafeteria now.
>   (look)

1. Ali _____ a letter now.
     (write)

2. He _____ in the school cafeteria now.
     (sit)

3. He _____ a couple with a baby.
     (see)

4. He often _____ to the cafeteria between classes.
     (go)

5. He _____ to his family once a week.
     (write)

6. He _____ that his family _____ to know about
     (think)   (want)
Canadian customs.

7. He _____ at a young man and woman. They_____.
     (look)   (kiss)

8. This behaviour _____ bad in his country.
     (look)

9. He _____ about Canadian customs now.
     (think)

10. Two women _____ now.
     (smoke)

11. Women in Ali's country never _____ in public.
     (smoke)

12. Canadian customs _____ strange to him.
     (seem)

EXERCISE 16 Read each sentence. Write the negative form of the underlined word, using the word(s) in parentheses ( ).

> EXAMPLES: Ali _____*is looking*_____ at Canadians. (people from his country)
>
> *Ali isn't looking at people from his country.*
>
> He _____*knows*_____ about Arab customs. (Canadian customs)
>
> *He doesn't know about Canadian customs.*

1. The father <u>is feeding</u> the baby. (the mother)

   _____

2. Ali'<u>s sitting</u> in the cafeteria. (in class)

   _____

3. He <u>understands</u> Arab customs. (Canadian customs)

   _____

4. Canadian men and women sometimes <u>kiss</u> in public. (Arab)

   _____

5. Canadians <u>use</u> their hands to eat a hamburger. (to eat spaghetti)

   _____

6. A man <u>is wearing</u> an earring in one ear. (in both ears)

   _____

7. Canadians <u>seem</u> strange to him. (Arabs)

   _____

8. Canadian men <u>like</u> to take care of the baby. (Ali)

   _____

9. Canadian women often <u>wear</u> shorts in the summer. (Muslim women/never)

   _____

EXERCISE 17   Read each sentence. Then write a *yes/no* question about the words in parentheses ( ). Write a short answer.

> **EXAMPLES: Canadian women sometimes wear earrings. (Canadian men/ever)**
>
> *Do Canadian men ever wear an earring? Yes, they do.*
>
> **The women are wearing shorts. (the men)**
>
> *Are the men wearing shorts? No, they aren't.*

1. Ali is writing. (his homework)

2. He's watching people. (Canadian people)

3. He understands Arab customs. (Canadian customs)

4. Canadian men wear shorts in the summer. (Canadian women)

5. The man is eating. (a hot dog)

EXERCISE 18   Read each statement. The write a *wh-* question about the words in parentheses ( ). An answer is not necessary.

> **EXAMPLES: A young man is resting his feet on a chair. (why)**
>
> *Why is he resting his feet on a chair?*
>
> **Ali lives in Canada. (where/his family)**
>
> *Where does his family live?*

1. Ali is writing a letter (to whom) OR (who ... to)

2. Ali wants to know about Canadian customs. (why)

_____

3. Two women are putting on makeup. (where)

_____

4. Canadian men and women touch and kiss in public. (why)

_____

5. Ali writes to his family. (how often)

_____

6. The man isn't using a fork. (why/not)

_____

7. Women don't wear shorts in some countries. (why)

_____

8. Canadians often wear blue jeans. (why)

_____

9. "Custom" means tradition or habit. (what/"behaviour")

_____

EXPANSION ACTIVITIES

DISCUSSION In a small group or with the entire class, discuss behaviour that is strange to you. What Canadian behaviour or customs are not polite in your country?

OUTSIDE ACTIVITY Go to the school cafeteria, student union, or other crowded place. Sit there for a while and look for unusual behaviour. Write down some of the unusual things you see. Report back to the class.

EDITING ADVICE

1. Include *be* with a continuous tense.

   He *is* working now.

2. Use the *-s* form when the subject is *he, she, it*.

   He *has* ~~have~~ a new car. He like*s* to drive.

3. Don't use *be* with a simple present tense verb.

   I ~~'m~~ need a new computer.

4. Use the correct word order in a question.

   Where *are you* ~~you're~~ going?

   Why *don't you* ~~you don't~~ like Toronto?

5. Use *do* or *does* in a simple present tense question.

   Where *does* ~~lives~~ your mother *live*?

6. Don't use the *-s* form after *does*.

   Where does he take~~s~~ the bus?

7. Don't use the present continuous with a nonaction verb.

   She *has* ~~is having~~ her own computer.

NOTE: For Canadian English, include *do* or *does* in negatives and questions with the verb *have*.

BRITISH: I *haven't* a car.

CANADIAN: I *don't have* a car.

BRITISH: *Have you* any money?

CANADIAN: *Do you have* any money?

SUMMARY OF LESSON SEVEN

Uses of Tenses

Simple Present Tense	
General truths	Canadians speak English or French. Many speak both languages. Wheat grows on the prairies.
Regular activity, habit	I always speak English in class. I sometimes eat in the cafeteria.
Customs	Canadians shake hands. Japanese people bow.
Place of origin	Michael comes from Russia. Marek comes from Poland.
With nonaction verbs	She has a new car. I like Canada.
Present Continuous (with action verbs only)	
Now	We're reviewing now. I'm looking at page 171 now.
A long action in progress at this general time	Reiko is learning how to play the guitar.
A descriptive state	She's wearing shorts. He's sitting near the door. The teacher's standing.

LESSON SEVEN TEST/REVIEW

Part 1   Find the mistakes in the following sentences and correct them. Not every sentence has a mistake. Change sentences that use British English to Canadian English. If the sentence is correct, write **C**.

> EXAMPLES: **She's ~~owning~~ a new bike now.**   *owns*
>
> **I'm not studying math this term.**   *C*

1. Why you aren't listening to me?

2. Usually I'm go home after class.

3. I think that he's having trouble with this lesson.

4. She's thinking about her family now.

5. Does she needs help with her homework?

6. What kind of car do you have?

7. Why he's studying now?

8. Has he any children?

9. He's wearing jeans now.

10. My teacher speak English well.

11. I'm speak my native language at home.

12. The baby sleeping now.

13. When begins summer?

14. Where does your family live?

Part 2   This is a conversation between two students, Alicia (A) and Teresa (T), who meet in the school library. Fill in each blank with the simple present or the present continuous of the verb in parentheses ( ).

T.   Hi, Alicia.

A.   Hi, Teresa. What ____*are you doing*____ here?
       (you/do)

T.   I _____ for a book on Canadian geography. What about you?
       (1 look)

A.   I _____ a book. _____ to go for a cup of coffee?
       (2 return)   (3 you/want)

T.   I can't. I _____ for my friend. We _____ on a
            (4 wait)   (5 work)

geography project together, and we _____ to finish it by
                                        (6 need)

next week.

A.   _____ your geography class?
          (7 you/like)

T.   Yes. I especially _____ the teacher, Bob.
                          (8 like)

He's a handsome young man. He's very casual. He always _____
                                                            (9 wear)

jeans and a T-shirt to class. He _____ an earring in one ear.
                                      (10 have)

A.   That _____ very strange to me. I _____ that
              (11 seem)   (12 think)

teachers in Canada are very informal. How _____ the class?
                                              (13 Bob/teach)

By lecturing?

T.   No. We _____ in small groups, and he _____ us
            (14 usually/work)   (15 help)

by walking around the classroom.

A.   _____ hard tests?
          (16 he/give)

No. He _____ in tests.
          (17 not/believe)

A.   Why _____ in tests?
            (18 he/not/believe)

T.   He _____ that students get too nervous during a test.
          (19 think)

He _____ it's better to work on projects. This week we
        (20 say)

_____ on city maps.
    (21 work)

A. That _____ interesting.
　　　　　　(22 sound)

T. Why _____ me so many questions about my teacher?
　　　　　(23 you/ask)

A. I _____ about taking a geography course next term.
　　　(24 think)

T. Bob's very popular. Be sure to register early because his classes always

_____ quickly. Oh. I _____ my friend now.
　　(25 fill)　　　　　　　　　　　　　(26 see)

She _____ towards us. I have to go now.
　　　(27 walk)

A. Good luck on your project.

T. Thanks. Bye.

Part 3　　Fill in each blank with the negative form of the underlined word.

EXAMPLE: Teresa is in the library. She _____isn't_____ at home.

1. Alicia wants to go for a cup of coffee. Teresa _____ to go for a
   cup of coffee.

2. Teresa is looking for a book. Alicia _____ for a book.

3. They are talking about school. They _____ about the news.

4. They have time to talk now. They _____ time for a cup of coffee.

Part 4　　Read each sentence. Then write a *yes/no* question about the words in
parentheses ( ). Write a short answer.

Example: Teresa is looking for a book. (a geography book)

　　　　Is she looking for a geography book? Yes, she is.

1. Bob likes projects. (tests)

_____

2. Alicia has time now. (Teresa)

_____

3. They are talking about their classes. (their teachers)

_____

4. Bob wears jeans to class. (ever/a suit)

_____

Part 5   Read each sentence. Then write a question with the words in parentheses ( ). An answer is not necessary.

> EXAMPLE: **Bob is popular. (Why)**
>
> _Why is he popular?_ _____

1. Bob sounds interesting. (Why)

_____

2. Bob doesn't like tests. (Why)

_____

3. Teresa and her friend are working on a project. (What kind of project)

_____

4. Teresa studies in the library. (How often)

_____

5. Teresa is looking for a book. (What kind)

_____

LESSON EIGHT

GRAMMAR

Future Tenses—*Will* and *Be Going To*
Review and Comparison of Tenses

CONTEXT

Jobs of the Future

Lesson Focus   Future Tenses—*Will* and *Be Going To*

We have two ways of talking about the future. We can either use *will* or *be going to* plus a base form to talk about the future.

> We *will study* the future tense.
> The teacher *is going to explain* the grammar.

Before you read:

1. Are you planning a career? (Or are you planning to change careers?) What field are you interested in?
2. What is a good career in your country?

Read the following article. Pay special attention to the future verbs.

JOBS OF THE FUTURE

Some job opportunities are increasing; others are decreasing. In Canada, jobs in the sciences are growing. As a result, we **will need** more biologists to do medical research. Technology is advancing rapidly, so jobs in high-technology fields **will grow**. The government predicts that we **will need** more computer analysts. However, many workers **will lose** their jobs as a result of high technology. Factory workers and telephone operators **will have** a hard time finding a job because computers and robots can do their jobs.

There **will be** an increase in service jobs. Some opportunities that **are going to increase** are jobs for legal assistants, physical therapists, computer repairers, and travel agents.

Students who are planning their future careers should look at a two-volume government publication called *Job Futures: Occupational Outlooks*. (You can find this book in the reference section of a library. It is also available on the Internet.) This book reports on the job opportunities of the future. It tells what areas **will need** more workers. In areas that are growing, there **will be** a shortage[1] of workers, and it **will not be** difficult to find a job. In areas that are getting smaller, there **are going to be** too many workers and not enough jobs. Another reference book that helps people with their career choice is *The National Occupational Classification Career Handbook*. This book explains how good a job is.

It is important to choose a career that **is going to offer** many jobs in the future.

---

[1]A *shortage* means there isn't enough of something.

8.1   Forms of *Will* and *Be Going To*

There are two ways to form the future tense.

Subject	*Will*	*(Not)*		Verb	Complement
I	will			become	a travel agent.
Some workers	will	not		find	a job.

Subject	*Be*	*(Not)*	*Going to*	Verb	Complement
I	am		going to	study	computer programming.
You	are	not	going to	lose	your job.

Language Notes

1. We use *will* with all persons to form the future tense.

    I *will* find a job.   He *will* find a job.

2. We can make a contraction with the subject pronoun and *will*.

I will	I'll
You will	You'll
He will	He'll
She will	She'll } help you find a job.
It will	It'll
We will	We'll
They will	They'll

3. The negative contraction of *will not* is *won't*.

    Factories *won't* need so many workers.

4. In informal speech, *going to* before another verb often sounds like "gonna." We don't write "gonna." Listen to your teacher's pronunciation of *going to* in the following sentences.

He's *going to* buy a new car. (He's "gonna" buy a new car.)
She's *going to* return in[2] an hour. (She's "gonna" return in an hour.)

Only *going to* before another verb sounds like "gonna."

    He's *going to* study law.

We don't pronounce "gonna" at the end of a sentence.

    Is he eating lunch? No, but he's *going to.*

5. We often shorten *going to go* to *going.*

    He's *going to go* to the bookstore. =
    He's *going* to the bookstore.

6. Compare the present and future with *there.*

There *are* a lot of factory workers today.
There *will be* a lot of service workers in the future.
There *are* five advanced classes this term.
Next term there *are going to be* only four advanced classes.

EXERCISE 1   Fill in each blank with an appropriate verb in the future tense. Use *will*.

    EXAMPLE: Robots _____*will do*_____ **the job of today's workers.**

    1. Many factory workers _____ their jobs.

---

[2]We often use the preposition *in* with the future to mean *after*.

2. If you look at *Job Futures*, you _____ more information about the jobs of the future.

3. In the future, there _____ too many factory workers and not enough jobs.

EXERCISE 2   Fill in each blank with an appropriate verb in the future tense. Use *be going to*.

   EXAMPLE: **Many telephone operators** ____*are going to lose*____ **their jobs.**

   1. Jobs for computer analysts _____ .

   2. Factories _____ more computers and robots in the future.

   3. There _____ more service jobs in the future.

Language Notes

1. We use *will* or *be going to* for predictions.

   Job opportunities *are going to* change.
   We *won't* need so many factory workers.
   Factories *are going to* use computers and robots, not workers.
   There *will* be an increase in service jobs.
   There *isn't going to* be an increase in factory jobs.

2. When we have a plan to do something, we usually use *be going to*.

   My brother *is going to* become a biologist. (He already has this plan.)
   On Saturday, I'm *going (to go) to* the library. I'm *going to* look at *Job Futures*. (I already have this plan.)

EXERCISE 3   Tell if you have plans to do these things or not. Use *be going to*.

   EXAMPLE: **meet a friend after class**
             I'm (not) going to meet a friend after class.

   1. get something to eat after class
   2. watch TV tonight
   3. eat dinner at home tonight
   4. go to the library this week
   5. go shopping for groceries this week
   6. stay home this weekend
   7. take a vacation this year
   8. move (to a different apartment) this year
   9. buy a car this year

EXERCISE 4   Tell if you predict these things will happen or not in this class. Use *will*.

> **EXAMPLE: we/finish this lesson today**
> **We won't finish this lesson today.**

1. the teacher/give a test soon
2. the test/be hard
3. most students/pass the test

4. I/pass the test
5. the teacher/give everyone an A
6. my English/improve

EXERCISE 5   With a partner or in a small group, tell if you predict that these things will happen or not in the next 50 years. Use *will*.

> **EXAMPLE: people/have more free time**
> **I think people won't have more free time. They will spend more time at their jobs and less time with their families.**

1. there/another world war
2. the economy of Canada/get worse
3. people in Canada/have fewer children
4. Canadians/live longer
5. health care/improve
6. cars/use solar energy[3]
7. (add your own prediction) _____

8.2   Questions with *Be Going To* and *Will*

Compare statements and questions with *be going to*:

Wh-Word	*Be*	Subject	*Be*	*Going to*	Verb	Complement	Short Answer
		They	are	going to	leave	soon.	
	Are	they		going to	leave	tomorrow?	No, they aren't.
When	are	they		going to	leave?		
Why	aren't	they		going to	leave	tomorrow?	
		Who	is	going to	leave?		

---

[3]*Solar energy* comes from the sun.

Compare statements and questions with *will*:

Wh-Word	*Will*	Subject	*Will*	Verb	Complement	Short Answer
		She	will	eat	lunch.	
	Will	she		eat	a sandwich?	Yes, she will.
What	will	she		eat	for lunch?	
Why	won't	she		eat	a salad?	
		Who	will	eat	lunch?	

EXERCISE 6   Ask another student a *yes/no* question with *are you going to* about a later time today. Then ask a *wh-* question with the words in parentheses ( ) whenever possible.

> EXAMPLE: **listen to the radio (when)**
> **A. Are you going to listen to the radio tonight?**
> **B. Yes, I am.**
> **A. When are you going to listen to the radio?**
> **B. After dinner.**

1. watch TV (what show)
2. listen to the radio (when)
3. read the newspaper (what newspaper)
4. eat dinner (with whom) OR (who ... with)
5. take a shower (when)
6. go shopping (why)

EXERCISE 7   Ask another student a *yes/no* question with *will* and the words given. Then ask a *wh-* question with the words in parentheses ( ) whenever possible.

> EXAMPLE: **study another English course after this one (which course)**
> **A. Will you study another English course after this one?**
> **B. Yes, I will.**
> **A. Which course will you study?**
> **B. I'll study level 4.**

1. go back to your country (when) (why)
2. study something new (what)
3. look for a job (when)
4. get an A in this course (what grade)
5. transfer to another school (why) (which school)
6. visit other Canadian cities (which cities)
7. buy a computer (why) (what kind)

8.3   Future Tense + Time/*If* Clause[4]

Notice the verb tenses in the following future sentences:

Time Clause (simple present)	Main Clause (future)
When I *find* a job,	I *won't have* so much free time.

If Clause (simple present)	Main Clause (future)
If he *leaves* the country,	he's *going to need* a passport.

Main Clause (future)	Time Clause (present)
I'*ll go* to the university	after I *finish* community college.

Main Clause (future)	*If* Clause (present)
I'*m going to buy* a car	if I *find* a good job.

Language Notes

The above sentences have two clauses. We use the future tense only in the main clause; we use the simple present tense in the time clause/*if* clause.

EXERCISE 8   Complete each statement about the future.

EXAMPLE: When computers replace workers, *many people will become unemployed.*

1. If service jobs increase, _____

2. If students don't prepare themselves for the future, _____

   _____

3. When you go to the library, the librarian _____

   _____ books on jobs.

4. If Canadian workers lose their jobs, _____

   _____

---

[4]A *clause* is a group of words that has a subject and a verb. Some sentences have more than one clause.

EXERCISE 9   Complete each statement.

EXAMPLES: **When this class is over,** *I'll go home.*

When this class is over, *I'm going to get something to eat.*

1. When this term is over, _____

2. When this class is over, _____

3. When I get home today, _____

4. When I graduate (or finish my course at this school), _____

_____

5. When I return to my country/become a citizen, _____

6. When I retire, _____

7. When I speak English better, _____

EXERCISE 10   Complete each statement.

EXAMPLES: **If I drink too much coffee,** *I won't sleep tonight.*

If I drink too much coffee, *I'm going to feel nervous.*

1. If I practise English, _____

2. If I don't study, _____

3. If I don't pay my rent, _____

4. If I pass this course, _____

5. If we have a test next week, _____

6. If the teacher is absent tomorrow, _____

7. If I find a good job, _____

EXERCISE 11   On the first day of class, a teacher is explaining the course to the students. Fill in the blanks to complete this conversation between a teacher (T) and his students (S).

T: In this course, you ____*are going to study*____ English grammar. You
                                    (study)

_____ a few short compositions. Tomorrow, I _____
        (1 write)   (2 give)

you a list of assignments. Do you have any questions about this course?

S: Yes. How many tests _____?
(3 have)

T: You will have 14 tests, one for each lesson in the book. If you're absent from a test, you can make it up.[5] If you don't make it up, _____ an
(4 get)
F on that test.

S: _____ us about the tests ahead of time?
(5 tell)

T: Oh, yes. I'll always tell you about a test a few days before.

S: When _____ the midterm exam?
(6 give)

T: I'm going to give you the midterm exam in March.

S: _____ very hard?
(7 be)

T: If you _____, it won't be hard.
(8 study)

S: What _____ in this course?
(9 study)

T: You'll study verb tenses, count and noncount nouns, and comparison of adjectives.

S: _____ everything in this book?
(10 finish)

T: Yes, I think we'll finish everything.

S: _____?
(11 over)

T: The term will be over[6] in June. Tomorrow I _____ you a
(12 give)
course outline with all this information.

EXERCISE 12   Write a question to ask your teacher about this course.

EXAMPLES: _Will there be a test on this lesson?_ OR _When will you give us the next test?_

_____

_____

[5]If you are absent on the day of the test, the teacher expects you to take it at a later time.
[6]To *be over* means to be finished.

EXERCISE 13   A young women (A) is going to leave her country to go to Canada. Her friend (B) is asking her questions. Fill in each blank to complete this conversation.

A. I'm so happy! I'm going to Canada.

B. When _are you going to leave_ ?

A. I'm going to leave next month.

B. So soon? _____ anything before you _____?
                       (1 buy)   (2 leave)

A. Yes. I'm going to buy warm clothes for the winter. I hear the winter there is very cold.

B. What city _____?
                       (3 be)

A. I'll be in London, Ontario.

B. Where _____?
                       (4 live)

A. I'm going to live in a residence.

B. _____ in Canada?
              (5 work)

A. No, I'm not going to work. I have a scholarship. I'm going to study at the University of Western Ontario.

B. What _____?
                       (6 study)

A. I'm going to study to be a computer analyst.

B. When _____ to our country?
                       (7 return)

A. I _____ when I _____.
              (8 return)   (9 graduate)

B. When _____?
                       (10 you/graduate)

A. In four years.

B. That's a long time! _____?
                                         (11 miss)

A. Of course, I'll miss you.

B. _____?
              (12 write)

A. Of course, I'll write you.

EXERCISE 14   Check (✔) the activities that you plan to do soon. Find a partner. Ask your partner for information about the items he or she checked off. Report something interesting to the class about your partner's plans.

Example: ___✔___ move
   When are you going to move?
   Why are you going to move?
   Are your friends going to help you?
   Are you going to rent a truck?
   Where are you going to move to?

1. _____ get married

2. _____ go back to my country

3. _____ spend a lot of money

4. _____ write a letter

5. _____ buy something (a computer, a VCR, a TV, an answering machine, etc.)

6. _____ go to a party

7. _____ have a job interview

8. _____ transfer to another college or university

9. _____ become a citizen

10. _____ eat in a restaurant

11. _____ _____

EXERCISE 15   A young woman is planning to get married. Her friend is asking her questions about her plans. Fill in each blank to complete this conversation.

A. I'm getting married!

B. That's wonderful! Congratulations. _Are you going to have_ a big wedding?

A. No, we're going to have a small wedding. We _____ about
                                              (1 invite)
   50 people.

B. Where _____ ?
            (2 be)

A. It'll be at St. Peter's Church. We _____ a reception[7] at a
(3 have)

Korean restaurant after the wedding.

B. _____ a wedding dress?
(4 buy)

A. No, I _____ my sister's dress for the wedding. Then, for
(5 use)

the reception, I _____ a traditional Korean dress.
(6 wear)

B. Where _____ after you get married?
(7 live)

A. For a few years, we _____ with Kim's parents. When Kim
(8 live)

_____ university and _____ a job, we
(9 finish)   (10 get)

_____ our own apartment.
(11 get)

B. You're going to live with your in-laws? I can't believe it.

A. In my country, it's common. My in-laws are very nice. I'm sure it

_____ a problem. We _____ children
(12 not/be)   (13 not have)

right away.

B. _____ come here for the wedding?
(14)

A. No, my parents aren't going to come. But a month after the wedding, we

_____ a trip to Korea, and Kim can meet my parents there.
(15 take)

B. _____ married?
(16 get)

A. On May 15. I hope you'll be able to attend. We _____ you
(17 send)

an invitation.

B. I _____ glad to attend.
(18 be)

---

[7]A *reception* is a party.

8.4   Review and Comparison of Tenses

Compare the forms of three verb tenses.

Simple Present	Present Continuous	Future
I work.	I'm working.	I will work. I'm going to work.
I don't work.	I'm not working.	I won't work. I'm not going to work.
Do you work? Yes, I do.	Are you working? Yes, I am.	Will you work? Yes, I will. Are you going to work? Yes, I am.
Where do you work?	Where are you working?	Where will you work? Where are you going to work?
Why don't you work?	Why aren't you working?	Why won't you work? Why aren't you going to work?
Who works?	Who is working?	Who will work? Who is going to work.

EXERCISE 16   Read the following letter. Fill in each blank with the simple present, the present continuous, and the future tenses.

Dear Judy,

Please excuse me for not writing sooner. I rarely _____*have*_____ time to sit
                                                        (have)
and write a letter. My husband _____ on his car now, and the baby
                                        (1 work)
_____. So now I _____ a few free moments.
   (2 sleep)   (3 have)

I _____ a student now. I _____ to Seneca College twice
         (4 be)   (5 go)
a week. The school _____ a few blocks from my house. I usually
                            (6 be)

_____ to school, but sometimes I _____. My mother usually
   (7 walk)   (8 drive)

_____ the baby when I'm in school. This term I _____
   (9 watch)   (10 study)

English and math. Next term I _____ a computer course. I
                                                    (11 take)

_____ knowledge about computers _____ me find a good job.
        (12 think)   (13 help)

    When the term _____ over, we _____ to the U.S. for
                            (14 be)   (15 go)

vacation. We _____ my husband's sister. She _____ in
                    (16 visit)   (17 live)

Philadelphia. We _____ the winter holiday with her family this year. When
                            (18 spend)

we _____ to Philadelphia, I _____ you a postcard.
            (19 get)   (20 send)

    Please write and tell me what is happening in your life.

    Love,

    Barbara

EXERCISE 17   Fill in each blank with the negative form of the underlined verb.

    EXAMPLE: Barbara's a student. She _____*isn't*_____ a teacher.

    1. She's <u>writing</u> a letter now. She _____ a composition.

    2. Her mother sometimes <u>takes</u> care of her baby. Her father _____
       care of her baby.

    3. They<u>'re going to visit</u> her husband's sister. They _____ her
       mother.

    4. She <u>goes</u> to Seneca College. She _____ to Humber College.

    5. Barbara and her husband <u>live</u> in Canada. They _____ in the U.S.

    6. Her family <u>will go</u> to Philadelphia. They _____ to New York.

EXERCISE 18   Read each statement. Then write a *yes/no* question with the words in
parentheses ( ). Write a short answer, based on the letter.

    EXAMPLE: Barbara's studying English. (math)

        Is she studying math? Yes, she is. _____

    1. The baby's sleeping. (her husband)

    _____

2. She sometimes drives to school. (ever/walk to school)

_____

3. She's going to take a computer course next term. (a math class)

_____

4. She'll go to the U.S. (Philadelphia)

_____

5. She's going to send Judy a postcard. (a letter)

_____

6. She sometimes writes letters. (write a letter/now)

_____

7. Her sister-in-law lives in the U.S. (in New York)

_____

EXERCISE 19   Read each statement. Then write a *wh-* question with the words in parentheses ( ). Write an answer, based on the letter.

    EXAMPLE: She goes to college. (Where)

        A. *Where does she go to college?*

        B. *She goes to Seneca College.*

1. Her baby's sleeping. (What/her husband/do)

    A. _____

    B. _____

2. She's taking two courses this term. (What courses)

    A. _____

    B. _____

3. Someone watches her baby. (Who)

    A. _____

    B. _____

4. She's going to take a course next term. (What course)

   A. _____

   B. _____

5. They'll go on vacation for the winter holiday. (Where)

   A. _____

   B. _____

6. Her husband's sister lives in another city. (Where/she)

   A. _____

   B. _____

7. She doesn't usually drive to school. (Why)

   A. _____

   B. _____

EXPANSION ACTIVITIES

PROVERB   The following proverb uses the future tense. Discuss the meaning of the proverb. Do you have a similar proverb in your language?

When the cat's away, the mice will play.

OUTSIDE   1. Go to the library, or get on the Internet. Find *Job Futures:*
ACTIVITIES   *Occupational Outlooks.* Look for a career that interests you. Find out about the future of this career. Report back to the class.

2. Interview a Canadian about his job. What does this person do at his job? Is he worried about the future of his job? Why? Is he going to retire or change jobs soon?

3. Interview a Canadian about her concerns about the future. What is she worried about? Ask her to tell you about her family, standard of living, the economy, the political situation, etc.

EDITING ADVICE

1. Don't use *be* with a future verb.

   I will ~~be~~ go.

2. You need *be* in a future sentence that has no other verb.

   He will _^angry. *be*

   There will _^a party soon. *be*

3. Don't combine *will* and *be going to*.

   He ~~will~~ going to leave. *is*   *Or He will leave.*

4. Don't use the present tense for a future action.

   I'm going home now. I _^see you later. *'ll*

5. Don't use the future tense after *when* or *if.*

   When they ~~will~~ go home, they will watch TV.

6. Use a form of *be* with *going to*.

   He _^going to help me. *is*

7. Use *to* after *going*.

   I'm going _^study on Saturday. *to*

LESSON EIGHT TEST/REVIEW

Part 1   Fill in each blank with the simple present, the present continuous, or the future tense of the verb in parentheses ( ). Use the affirmative form.

EXAMPLES: **We** _____*are filling*_____ **in the blanks now.**
                                (fill)

   I always _____*drink*_____ **coffee in the morning.**
                                   (drink)

1. We always _____ at the end of each lesson.
                        (review)

2. Now we _____ verb tenses.
                    (review)

3. We always _____ English in class.
                        (speak)

4. The students _____ the answers now.
                            (write)

5. I _____ to improve my English.
            (want)

6. Next week we _____ Lesson Nine.
                            (begin)

7. When we _____ this test, we _____ a break.
                    (finish)   (take)

Part 2   Fill in each blank with the negative form of the underlined verb.

EXAMPLE: **It's easy to find a low-paying job. It** _____*isn't*_____ **easy to find a good job.**

1. There <u>will be</u> jobs for computer analysts. There _____ a lot of jobs for factory workers.

2. Factory workers <u>are losing</u> their jobs. Computer repairers _____ their jobs.

3. *Job Futures* <u>explains</u> about the future of many occupations in Canada. It _____ about jobs in other countries.

4. A legal assistant <u>works</u> for a lawyer. A legal assistant _____ without a lawyer.

5. Some job opportunities <u>are growing</u>. Jobs for factory workers
   _____ .

6. The jobs of the future <u>are going to be</u> different. They _____ the
   same as now.

7. A travel agent <u>has</u> an interesting job. A factory worker _____ an
   interesting job.

8. Technology <u>is</u> a growing field. Manufacturing _____ a growing
   field.

Part 3 Read each statement. Write a *yes/no* question with the words in parentheses
( ). Write a short answer.

    EXAMPLES: Doctors make a lot of money. (nurses)

       Do nurses make a lot of money? No, they don't.

    I'm looking for a job. (you)

       Are you looking for a job? Yes, I am.

1. I'm studying to be a doctor. (you)

   _____

2. Medicine is a good career. (factory work)

   _____

3. Factory workers will lose their jobs. (computer analysts)

   _____

4. Computer jobs are increasing. (factory jobs)

   _____

5. I'm going to look for a new job. (you)

   _____

6. We'll need more biologists in the future. (more legal assistants)

   _____

7. Job opportunities are going to change. (educational opportunities)

_____

8. A lawyer needs a university education. (a biologist)

_____

Part 4   Read each statement. Then write a *wh-* question with the words in parentheses
( ). No answer is necessary.

> **EXAMPLES: Jobs will be different in the future. (why/they)**
>
>   *Why will they be different?*_____
>
>   **She works as a pharmacist. (where/she)**
>
>   *Where does she work?*_____

1. I'm looking for a job. (why/you)

_____

2. I'll find a job. (where/you)

_____

3. There won't be any manufacturing jobs. (why)

_____

4. My sister is going to study law. (why/she)

_____

5. The newspaper has job listings. (where/the newspaper)

_____

6. The job listings are in the help-wanted section. (where/the movie listings)

_____

7. I don't have a good job. (why/you)

_____

8. Job opportunities are changing. (why/they)

_____

Part 5   Find the mistakes with future verbs and correct them. Not every sentence has a mistake. If the sentence is correct, write **C**.

EXAMPLES: I w~~ill~~ *am* going to buy a newspaper.

If you're too tired to cook, I'll do it.   *C*

1. When you will write your composition?

2. We will be buy a new car soon.

3. Will you going to eat dinner tonight?

4. When he will leave, he will turn off the light.

5. I going to take a vacation soon.

6. Is he going to use the computer?

7. They're going graduate soon.

8. I will happy when I will know more English.

9. I'm going on vacation. I will going to leave next Friday.

10. I'll write you a letter when I arrive.

11. There will a test soon.

12. I'll help you tomorrow.

LESSON NINE

GRAMMAR

Simple Past Tense

CONTEXT

The Ice Storm of '98
Standard Time
John Lennon

Lesson Focus Simple Past Tense

We use the simple past tense to talk about an action that is completely in the past. It usually refers to a specific time in the past.

Some verbs are regular in the past tense and some are irregular; *be* has two forms in the past—*was* and *were*.

World War II *started* in 1939.   It *ended* in 1945.
Many people *lost* their lives during the war.   It *was* a very tragic time.

We often use a past time expression with the simple past tense.

My brother got a job *last week*.
My parents came to Canada a long time *ago*.[1]

Before you read:

READING

1. Were you ever in the middle of a natural disaster such as a flood, fire, earthquake, hurricane, tornado, or winter storm?
2. Describe one natural disaster that you know about from the newspaper or TV.

Read the following article. Pay special attention to the past forms of *be*.

THE ICE STORM OF '98

The ice storm of January 1998 **was** the worst winter storm of the century for Canadians. For five days there **was** freezing rain throughout southwestern Quebec and into eastern Ontario. Millions of people **were** without power, some for several weeks. Farmers in rural[2] areas **were** unable to keep their animals alive without electricity in the barns, and losses **were** enormous. During the worst of the power failure, 1.46 million households in Quebec had no electricity.

The entire downtown area of Montreal **was** in the dark for several days, shutting down most stores, businesses, and offices. Students **were** unable to go to school. Once the actual storm ended and the sun began to melt the ice, there **was** a danger from ice falling from rooftops. It **wasn't** safe to walk outside, especially where there **were** tall buildings.

---

[1]*Ago* means before now.

[2]*Rural* means relating to the countryside. It often refers to farming. Rural is the opposite of *urban*, which means relating to the city.

Hydro[3] repair crews worked 24 hours a day to restore power. Many hydro workers who volunteered to help **were** from the U.S. Over ten thousand Canadian army troops **were** also on hand to help clear fallen tree branches from the streets. They also worked to remove ice from rooftops and power lines.

For many people, the ice storm **was** a time to share food and warmth. There **was** a special telephone number where people who had electricity could offer shelter to those who **were** without power. Over 250 schools and community centres became shelters for people who **were** without electricity. There **was** even a special shelter for pets such as dogs, cats, and birds. However, many people **were** unwilling to leave their homes. As the days went by and the temperatures dropped to –19° C, police and army officers **were** in every community, convincing people who **were** still without heat to go to a shelter. There **were** over 20 deaths resulting from the ice storm disaster.

After the worst **was** over and power came back to most areas, there **was** a special news broadcast on TV to show people all the news they missed during the actual storm. Most people agree that Ice Storm '98 **was** one of the most difficult experiences of their lives.

9.1   Past Tense of *Be*

The past of *be* uses two forms: *was* and *were*.

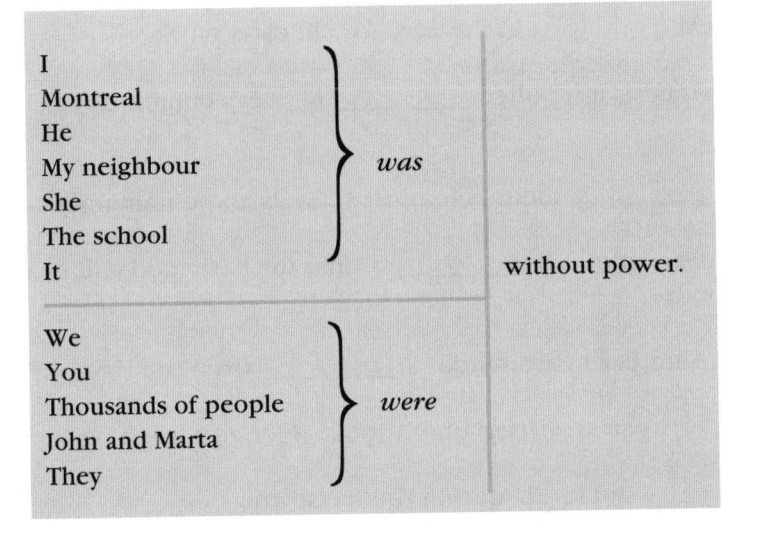

I		
Montreal		
He		
My neighbour	*was*	
She		
The school		
It		without power.
We		
You		
Thousands of people	*were*	
John and Marta		
They		

---

[3]*Hydro* means the public utility that provides electricity. It comes from the Latin word for "water," as much of the electricity in Canada comes from water power.

1. To make a negative statement, put *not* after *was* or *were*.

> I *was not* in a shelter.
> Many people *were not* safe in their homes.

You can make a contraction with *was* or *were* and *not*.

> She *wasn't* safe at home.
> Students *weren't* able to go to school.

2. We use *be* with a classification, a description, a location, a place of origin, with *born*, and with *there*.

Classification:	My cousin was *an ice storm victim.*
Description:	My cousin was *afraid.*
Location:	My cousin was *in Montreal.*
A Place of Origin:	Some volunteer hydro workers were *from the U.S.*
With *Born*:	My daughter was *born in 1974.*
With *There*:	*There* was a special shelter for pets during the ice storm.

EXERCISE I   Fill in each blank with *was* or *were*.

EXAMPLE: Many people _____were_____ afraid during the ice storm of '98.

1. The ice storm of '98 _____ one of the worst natural disasters in Canadian history.

2. Montreal _____ in the dark for almost a week.

3. Army officers and police _____ in every community helping to restore order.

4. There _____ shelters in most schools and community centres.

5. The ice storm of '98 _____ a time to share food and heat with neighbours.

6. Many volunteer hydro workers _____ from the U.S.

7. _____ you surprised that it took so long to bring back power?

8. I _____ in Florida during the ice storm.

9. I _____ very lucky to miss the storm.

10. The damage to trees, houses, and cars _____ very great.

EXERCISE 2   Read each statement. Then write a negative statement with the words in parentheses ( ).

> EXAMPLE: **January was the month of the great ice storm of 1998. (July)**
>
> *July wasn't the month of the great ice storm of 1998.*

1. Canadian army personnel were in Montreal during the ice storm. (U.S. army personnel)

   _____

2. Shelters were safe places for ice storm victims. (homes without power)

   _____

3. Downtown Montreal was without power for several days. (downtown Toronto)

   _____

4. There was freezing rain for five days. (heavy snow)

   _____

5. Office workers were able to stay away from work. (hydro workers)

   _____

6. Most people were afraid during the ice storm. (very few people)

   _____

 **9.2   Questions with *Was/Were***

Compare statements and questions with *was* and *were*.

Wh-Word	*Was/Were*	Subject	*Was/Were*	Complement	Short Answer
		Many people	were	afraid during the ice storm.	
	Were	many people		afraid during the ice storm?	Yes, they were.
Why	were	many people		afraid during the ice storm?	
		My cousin	wasn't	in Montreal.	
Why	wasn't	she		in Montreal?	
		She	was	in Florida.	
		Who	was	in Florida?	

EXERCISE 3   Read each statement. Then write a *yes/no* question with the words in parentheses ( ). Give a short answer.

> **EXAMPLE: January was the month of the great ice storm of 1998. (July)**
>
> *Was July the month of the great ice storm of 1998? No, it wasn't.*

1. Some parts of Quebec and Ontario were without power during the ice storm. (Manitoba and Saskatchewan)

2. The Manitoba flood of 1997 was a huge natural disaster. (the ice storm of 1998)

3. There was freezing rain for five days. (heavy snow)

4. Hydro workers from across Canada were in Quebec to help. (hydro workers from Australia)

5. Businesses were in financial trouble as a result of the ice storm. (farmers)

6. You are in class today. (yesterday)

7. I was interested in the story about the ice storm. (you)

8. I wasn't born in Canada. (you)

EXERCISE 4   With a partner or in a small group, discuss your answers to these questions.

1. Where were you born?
2. Were you happy or sad when you left your country?
3. Who was with you on your trip to Canada?
4. Were you happy or sad when you arrived in Canada?
5. What was your first impression of Canada?
6. Were you tired when you arrived?

7. Who was at the airport to meet you?

8. How was the weather on the day you arrived?

EXERCISE 5   Read each statement. Then write a *wh-* question with the words in parentheses ( ). Answer the question.

EXAMPLE: **Many people were afraid during the ice storm. (why)**

A. *Why were many people afraid during the ice storm?*

B. *They were without heat and light.*

1. Farmers' losses were enormous. (why)

    A. _____

    B. _____

2. The Manitoba flood was in 1997. (when/ice storm in eastern Canada)

    A. _____

    B. _____

3. It wasn't safe to walk in the downtown area after the ice storm. (why)

    A. _____

    B. _____

4. Some of the volunteer hydro crews weren't from Canada. (what nationality)

    A. _____

    B. _____

5. Many households in Quebec were without power. (how many)

    A. _____

    B. _____

6. Some people were not able to stay in their homes during the power failure. (where)

    A. _____

    B. _____

9.3 Simple Past Tense of Regular Verbs

We add *-ed* to the base form to make the simple past tense of regular verbs in affirmative sentences:

Base Form	Past Form
start	started
work	worked
play	played

The past form is the same for all persons.

Subject	Past Form
I	
You	
We	
They	worked.
He	
She	
It	

Before you read:

1. Do you know of any inventions or discoveries by famous people in your country?
2. What time is it in your country right now? Is there a time difference between your hometown and where you live today?

Read the following article. Pay special attention to the past tense verbs.

STANDARD TIME

Before the invention of Standard Time, clocks in every town and city **operated** according to local time. When the sun was exactly overhead, it was noon. In a large country such as Canada, 12 p.m. **varied** considerably from city to city. For example, noon in Toronto was 13 minutes later than in Kingston, and 23 minutes later than in Montreal. Local times were convenient in an agricultural society where most people **lived** and **worked** in one place. But as people **started** to travel across the country by train, their attitude towards time **changed**. Each station stop **required** an adjustment to the railway engineer's watch.   Some people **carried** several watches that **showed** the time for each city along the way. It was very confusing and inefficient!

Sir Sandford Fleming was born in Scotland and **immigrated** to Canada in 1845. He **worked** as a map maker, surveyor, and engineer on several Canadian railways. In 1871, he became the chief engineer for the Canadian Pacific Railway, which **crossed** the entire country. Because he **recognized** the confusion that local times **created** for railway travel, he **proposed** a world map with 24 time zones. Within each time zone, there was a single time, and there was one hour's difference between neighbouring time zones. Many scientists and politicians **resisted** Fleming's plan at first, but in 1884, the International Prime Meridian Conference in Washington, D.C., **approved** Standard Time, which **started** on January 1, 1885. International travel and communications were much more convenient as a result of Sir Sandford Fleming's invention.

Canada has six time zones with a four-and-a-half-hour time difference from coast to coast. For example, if it is 12 noon in Vancouver (Pacific Standard Time), it will be 1 p.m. in Calgary and Edmonton (Mountain Standard Time), 2 p.m. in Regina and Winnipeg (Central Standard Time), 3 p.m. in Toronto, Ottawa, and Montreal (Eastern Standard Time), 4 p.m. in Halifax and Charlottetown (Atlantic Standard Time), and 4:30 p.m. in St. John's, Newfoundland (Newfoundland Standard Time).

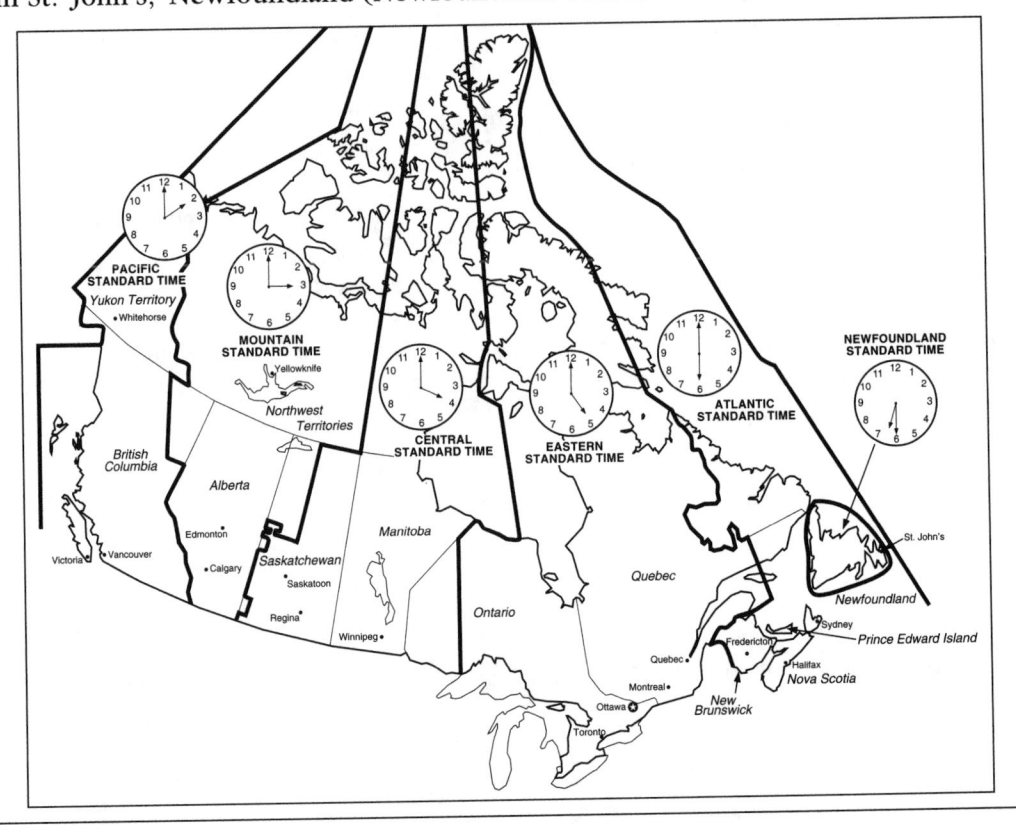

9.4 Spelling and Pronunciation of the Past Tense of Regular Verbs

The past form of regular verb ends in -*ed*. The chart below shows the spelling of the -*ed* form. Fill in the last examples.

Rule	Verbs	-*ed* Form
Add -*ed* to the base form to make the past tense of most regular verbs.	work	work*ed*
	resist	resist*ed*
	cross	*crossed* _____
	start	_____
When the base form ends in *e*, add -*d* only.	change	change*d*
	live	live*d*
	create	_____
	recognize	_____
When the base form ends in a consonant + *y*, change the *y* to *i* and add -*ed*.	carry	carr*ied*
	worry	worr*ied*
	study	_____
	hurry	_____
When the base form ends in a vowel + *y*, do not change the *y*.	destroy	destroy*ed*
	stay	stay*ed*
	play	_____
	enjoy	_____
In a one-syllable word, when the base form ends in consonant-vowel-consonant (CVC), double the final consonant and add -*ed*.	s t o p ↓↓↓ CVC	stop*ped*
	p l u g ↓↓↓ CVC	plug*ged*
	grab	_____
	hug	_____
Exceptions: Do not double final *w* or *x*.	sew	sew*ed*
	fix	fix*ed*
	show	_____
	tax	_____

Rule	Verbs	*-ed* Form
For a two-syllable word, double the final consonant only if the base form ends in consonant-vowel-consonant and the last syllable is stressed.	occúr	occur**red**
	permít	permit**ted**
	refér	_____
	admít	_____
When the last syllable of a two-syllable word is not stressed, do not double the final consonant.[4]	ópen	open**ed**
	háppen	happen**ed**
	lísten	_____
	óffer	_____

The past tense with *-ed* has three pronunciations. Listen to your teacher's pronunciation.

1. We pronounce a/**t**/ if the base form ends in a voiceless sound: /p, k, f, θ, s, š, č/.

jumped—jumped	kissed—kissed
cook—cooked	wash—washed
cough—coughed	watch—watched

2. We pronounce an extra syllable /**Id**/ if the base form ends in a /t/ or /d/ sound.

wait—waited	add—added
hate—hated	need—needed
want—wanted	decide—decided

3. We pronounce a /**d**/ if the base form ends in a voiced sound.

rub—rubbed	name—named
drag—dragged	learn—learned
love—loved	bang—banged
bathe—bathed	call—called
use—used	fear—feared
massage—massaged	free—freed
charge—charged	glue—glued

EXERCISE 6   Write the past tense of these regular verbs. (Accent marks show you where a word is stressed.)

EXAMPLES: learn ____*learned*____   **clap** ____*clapped*____

love ____*loved*____   **listen** ____*listened*____

1. play _____   4. want _____

2. study _____   5. like _____

3. decide _____   6. show _____

_____

[4]Although this rule is true for American English, there are several exceptions to it in Canadian English; for example, trável, travelled; prógram, programmed; lábel, labelled. See footnote 4 on page 153.

7. look _____   14. start _____

8. stop _____   15. follow _____

9. háppen _____   16. prefér _____

10. carry _____   17. like _____

11. enjoy _____   18. mix _____

12. drag _____   19. admít _____

13. drop _____   20. devélop _____

EXERCISE 7   Fill in each blank with the past tense of the verb in parentheses ( ). Use correct spelling.

> **EXAMPLE: Sir Sandford Fleming** _invented_ **Standard Time over one hundred**
>   (invent)
> **years ago.**

1. Sir Sandford Fleming _____ for the Canadian Pacific Railway.
                                    (work)

2. Local times _____ considerably from city to city across Canada.
                            (vary)

3. Many travellers _____ several watches.
                                (carry)

4. Local times _____ confusion for travellers.
                            (create)

5. Each station stop _____ an adjustment to the railway engineer's watch.
                                (require)

6. Sir Sandford Fleming _____ a world map with 24 time zones.
                                    (propose)

7. Many scientists _____ Fleming's ideas at first.
                                (resist)

8. In 1884, the International Prime Meridian Conference _____ Standard
   (accept)

   Time.

9. Standard Time _____ the way people thought about time.
   (change)

EXERCISE 8   Fill in each blank with the correct form of the verb in parentheses ( ). Use
correct spelling. Read your answers out loud. Use correct pronunciation.

    EXAMPLE: The ice storm of '98 _destroyed_ **many trees and power lines.**
                                                                        (destroy)

1. For five days, freezing rain _____ trees and power lines with ice.
   (cover)

2. Falling branches of trees _____ hydro workers from repairing power
   (prevent)
   lines.

3. The government _____ schools and businesses to close[5] until the
   (ask)
   crisis was over.

4. Thousands of farm animals _____ from the cold.
   (die)

5. Canadian soldiers _____ restore order after the ice storm.
   (help)

6. Many hydro workers _____ from the U.S. to help in the crisis.
   (travel)

7. Many people without power _____ to leave their homes.
   (refuse)

8. Shelters _____ warmth and food to thousands of ice storm victims.
   (provide)

9. When the sun _____ the ice, there was danger from falling ice "bombs."
   (melt)

10. Sometimes the police _____ people from their homes to shelters.
    (transport)

_____

[5]A verb after _to_ does not use the past form.

9.5   Simple Past Tense of Irregular Verbs

An irregular verb is a verb that doesn't use the -*ed* ending for the past tense. Here is a list of common irregular verbs, grouped according to the type of change. For an alphabetical list of irregular verbs, see Appendix D.

Verbs with No Change	
bet	hurt
cost	let
cut	put
fit	quit
hit	shut

Verbs Ending in -*d* That Have -*t* for the Past Form	
bend—bent	send—sent
build—built	spend—spent
lend—lent	

Verbs with a Vowel Change	
feel—felt	bring—brought
keep—kept	buy—bought
leave—left	catch—caught
lose—lost	fight—fought
mean—meant[6]	teach—taught
sleep—slept	think—thought
break—broke	begin—began
choose—chose	drink—drank
freeze—froze	ring—rang
steal—stole	sing—sang
speak—spoke	sink—sank
wake—woke	swim—swam
dig—dug	drive—drove
hang—hung	ride—rode
win—won	shine—shone
	write—wrote

[6]There is a change in the vowel sound. *Meant* rhymes with *sent*.

Verbs with a Vowel Change *(continued)*	
blow—blew draw—drew fly—flew grow—grew know—knew throw—threw	bleed—bled feed—fed lead—led meet—met read—read[7]
sell—sold tell—told	find—found wind—wound
shake—shook take—took mistake—mistook	lay—laid pay—paid say—said[8]
tear—tore wear—wore	bite—bit hide—hid light—lit
become—became come—came eat—ate	fall—fell hold—held
give—gave forgive—forgave lie—lay	run—ran sit—sat see—saw
forget—forgot get—got shoot—shot	stand—stood understand—understood
	hear—heard

Miscellaneous Changes	
be—was/were do—did go—went	have—had make—made

---

[7]The past form of *read* is pronounced like the colour *red*.

[8]*Said* rhymes with *bed*.

R
E   **Before you read:**
A
D   1. What kind of music do you like?
        2. What kind of music is popular in your country?

N   Read the following article. Pay special attention to the past tense of regular and
G   irregular verbs.

The Beatles

← John Lennon

JOHN LENNON

John Lennon **was** a talented musician. He **became** rich and famous. However, when he **was** young, it **seemed** that he was going to be a failure.

John **was** born in Liverpool, England, in 1940 to a working-class family. Soon after he **was** born, his father **abandoned** him. His mother **sent** John to live with her sister when she **left** with a new boyfriend. John **became** the leader of a street gang. He **spent** a lot of time on the streets, where he **stole** things. A teacher once **wrote** on his report card that he **had** no future.

John's mother **lived** not far from him, and she **visited** him from time to time. When John **was** 13, his mother **brought** him a guitar when she **came** to see him. She **taught** him how to play a few chords. John **got** together with some classmates and **formed** a rock group. The group **changed** names over the years, but it eventually **became** known as the Beatles

John and the Beatles **became** popular all over the world in the 1960s. They **were** the most popular musical group for more than a decade. They **got** rich from all the records they sold.

The Beatles greatly **influenced** the music and popular culture of the 1960s and 1970s. They **had** long hair, and young men **started** to grow their hair long to imitate the Beatles.

In 1968, Lennon **married** a Japanese woman, Yoko Ono. In 1970, the Beatles **broke** up, and he **began** to perform with his wife.

On December 8, 1980, Mark Chapman, an unemployed amateur guitarist, **went** to the New York building where Lennon **lived** with his wife and young son. Chapman **waited** outside Lennon's building. When Lennon **came** out, Chapman **fired** several shots and **killed** Lennon. This **was** a great tragedy for Beatles fans. Lennon's fans all over the world **cried** while radio stations **played** music by Lennon and the Beatles.

EXERCISE 9   Fill in each blank with the past form of the verb in parentheses ( ).

EXAMPLE: **John Lennon** _____*was*_____ **born in England.**
                                          (be)

1. His parents _____ him when he was young.
                        (leave)

2. He _____ to live with an aunt.
           (go)

3. He _____ a street gang.
          (lead)

4. He _____ things when he was a child.
          (steal)

5. A teacher _____ on his report card that he _____
                     (write)   (have)
    no future.

6. John's mother _____ to visit him.
                         (come)

7. She _____ him a guitar.
             (bring)

8. John Lennon and the Beatles _____ popular all over the world.
                                          (become)

9. Many young men _____ their hair to imitate the Beatles.
                            (grow)

10. Lennon _____ and _____ Yoko Ono.
                 (meet)   (marry)

11. The Beatles _____ up.
                       (break)

12. Mark Chapman _____ and _____ Lennon.
                          (shoot)   (kill)

13. Lennon's fans _____ when they _____ of his death.
                          (cry)   (hear)

9.6 Negative Forms of Past Tense Verbs

In a negative statement, we use *didn't* + the base form for all verbs, regular or irregular (except *be*). We don't use the past form.

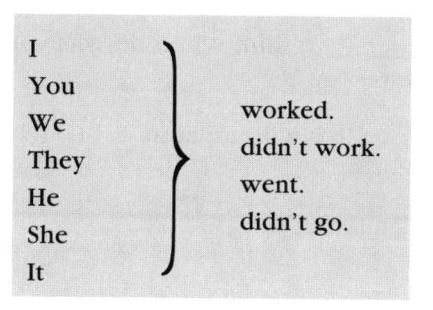

I
You
We
They
He
She
It
}
worked.
didn't work.
went.
didn't go.

Language Notes

Compare the affirmative and negative sentences below:

The ice storm *hit* Quebec and eastern Ontario.
It *didn't hit* the western part of Canada.

John Lennon *lived* with his aunt.
He *didn't live* with his mother.

John Lennon's mother *came* to visit him.
His father *didn't come* to visit him.

He *sang* rock music.
He *didn't sing* opera.

EXERCISE 10 Fill in each blank with the negative form of the underlined verb.

EXAMPLE: **John Lennon played the guitar. He** ___*didn't play*___ **the violin.**

1. John Lennon <u>lived</u> with his aunt. He _____ with his mother.

2. His mother <u>left</u> with her boyfriend. She _____ with her husband.

3. John <u>spent</u> a lot of time on the streets. He _____ a lot of time in the library.

4. John <u>was</u> a bad student. He _____ a good student.

5. His teacher <u>said</u> bad things about him. She _____ good things.

6. His mother <u>gave</u> him a guitar. His aunt _____ him a guitar.

7. His mother <u>taught</u> him to play a few chords. His aunt _____ him.

8. John <u>became</u> a famous musician. He _____ a criminal.

9. He <u>played</u> with three other musicians. He _____ alone.

10. The Beatles <u>were</u> popular all over the world. They _____ popular just in England.

11. In the 1970s, John Lennon <u>performed</u> with his wife. He _____ with the Beatles anymore.

12. Mark Chapman <u>went</u> to New York. He _____ to London.

13. He <u>waited</u> outside Lennon's apartment building. He _____ in the apartment.

14. He <u>had</u> a gun. He _____ a knife.

15. He <u>killed</u> Lennon. He _____ Lennon's wife.

EXERCISE 11   Check (✔) what was true for you before you came to Canada. Find a partner and compare your list to your partner's list. Report to the class something interesting you learned about your partner.

> EXAMPLES: **Marek studied English with a private teacher for three months before he came to Canada.**
>
> **Tran went to Thailand before he came to Canada. He stayed there for one week.**

1. _____ change my money for dollars

2. _____ get a passport

3. _____ apply for a visa

4. _____ study English

5. _____ sell my furniture, my house, etc.

6. _____ say goodbye to my friends

7. _____ buy an English dictionary

8. _____ have a clear idea about life in Canada

9. _____ be afraid about the future

10. _____ go to another country

11. _____ understand English well

12. _____ know a lot of Canadians

13. _____ _____

14. _____ _____

EXERCISE 12   Tell if you did or didn't do these things in the past week. Add some information to tell more about each item.

> EXAMPLE: **go to the movies**
>
> **I went to the movies last weekend with my brother. We saw a great movie.**
>
> OR
>
> **I didn't go to the movies this week. I didn't have time.**

1. receive a letter
2. write a letter
3. go to the library
4. do my laundry
5. buy groceries
6. make a long-distance phone call

7. buy a lottery ticket
8. work hard
9. look for job
10. rent a video
11. _____
12. _____

EXERCISE 13   Tell if these things happened or didn't happen after you arrived in Canada. If affirmative, tell when.

> EXAMPLE: **find an apartment**
>
> **I found an apartment two weeks after I arrived in Canada.**
>
> OR
>
> **I didn't find an apartment right away. I lived with my cousins for two months.**

1. find a job
2. register for English classes
3. rent an apartment
4. buy a car

5. get a social insurance card.
6. get a driver's licence
7. visit a museum
8. _____

9.7 Questions with Past Tense Verbs

Compare statements and questions with the simple past tense:

Wh- Word	Did	Subject	Verb	Complement
		The ice storm	ended.	
	Did	the ice storm	end	after five days?
When	did	the ice storm	end?	
		The ice storm	didn't destroy	every tree.
Why	didn't	the ice storm	destroy	every tree?
		Lennon's mother	brought	him an instrument.
	Did	she	bring	him a guitar?
Why	did	she	bring	him a guitar?
		Someone	killed	Lennon.
	Who		killed	Lennon?
		Several people	died	in the ice storm.
	How many people		died	in the ice storm?

Language Notes

1. In all *yes/no* questions, use *did* + the base form for all verbs, regular or irregular (except *be*). Use *did* in a short answer.

   John Lennon *married* Yoko Ono.
   Did he *marry* an American woman? No, he *didn't*.

   John Lennon *became* popular in England.
   Did he *become* popular in the rest of the world? Yes, he *did*.

2. Most *wh-* questions use *did* + the base form.

   The ice storm *hit* in January '98.
   Where *did* the ice storm *hit*?

   The army *came* to Montreal.
   When *did* the army *come* to Montreal?

   The hydro repair crews *didn't restore* power immediately.
   Why *didn't* the hydro repair crews *restore* power immediately?

   Lennon *played* the guitar.
   With whom *did* he *play* the guitar? (formal word order)
   Who *did* he *play* the guitar with? (informal word order)

3. When we ask a *wh-* question about the subject, we use the past form, not the base form.

   Subject Questions:

Who		
What	+ Past Form ... ?	
How Many		
Which noun		

   Something *caused* the power failures.
   What *caused* the power failures?

   Someone *gave* Lennon a guitar.
   Who *gave* Lennon a guitar?
   Which relative *gave* Lennon a guitar?

EXERCISE 14   Use these questions to interview a partner about the time when he or she lived in his or her country. Report some interesting information about your partner to the class.

    1. Did you study English in your country?
    2. Did you live in a big city?
    3. Did you live with your parents?
    4. Did you know a lot about Canada?
    5. Were you happy with the political situation?
    6. Did you finish high school?
    7. Did you own a car?
    8. Did you have a job?
    9. Did you think about your future?
   10. Were you happy?
   11. _____

EXERCISE 15   Read each statement. Then write a *yes/no* question with the words in parentheses ( ). Write a short answer. The first word of the answer is given.

   EXAMPLE: John Lennon's father abandoned him. (his mother) (yes)

   Did his mother abandon him? Yes, she did.

   1. John Lennon was born in England. (London) (no)

   _____

   2. He stole things. (a guitar) (no)

   _____

   3. His mother visited him. (his father) (no)

   _____

   4. Lennon played music with the Beatles. (with his wife) (yes)

   _____

   5. The Beatles were born in England. (John's wife) (no)

   _____

   6. The Beatles had long hair in the 1960s. (many young men) (yes)

   _____

7. Lennon performed with the Beatles. (with his wife) (yes)

_____

8. Lennon lived in New York. (in an apartment) (yes)

_____

9. Mark Chapman went to Lennon's building. (inside the building) (no)

_____

10. Chapman killed Lennon. (Lennon's wife) (no)

_____

EXERCISE 16   Fill in each blank to complete the question and answer.

   EXAMPLE: What did the ice storm of '98 destroy?

   It _____destroyed_____ trees and power lines.

1. When did the ice storm hit Montreal?

   It _____ Montreal in January 1998.

2. How long did the ice storm _____?

   It lasted for five days.

3. How _____ people keep warm during the power failures?

   They _____ warm by staying with friends or going to shelters.

4. Who _____ clear up the damage and restored order?

   The Canadian army helped clear up the damage and restored order.

5. How many people _____ as a result of the ice storm?

   Over 20 people died as a result of the ice storm.

6. Where _____?

   Sir Sandford Fleming _____ born in Scotland.

7. When _____?

   He came to Canada in 1845.

8. What _____ the International Prime Meridian Conference approve in 1884?

   They _____ Standard Time in 1884.

9. Who _____ Standard Time?

   Sir Sandford Fleming invented Standard Time.

10. What railway company _____ ?

    Fleming worked for the Canadian Pacific Railway.

EXERCISE 17   Read each statement. Then write a question with the words in parentheses
( ). Answer with a complete sentence. (The answers are at the bottom of page 222.)

EXAMPLE: **John Lennon wasn't born in Canada. (Where)**

   Where was he born? _____

   He was born in England. _____

1. John Lennon was born in England. (When)

   A. _____

   B. _____

2. His father abandoned him. (When)

   A. _____

   B. _____

3. John didn't live with his mother. (Who ... with) OR (With whom ...)

   A. _____

   B. _____

4. His mother went away. (Who ... with) OR (With whom ...)

   A. _____

   B. _____

5. A teacher wrote something on his report card. (What)

   A. _____

   B. _____

6. His mother brought him a present. (What)

   A. _____

   B. _____

7. Somebody taught him to play the guitar. (Who)

   A. _____

   B. _____

8. John formed a group. (What kind of)

   A. _____

   B. _____

9. John Lennon became popular. (Where)

   A. _____

   B. _____

10. John married Yoko. (When)

   A. _____

   B. _____

11. The Beatles broke up. (When)

   A. _____

   B. _____

12. John began to perform with his wife. (When)

   A. _____

   B. _____

13. John lived with his wife and son. (Where)

   A. _____

   B. _____

14. Somebody went to John's building on December 8, 1980. (Who)

   A. _____

   B. _____

15. His fans cried. (Why)

   A. _____

   B. _____

EXERCISE 18   Check (✔) and read aloud a statement that is **true** for you. Another student will ask a question with the words in parentheses ( ). Answer the question.

       EXAMPLES: ___✔___ **I did my homework. (where)**
                           Where did you do your homework?
                           I did my homework in the library.

                  ___✔___ **I got married. (when)**
                  When did you get married?
                  I got married six years ago.

1. _____ I graduated from high school (when)

2. _____ I studied biology. (when)

3. _____ I bought an English dictionary. (where)

4. _____ I left my country. (when)

5. _____ I came to Canada. (why)

6. _____ I brought my clothes to Canada. (what else)

7. _____ I rented an apartment. (where)

8. _____ I started to study English. (when)

9. _____ I chose this institution. (why)

10. _____ I found an apartment. (when)

11. _____ I needed to learn English. (what else)

12. _____ I got married. (when)

Answers to Exercise 17:

1. In 1940	6. A guitar	11. In 1970
2. Soon after he was born	7. His mother	12. After the Beatles broke up
3. His aunt	8. A rock group	13. In New York
4. With a boyfriend	9. All over the world	14. Mark Chapman
5. He had no future	10. In 1968	15. Because Lennon died

Exercise 19   Check (✔) which of these things you did when you were a child. Find a partner and compare your list to your partner's list. Ask your partner about the items he or she checked. Report to the class something interesting you learned about your partner.

1. _____ I attended public school.

2. _____ I enjoyed school.

3. _____ I got good grades in school.

4. _____ I took music lessons.

5. _____ I lived with my grandparents.

6. _____ I got an allowance.[9]

7. _____ I had a pet.

8. _____ I lived on a farm.

9. _____ I played with dolls/played soccer.

10. _____ I studied English.

11. _____ I had a bike.

12. _____ I thought about my future.

13. _____ _____

EXERCISE 20   Fill in each blank in this conversation between two students about their past.

A. I ____was born____ in Hong Kong. I _____ to Canada 10 years ago.
     (born)   (1 come)

Where _____ born?
      (2 be)

B. In El Salvador. But my family _____ to Guatemala when I
                                    (3 move)

_____ 10 years old.
   (4 be)

A. Why _____ to Guatemala?
         (5 move)

B. We _____ afraid to stay in El Salvador.
        (6 be)

A. Why _____ afraid?
        (7 be)

B. Because there _____ a war in El Salvador.
         (8 be)

---

[9]An *allowance* is money children get from their parents, usually once a week.

A. How long _____ in Guatemala?
(9 stay)

B. We stayed there for about five years. Then I _____ to Canada.
(10 come)

A. What about your family? _____ to Canada with you?
(11 come)

B. No, they _____ . I _____ a job, _____
(12 auxiliary)   (13 find)   (14 save)

my money, and _____ them here later.
(15 brought)

A. My parents _____ with me either. But my older brother did.
(16 not/come)

I _____ to go to school as soon as I _____ .
(17 start)   (18 arrive)

B. Who _____ you while you were in school?
(19 support)

A. My brother _____ .
(20 auxiliary)

B. I _____ to go to school right away because I _____ to
(21 not/go)   (22 have)

work. Then I _____ a grant and _____ to go to
(23 get)   (24 start)

Prince Albert College.

A. Why _____ Prince Albert College?
(25 choose)

B. I choose it because it has a good ESL program.

A. Me too.

EXPANSION ACTIVITIES

FAMOUS QUOTE

I came, I saw, I conquered.—Julius Caesar

OLD QUESTION

The following old question uses the past tense in a subject question. Do you have this question in your language too?

Which came first, the chicken or the egg?

OUTSIDE ACTIVITIES

1. Interview a Canadian about a vacation he or she took. Find out where he or she went, with whom, for how long, and other related information.

2. Go to the library to find out about a famous person who interests you. Write a short report about this person's life. (Ideas: Princess Diana, Mother Teresa, Mohandas Gandhi, Josef Stalin, Anwar Sadat, the Dalai Lama, Che Guevara)

DISCUSSIONS

1. In a small group or with your entire class, discuss your first experiences in Canada. What were your first impressions? What did you do in your first few days in Canada?

   EXAMPLE: **I lived with my cousins. They helped me find an apartment. I didn't have money to buy furniture. They lent me money. At first I wasn't happy. I didn't go out of the house much ...**

2. Find a partner to interview. Ask questions about the circumstances that brought him or her to Canada and the conditions of his or her life after he or she arrived. Write your conversation. Use Exercise 20 as your model.

   EXAMPLE: **A. When did you leave your country?**
   B. I left Ethiopia five years ago.
   A. Did you come directly to Canada?
   B. No, first I went to Sudan.
   A. Why did you leave Ethiopia?

SUMMARY OF LESSON NINE

The Simple Past Tense

1. *Be*

I He She It	was in Paris.	We You They	were in Paris.
There was a problem		There were many problems.	

He was in *Poland.*	They *were* in France.
He *wasn't* in Russia.	They *weren't* in England.
Was he in Hungary?	*Were* they in Paris?
No, he *wasn't.*	No, they *weren't.*
Where *was* he?	When *were* they in France?
Why *wasn't* he in Russia?	Why *weren't* they in Paris?
Who *was* in Russia?	How many people *were* in France?

NOTE: Use *be* with *born.*

> Where *were* you born?
> I *was* born in India.

2. Other Verbs

Regular Verb (work)	Irregular Verb (buy)
She *worked* on Saturday.	They *bought* a car.
She *didn't work* on Sunday.	They *didn't buy* a motorcycle.
Did she *work* in the morning?	*Did* they *buy* a Japanese car?
Yes, she *did.*	No, they *didn't.*
Where *did* she *work*?	What kind of car *did* they *buy*?
Why *didn't* she *work* on Sunday?	Why *didn't* they *buy* a Japanese car?
Who *worked* on Sunday?	How many people *bought* a Japanese car?

NOTE: The verb *to* does not use the past form.

> She wanted to *leave.*
> They had to *work.*

LESSON NINE TEST/REVIEW

Part 1   Find the mistakes with past tenses (including mistakes in spelling), and correct them. Not every sentence has a mistake. If the sentence is correct, write **C**.

> EXAMPLE: John Lennon ~~were~~ *was* a good musician.

1. John Lennon born in England.

2. He spended a lot of time on the streets.

3. John didn't liked school.

4. John's mother teached him to play the guitar.

5. He began to play the guitar when he 13 years old.

6. John wanted to be a musician.

7. He enjoied popular music.

8. The Beatles were popular all over the world.

9. He marryed a Japanese woman.

10. He lived in New York with his wife and son.

11. Mark Chapman went to Lennon's apartment and shoot him.

12. He died at the age of 40.

Part 2   Write the past tense of each verb.

> EXAMPLES: live _____*lived*_____   feel _____*felt*_____

1. eat _____

2. see _____

3. get _____

4. sit _____

5. hit _____

6. make _____

7. take _____

8. find _____

9. say _____

10. read _____

11. drink _____

12. build _____

13. stop _____

14. leave _____

15. buy _____

16. think _____

17. run _____

18. carry _____

19. sell _____

20. stand _____

Part 3   Fill in each blank with the negative form of the underlined verb.

> **EXAMPLE:** **Sir Sandford Fleming worked for the Canadian Pacific Railway.**
>
> **He _____*didn't work*_____ for the Hudson's Bay Company.**

1. There <u>were</u> Canadian soldiers in Quebec during the ice storm. There
   _____ any British soldiers.

2. Montreal <u>had</u> a big ice storm in 1998. Toronto _____ a big ice storm.

3. Sir Sandford Fleming <u>was</u> a railway engineer. He _____ a doctor.

4. Before 1885, each city <u>used</u> its own local time. People _____
   Standard Time.

5. Many people <u>went</u> to shelters during the ice storm. They _____ to
   their homes.

6. Volunteer hydro crews from the U.S. <u>came</u> to Quebec during the ice storm.
   American soldiers _____ to Quebec.

Part 4   Read each statement. Write a *yes/no* question about the words in parentheses
( ). Write a short answer.

> **EXAMPLE:** **Sir Sandford Fleming invented Standard Time. (Albert Einstein)**
> **(no)**
>
> *Did Albert Einstein invent Standard Time? No, he didn't.*

1. Montreal had a big ice storm in 1998. (Vancouver) (no)

   _____

2. Sir Sandford Fleming was an engineer. (John Lennon) (no)

   _____

3. Several people died as a result of the ice storm. (farm animals) (yes)

   _____

4. John Lennon was born in England. (London) (no)

   _____

5. His aunt took care of him. (his father) (no)

   _____

6. Young people liked the Beatles' musical style. (hair style) (yes)

_____

7. Lennon wrote music. (classical music) (no)

_____

8. He made a lot of records. (a lot of money) (yes)

_____

9. His second wife was from Japan. (his first wife) (no)

_____

10. He spent his last years in the U.S. (in New York) (yes)

_____

Part 5   Write a *wh-* question about the words in parentheses ( ). It is not necessary to answer the questions.

> **EXAMPLE: Sir Sandford Fleming became famous for his invention of Standard Time. (why/John Lennon)**
>
> *Why did John Lennon become famous?* _____

1. Sir Sandford Fleming was born in Scotland. (where/John Lennon)

_____

2. Alexander Graham Bell invented the telephone. (what/Sir Sandford Fleming)

_____

3. Alexander Graham Bell invented the telephone. (who/Standard Time)

_____

4. Several people died in the ice storm of 1998. (how many people)

_____

5. I came to Canada in 1974. (when/Sir Sandford Fleming)

_____

6. Students were unable to go to school during the ice storm. (why)

_____

7. Thousands of people stayed in shelters during the ice storm. (where)

_____

8. Lennon didn't do well in school. (why)

_____

9. Lennon's parents abandoned him. (why)

_____

10. Lennon lived in New York (with whom) OR (who ... with)

_____

LESSON TEN

GRAMMAR

Imperatives
Infinitives
Modals

CONTEXT

Change of Address
Traffic Tickets
Driving Regulations

Lesson Focus   Imperatives; Infinitives; Modals

- We use imperative sentences to make requests, commands, and instructions to other people.

  Stay here.   *Be* good.   *Open* your book.

- The infinitive is *to* + the base form of the verb.

  I want *to leave*.   I need *to go* home.

- We use modal auxiliaries to add certain meanings to verbs.

  I *can* read this paragraph easily.   You *should* help your roommate.

Before you read:

1. In your country, did your family move from one place to another, or did you live in the same place for most of your life?
2. If you've ever moved, how did you let your friends know about your move?

Change-of-Address Notification Form

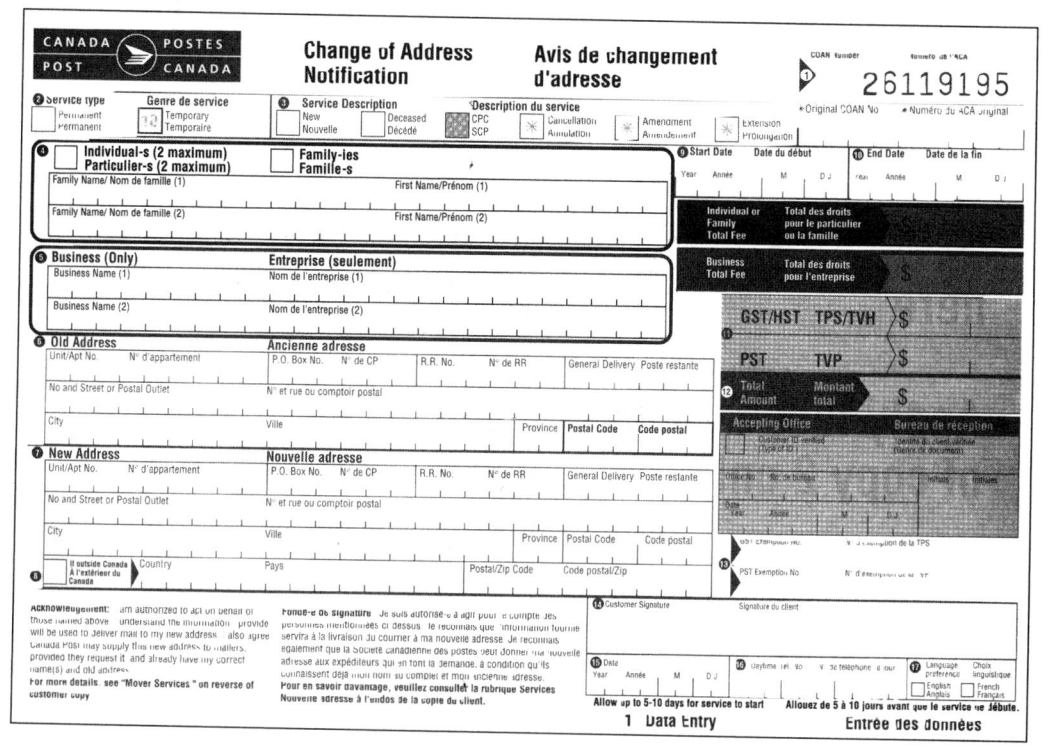

Read the following article. Pay special attention to the imperative forms.

CHANGE OF ADDRESS

If you move to a different address, **inform** the post office. **Ask** the post office for a change-of-address notification form. **Read** the instructions carefully and **fill out** the form. **Return** this form to the post office.

Sign your name on line 14, but **print** all other information. **Don't write** in the grey areas numbered 11 and 12. These are for official use only. **Include** your old address as well as your new address. **Fill in** the starting date; this is the date when you want the Canada Post Corporation (Canada Post) to start delivering your mail to your new address. **Give** the form to the post office of your old address and **pay** the appropriate fee. Canada Post charges $30 to redirect your mail to a new address inside Canada and $60 to redirect mail to a U.S. or international address.

Before you move, **pick up** some change-of-address announcement cards from the post office. On one side of these cards, **print** the city, province, and postal code of your old address as well as your new address. **Include** the starting date of your new address. **Remember** to sign the cards. **Write** the name and address of the people who need to know that you are moving—friends, family, and business people—on the other side of each of these cards. **Mail** them as soon as possible. **Don't forget** to put a stamp on these cards.

On the day of the move, **put** your name on the new mailbox. **Don't leave** your name on the old mailbox. Within a short time, usually one week, your mail should start to arrive at your new address.

10.1 Using Imperatives

The subject of the imperative is *you,* but we don't include it in the statement.

Don't	Base Form	Complement
	Stay	here.
Don't	go	out.
	Be	on time.
Don't	be	late.

Language Notes

We use the imperative form in the following cases:

1. To give instructions.

   Print the information on the card.
   Don't print on line 14. *Sign* your name.

2. To make a request. *Please* makes the request more polite.

   Please mail this card for me.
   Take this form to the post office for me, please.

3. To make a command.

   Don't open my mail!
   Stand at attention!

4. In certain polite conversational expressions.

   Have a nice day (weekend).
   Have a good time.
   Make yourself at home.

5. In some angry expressions.

   Shut up!
   Mind your own business!

EXERCISE 1   Fill in each blank with an appropriate imperative verb (affirmative or negative) to give an instruction.

> EXAMPLE: **If you plan to move, _____*fill out*_____ a change-of-address notification form.**

1. _____ the information on all lines except 14.

2. _____ your name on line 14.

3. _____ the instructions carefully.

4. _____ your old address as well as your new one.

5. _____ the card to the post office of your old address.

6. _____ a number of change-of-address announcement cards.

7. _____ your name on the new mailbox.

8. _____ your name on the old mailbox.

EXERCISE 2   Parents often give their children rules with imperatives. Fill in each blank with an imperative, either affirmative or negative.

> EXAMPLES: _*Do*_____ **your homework.**
>
> _*Don't eat*_____ **so much candy.**

1. _____ to strangers.

2. _____ after school.

3. _____ before dinner.

4. _____ before you cross the street.

5. _____ your brothers and sisters.

6. _____ with matches.

7. _____ your grandparents.

8. _____ before you go to bed.

EXERCISE 3   Choose one of the activities from the following list (or choose a different one, if you like). Use imperatives to give instructions on how to do the activity.

> EXAMPLE: **how to get from school to your house**
>
> **Take the number 53 bus north on the corner of Elm Street. Ask the driver for a transfer. Get off at Park Avenue. Cross the street and wait for a number 18 bus.**

1. hang a picture

2. change a tire

3. fry an egg

4. prepare your favourite recipe

5. hem a skirt

6. write a cheque

7. make a deposit at the bank

8. tune a guitar

9. get a driver's licence

10. use a washing machine

11. prepare for a job interview

12. get from school to your house

13. get money from a bank machine (automatic teller)

14. record a TV show on your VCR

15. _____

hem ⟶

10.2 *Let's*

We use *let's* + the base form to make an invitation or suggestion. *Let's* includes the speaker in the invitation. (*Let's* is a contraction of *let + us*, but we always use the contracted form.)

Let's	*(Not)*	Base Form	Complement
Let's		get	married. I love you.
Let's		hurry.	
Let's	not	be	so quick to make a decision.

EXERCISE 4   Fill in each blank with an appropriate verb to complete this conversation.

   A.   I need a change-of-address notification form. I'm going to move on Saturday.

   B.   I need to buy some stamps. Let's _____*go*_____ to the post office together.

   A.   I don't have my car. My wife is using it.

   B.   The post office is not so far. Let's _____ .
                                         (1)

   A.   It looks like rain.

   B.   No problem. Let's _____ an umbrella.
                               (2)

   A.   I need to ask you about good movers.

   B.   Let's _____ about it now. The post office is going to close in
                    (3)
   20 minutes.

   A.   Let's _____ . I want to get there before it closes.
                   (4)

EXERCISE 5   Work with a partner. Write a few suggestions for the teacher or other students in this class. Read your suggestions to the class.

     EXAMPLES: *Let's review verb tenses.*

                   Let's not speak our native languages in class.

     1. _____

     2. _____

     3. _____

EXERCISE 6   Work with a partner. Write a list of command forms that the teacher often uses in class. Read your sentences to the class.

     EXAMPLES: *Open your books to page 10.*

                   Don't come late to class.

     1. _____

     2. _____

     3. _____

**R
E
A
D

N
G**

Before you read:

1. Did you (or your family) have a car in your country?
2. Are driving rules stricter in Canada or in your country?
3. Did you ever get a traffic ticket in Canada?

Read the following article. Pay special attention to infinitives.

TRAFFIC TICKETS

A driver can get a ticket for a moving violation or a nonmoving violation. In a moving violation, you break a rule while you are driving your car. Often you have to go to court for a moving violation. A nonmoving violation is not so serious. Parking in a no-parking zone is a nonmoving violation. It is usually not necessary **to go** to court. Usually, you can pay for this ticket by mail. However, if you get a lot of tickets and don't pay them, the city might decide **to put** a Denver boot on a wheel of your car until you pay these tickets. You can't continue **to drive** your car until you pay all your tickets and the city removes the Denver boot.

Denver boot →

tow truck →

If you see a street sign that says "NO PARKING TOW ZONE," do not park in this place. You may not find your car when you return. You will need **to contact** the police station **to find out** where your car is, and **pay** the ticket as well as the price of towing. Private businesses often have signs that say "PARKING FOR CUSTOMERS ONLY. VIOLATORS WILL BE TOWED." If you are not a customer and park in this place, your car may not be there when you return. You need **to call** the phone number on the sign and **ask** where your car is. It will probably be necessary for you **to pay** at least $50 to get your car.

No one likes **to get** a ticket or **pay** for towing. But sometimes people try **to break** the rules.

10.3 Verbs Followed by an Infinitive

We form the infinitive by adding *to* to the base form of a verb.

Subject	Verb	Infinitive	Complement
They	began	to drive	fast.
He	needs	to buy	a new car.
We	try	to obey	the law.

1. We often use an infinitive after the following verbs.

begin	hope	prefer
continue	like	promise
decide	love	start
expect	need	try
forget	plan	want

2. An infinitive never has an ending. It never shows the tense. Only the first verb shows the tense.

> I need *to go* to court next Monday.
> The police officer needed *to see* my licence.
> I'm trying *to drive* carefully.
> She doesn't want *to get* a ticket.

3. Sometimes a verb is followed by two infinitives. We usually omit "to" for the second infinitive.

> I need *to go* to court and *pay* a ticket.
> She likes *to sing* and *dance*.

4. In an infinitive, we often pronounce *to* like "ta," or, after a <u>d</u> sound or vowel sound, like "da." Listen to your teacher pronounce these sentences.

> Do you like *to dance*?
> I try *to exercise* every day.
> I decided *to leave*.
> I need *to talk* to you.

5. In fast, informal speech, *want to* is often pronounced "wanna." Listen to your teacher pronounce these sentences.

> I *want to* go home. = I "wanna" go home.
> Do you *want to* leave now? = Do you "wanna" leave now?

EXERCISE 7   Ask a question with "Do you want to ... ?" and the words given. Another student will answer. Then ask a *wh-* question with the words in parentheses ( ) whenever possible.

> EXAMPLE: **buy a car (why)**
> **A. Do you want to buy a car?**
> **B. Yes, I do.**   OR   **No, I don't.**
> **A. Why do you want to buy a car?**
> **B. I don't like public transportation.**

1. take a computer course next term (why)
2. move (why) (when)
3. return to your country (why) (when)
4. get a job/get another job (what kind of job)
5. become a Canadian citizen (why)
6. transfer to a different school (why)
7. take another English course next term (which course)
8. learn another language (which language)
9. review the last lesson (why)

EXERCISE 8   Ask a question with the words given in the present tense. Another student will answer.

> EXAMPLE: **like/travel**
> **A. Do you like to travel?**
> **B. Yes, I do.**   OR   **No, I don't.**

1. expect/pass this course
2. plan/graduate soon
3. plan/transfer to another
   academic institution
4. like/read
5. like/study grammar
6. try/understand Canadians
7. try/learn idioms
8. expect/return to your country

EXERCISE 9   Make a sentence about yourself with the words given. Use an appropriate tense. Find a partner, and compare your sentences to your partner's sentences.

EXAMPLES: **like/eat**

I like to eat pizza.

learn/speak

I learned to speak German when I was a child.

try/find

I'm trying to find a bigger apartment.

1. love/go

2. like/play

3. need/have

4. expect/get

5. want/go

6. plan/buy

7. need/understand

8. not need/have

9. try/learn

10.4 *It* + *Be* + Adjective + Infinitive

We use an infinitive in this pattern:

It	Be (Not)	Adjective	Infinitive Phrase
It	is	important	to know your rights.
It	was	necessary	to clean the apartment.
It	isn't	easy	to learn another language.
It	will be	hard	to find a better job.

Language Notes

We can use an infinitive after the following adjectives:

dangerous	good	possible	expensive
difficult	hard	necessary	impossible
easy	important	fun	

EXERCISE 10   Complete each statement.

EXAMPLE: It's expensive to own *a big car.*_____

1. It's important to learn _____

2. It's hard to pronounce _____

3. It's hard to lift _____

4. It's necessary to have _____

5. It's easy to learn _____

6. It's hard to learn _____

7. It isn't important to know _____

EXERCISE 11   Complete each statement with an infinitive phrase.

EXAMPLE: It's easy *to ride a bike.*_____

1. It's fun _____

2. It's impossible _____

3. It's possible _____

4. It's necessary _____

5. It's dangerous _____

6. It's hard _____

7. It isn't good _____

8. It isn't necessary _____

10.5 *Be* + Adjective + Infinitive

Some adjectives can be followed by an infinitive in this pattern:

Subject	*Be*	Adjective	Infinitive (Phrase)
I	am	happy	to be here.
You	are	lucky	to have a job.
She	is	ready	to leave.

Language Notes

We can use an infinitive after these adjectives:

afraid	happy	prepared	ready
glad	lucky	proud	sad

EXERCISE 12   Fill in each blank.

EXAMPLE: I'm lucky *to be in Canada.* _____

1. Canadians are lucky _____

2. I'm proud _____

3. I'm happy _____

4. I'm sometimes afraid _____

5. I'm not afraid _____

6. Are the students prepared _____

7. Is the teacher ready _____

10.6 Modals

Modals are auxiliary verbs. A base verb follows a modal.

Subject	Modal	(Not)	Main Verb (Base Form)
I You He She It We They	can could should will would may might must	(not)	go. stay. wait.

Observe statements and questions with a modal verb.

Wh- Word	Modal	Subject	Modal	Main Verb	Complement	Short Answer
What	Should should	He he he	should	study study study?	English. grammar?	Yes, he should.
How many aspirins	Can can	I I I	can	take take take?	a pill. an aspirin?	Yes, you can.
Why	can't	You you	can't	drive drive	a car. a car?	
		Someone Who	should should	close close	the window. the window?	

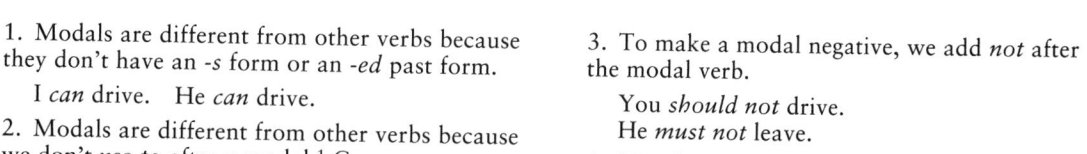

1. Modals are different from other verbs because they don't have an *-s* form or an *-ed* past form.

   I *can* drive.   He *can* drive.

2. Modals are different from other verbs because we don't use *to* after a modal.[1] Compare:

   He wants *to leave.*   He likes *to swim.*
   He *must* leave.   He *can* swim.

3. To make a modal negative, we add *not* after the modal verb.

   You *should not* drive.
   He *must not* leave.

4. We often use modals to ask for things in a polite way.

   Would you open the door, please?

---

[1]Exception: *ought to. Ought to* means *should.*

Before you read:

1. Do you have a driver's licence? When did you get your licence?
2. In your country, is there a national driver's licence?

Read the following article. Pay special attention to modal verbs.

DRIVING REGULATIONS

In Canada, driving regulations differ from province to province. There is no federal driver's licence. If you travel across Canada, you **can** use your driver's licence in other provinces and territories. While most laws are the same, there are some differences from province to province. For example, in some provinces, a driver **must** be 18 years old. In other provinces, someone who is 16 **can** get a licence; however, in some jurisdictions a driver **must** have parental consent to obtain a licence if he or she is under 18. Throughout Canada, the driver and front-seat passenger **must** wear a seat belt, but, in some provinces, the backseat passengers don't have to. Every province requires car owners to have liability insurance. Some provinces have stricter laws than others for drinking and driving. A driver who is caught drinking even a small quantity of alcohol while driving **could** have his or her licence suspended or **might** even go to jail. You **should** become acquainted with the differences in driving regulations if you plan on interprovincial driving. If you break a rule, you **might** get a ticket or you **might** have to go to court.

If you move to another province and become a resident there, you **can** use the driver's licence from your former jurisdiction for a few months. After this time period elapses, some provinces **may** require you to take a driver's test. In some others, you **can** exchange your old licence for one that is valid in your new province.

You **can** get more information about driving regulations from the office of the Ministry of Transportation in the capital city of the province in which you live.

Language Notes

Can

1. We use *can* for ability, possibility, or permission.

 A. Ability:

 I *can* drive a car.

 B. Possibility:

 If you drive too fast, you *can* get a ticket.

 C. Permission:

 You *can* park at a meter, but you *can't* park at a bus stop.
 You *can* use your driver's licence in another province for a few months.

2. The negative of *can* is *cannot*. The contraction is *can't*.

3. In affirmative statements, we usually pronounce *can* /kIn/. In negative statements, we pronounce *can't* /kænt/. Sometimes it is hard to hear the final *t*, so we must pay attention to the vowel sound to hear the difference. Listen to your teacher pronounce these sentences:

 I *can* go.   I *can* see you.
 I *can't* go.   I *can't* see you.

In a short answer, we pronounce *can* /kæn/.

 Can you help me later?
 Yes, I *can*.

4. We use *can* in the following idiomatic expression:

 I *can't afford* to buy a new car. I don't have enough money to buy a new car.
 I saved my money, and now I *can afford* to take a vacation.

EXERCISE 13   Fill in each blank with *can* or *can't* to tell about your abilities.

> **EXAMPLES: I ___can___ drive a car.**
>
> **I ___can't___ fly a plane.**

1. I _____ identify traffic signs.

2. I _____ pass a driving test in this province.

3. I _____ drive a car.

4. I _____ drive a truck.

5. I _____ change the oil in a car.

6. I _____ change a tire.

7. I _____ fill up a gas tank.

8. I _____ operate a motorcycle.

EXERCISE 14   Ask a question about a classmate's abilities with the words given. Another student will answer.

> **EXAMPLE: speak Arabic**
> **Can you speak Arabic?**
> **Yes, I can. OR No, I can't.**

1. write with your left hand
2. type 60 words per minute
3. use a word processor
4. play chess

5. ski
6. play the piano
7. speak Chinese
8. bake a cake

chess

EXERCISE 15   Write down one thing that you can do well. By going around the room and asking questions, find another student who has the same talent.

EXERCISE 16   Fill in each blank with *can* or *can't* to show permission or no permission.

> **EXAMPLE: You ___can't___ park at a bus stop.**

1. You _____ park at a parking meter.

2. You _____ park at a fire hydrant.

3. You _____ drive slowly on a highway.

4. You _____ turn right at a red light after stopping.

5. You _____ drive 90 kilometres on the highway.

6. You _____ drive without a driver's licence.

7. You _____ drive without insurance in this province.

8. You _____ drink and drive.

fire hydrant

Should

1. We use *should* to give advice or a warning.

   You *should* be careful when you drive.
   You *shouldn't* drive if you're sleepy.
   It's snowing hard today. She *shouldn't* drive.
   She *should* use public transportation.

2. The negative of *should* is *should not*. The contraction is *shouldn't*.

EXERCISE 17   Fill in each blank with *should* or *shouldn't* to give advice.

> **EXAMPLE: You** ___*should*___ **be careful when you drive.**

1. Pedestrians[2] _____ wear light-coloured clothing at night.

2. Pedestrians _____ always cross at a corner.

3. You _____ drive the maximum speed limit on icy roads.

4. If you drive long distances, you _____ stop and rest frequently.

5. Passengers _____ wear a seat belt.

6. You _____ check your motor oil about once a month.

7. You _____ smoke while filling up your gas tank.

8. If you drive slowly, you _____ use the left lane.

EXERCISE 18   Tell if children *should* or *shouldn't* do the following.

> **EXAMPLE: obey their parents**
> **Children should obey their parents.**

1. play with matches
2. study hard
3. watch adult movies
4. talk to strangers
5. go to their parents for advice
6. play in the street
7. respect older people

---

[2]A *pedestrian* is a person who is travelling on foot.

EXERCISE 19   Read each statement. Then ask a question with the word in parentheses
( ). Another student will answer.

>   **EXAMPLE: The students should do their homework. (why)**
>   **A. Why should they do their homework?**
>   **B. It helps them understand the lesson.**

1. The students should study the lessons. (why)
2. The teacher should take attendance. (when)
3. The students should bring their textbooks to class. (what else)
4. I should study modals. (why)
5. We should register for classes early. (why)
6. The teacher should speak clearly. (why)
7. The students shouldn't talk during a test. (why)
8. We shouldn't do the homework in class. (where)
9. The teacher should announce a test ahead of time. (why)

Must

1. We use *must* for laws and rules.

    You *must* have a licence plate on the back of
    your car.
    A driver *must* stop at a red light.

2. We use *must not* (*musn't*) for something that
is against the law or a rule.

    You *must not* park at a fire hydrant.
    You *musn't* pass in a no passing zone.

3. *Must not* and *cannot* have almost the same
meaning.

    You *must not* park at a fire hydrant. (It's
    against the law.)
    You *can't* park at a fire hydrant. (It's not
    permitted.)

EXERCISE 20   Fill in each blank with *must* or *must not.*

>   **EXAMPLES: You _____*must*_____ stop at a red light.**
>
>   **You _____*must not*_____ drive slowly on the expressway.**

1. You _____ pass a driving test if you want a driver's licence.

2. You _____ drive when you drink alcohol.

3. If a school bus stops in front of you, you _____ stop.

4. You _____ park at a bus stop.

5. You _____ put money in a parking meter during business hours.

6. You _____ drive over the speed limit.

7. You _____ use your turn signal before you make a turn.

EXERCISE 21   Name something.

> **EXAMPLE:**   **Name something you must have if you want to drive.**
> **You must have a licence.**

1. Name something you must have if you want to leave the country.
2. Name something you must not carry onto an airplane.
3. Name something you must not do in the classroom.
4. Name something you must not do during a test.
5. Name something you must not do or have in your apartment.
6. Name something you must do to enter a Canadian university.

Language Notes

Have to or *Must*

1. *Have to* and *must* both show necessity. Use *must* or *have to* for legal obligations. For personal obligations, *have to* is more common than *must*.

> You *must* have a driver's licence if you want to drive.
> You *have to* renew your licence every few years.
> I *have to* buy a new car. I'm having problems with my old car.

2. The negative of *have to* is *do not have to*. The contraction is *don't have to*.

3. In the negative, *have to* and *must* have different meanings.

> You *must not* drink and drive. (It is against the law; it's dangerous.)
> You *don't have to* go to court for a parking ticket. You can pay by mail. (It's not necessary to go to court.)

4. In fast speech, *have to* sounds like "hafta"; *has to* sounds like "hasta."

> I "hafta" go.
> He "hasta" go.

EXERCISE 22   Tell if you *have to* or *don't have to* do these things at this school. (Remember: *don't have to* means not necessary.)

> **EXAMPLES:**   **study before a test**
> **I have to study before a test.**
>
> **study in the library**
> **I don't have to study in the library. I can study at home.**

1. wear a suit to school
2. come to class on time
3. stand up to ask a question in class
4. do homework
5. notify the teacher if I'm going to be absent

6. call the teacher "professor"
7. raise my hand to answer
8. take a final exam
9. wear a uniform
10. _____

EXERCISE 23   Ask your teacher what he or she *has to* or *doesn't have to* do.

> **EXAMPLE: work on Saturdays**
> **A. Do you have to work on Saturdays?**
> **B. Yes, I do   OR   No, I don't.**

1. take attendance
2. give the students a grade
3. call the students by their last names
4. wear a suit

5. work in the summer
6. have a master's degree
7. work on Saturdays
8. _____

EXERCISE 24   Write four sentences about students and teachers in your country. Tell what they *have to* or *don't have to* do. Use the ideas from the previous exercises. Share your sentences with a small group or with the entire class.

> **EXAMPLE:**   *In my country, a student has to wear a uniform.*

1. _____

2. _____

3. _____

4. _____

Language Notes

Might/May

1. We use *might* or *may* to show possibility (like the word *maybe*). The result is possible but uncertain. Both *may* and *might* have about the same meaning.

> If you park at a bus stop, you *may* get a ticket.
> If you park at a bus stop, a tow truck *might* tow your car away.

2. We do not usually make a contraction for *may not* or *might not*.

> If you don't practise, you *might not* pass the driver's test.

3. If you use *will*, the result is certain. If you use *may* or *might*, the result is not certain.

> The provincial government *will* send you a notice when your licence is about to[3] expire.
> If you drink and drive, you *might* have an accident.

_____

[3]*About to* means ready to.

EXERCISE 25   Tell what *may* or *might* happen in the following situations. If you think the result is certain, use *will*.

> EXAMPLES: **If you don't put money in a parking meter,** *you might get a* *parking ticket.*
>
> **If you are absent from tests,** *you may not pass the course.*
>
> **If I don't pass the tests,** *I'll fail this course.*

1. If you drive too fast, _____

2. If you are driving on an icy street, _____

3. If you get a lot of tickets in one year, _____

4. If you move and don't inform the post office, _____

5. If I don't study before a test, _____

6. If I have some free time tonight, _____

7. If I don't lock the door of my house, _____

8. If I eat too much, _____

9. If I buy a lottery ticket, _____

10. If the weather is nice this weekend, _____

EXERCISE 26   Working in a small group, write a list of things a new student or a foreign student *should, must, might,* or *can* do.

> EXAMPLE: **A new student must fill out an application for admission.**
> **A foreign student should speak with the foreign student advisor.**

EXERCISE 27   With a partner, write a few instructions for one of the following situations.

> EXAMPLE: **using a microwave oven**
> **You shouldn't put anything metal in the microwave.**
> **You can set the power.**
> **You should rotate the dish in the microwave. If you don't, the food might not cook evenly.**

1. preparing for the TOEFL[4]
2. registering for this course

3. taking a test in this class
4. preparing for the driver's test in this province

---

[4]The *TOEFL* is the Test of English as a Foreign Language.

Before you read:

1. Do you have a chequing account?
2. Do you have a chequing account in your country?
3. Do most people in your country get paid by cash or by cheque?

teller

Read the following conversation between a bank teller (T) and a customer (C). Pay special attention to modals used for polite requests.

SCENE IN A BANK

T. **May** I help you?
C. I**'d like to** cash a cheque.
T. Do you have an account in this bank?
C. Yes, I do. I have a savings account.
T. **Could** you give me your account number, please?
C. Yes. Here it is.
T. **Would** you please sign your name on the back of the cheque?
C. **Can** I use your pen, please?
T. Of course. How **would you like** your cash?
C. **May** I have my cash in tens and twenties, please?
T. Yes. Here you are. **May** I help you with something else?
C. Yes. I**'d like to** open a chequing account.
T. You need to see a personal banker. **Why don't you** have a seat over there? A personal banker will be with you shortly.[5]
C. Thank you.

10.7 Using Modals for Polite Commands and Requests

To command someone to do something, we use an imperative.

> *Stand* at attention.
> *Don't* move! You're under arrest!
> *Shut* up!

A command is very strong, and sometimes impolite. We usually tell or ask someone to do something in a more polite way. We can do this by using modal auxiliaries in a question. We can also use *please* to be more polite.

---

[5]*Shortly* means very soon.

To request that someone do something:

Command:	*Sign* the cheque.
Polite Request:	*Would* ⎫ ⎬ you sign the cheque, please? *Could* ⎭

To ask for permission:

Command:	*Give* me your pen.
Polite Form:	*May* ⎫ ⎬ I use your pen, please? *Can* ⎭

Note: *May* is a little more polite than *can*.

Language Notes

1. A softer way to say *I want* is *I would like* (*I'd like*).

   I want to cash a cheque.
   I'd like to cash a cheque.
   How do you want your change?
   How *would* you *like* your change?

2. Another way to make a soft request or suggestion is with *Why don't you/we ...* ?

   Sit over there.
   Why don't you sit over there?
   Let's go to the bank.
   Why don't we go to the bank?

EXERCISE 28   Read the following conversation between a waiter (W) and a customer (C) in a restaurant. Change the underlined words to make the conversation more polite.

W. What <u>do you want</u> to order?   *would you like*

C. <u>I want</u> the roast chicken dinner.

W. Anything to drink?

C. Yes. <u>Bring</u> me a glass of wine.

W. What kind of wine <u>do you want</u>?

C. <u>Show</u> me the wine list.

W. Here you are, miss. <u>Order</u> the white wine.

C. Fine. You know, it's a little cold at this table. <u>Let me sit</u> at another table.

W. Of course. There's a nice little table in the corner. <u>Sit</u> over there.

C. Thanks, and <u>bring</u> me another glass of water.

W. Of course.

10.8 Contrasting Modals and Related Words

Review the meanings of modals and related words.

Ability, Possibility	*Can* you drive a truck? You *can* get a ticket for speeding.
Necessity, Obligation	A driver *must* have a licence. I *have to* buy a new car.
Permission	You *can* park at a meter. You *can't* park at a bus stop.
Possibility	I *may* buy a new car soon. I *might* buy a Japanese car.
Advice	You *should* buy a new car. Your old car is in terrible condition.
Permission Request	*May* I borrow your car? *Can* I have the keys, please?
Polite Request	*Would* you teach me to drive? *Could* you show me your new car?

Suggestion	*Why don't you* have a seat? I'll be with
	  you in a few minutes.
	We both need to go shopping. *Why*
	  don't we go together?

Want	What *would* you *like* to eat? I'*d like* a turkey sandwich.

EXERCISE 29   This is a phone conversation between a woman (W) and her mechanic (M). Fill in each blank with *can, should, may, might, would, could,* or *have to.* (In some cases, more than one answer is possible.)

W. This is Cindy Fine. I'm calling about my car.

M. I *can't* hear you. _____ you speak louder, please?
                                                    (1)

W. This is Cindy Fine. Is my car ready yet?

M. We're working on it now. We're almost finished.

W. When _____ I pick it up?
                        (2)

M. It will be ready by four o'clock.

W. How much will it cost?

M. $535.

W. I don't have that much money right now. _____ I pay by credit card?
                                                                        (3)

M. Yes. You _____ use any major credit card.
                        (4)

Later, at the mechanic's shop:

M. Your car's ready, ma'am. the engine problem is fixed. But you _____
                                                                                                (5)

change your brakes. They're not so good.

W. _____ I do it right away?
            (6)

M. No, you don't have to do it immediately, but you _____ do it within
                                                                                (7)

a month or two. If you don't do it soon, you _____ have an accident.
                                                                    (8)

W. How much will it cost to change the brakes?

M. It _____ cost about $150 or it _____ cost about $300, depending on
            (9)   (10)

whether you need all four brakes or just the front brakes changed.

W. I _____ like to make an appointment to take care of the brakes next week.
    (11)

  _____ I bring my car in next Monday?
  (12)

M. Yes. Monday is fine. You _____ bring it in early because we get very busy
                         (13)

later in the day.

W. OK. See you Monday morning.

EXPANSION ACTIVITIES

PROVERBS

1. The following proverbs contain modals. Discuss the meaning of each proverb. Do you have a similar proverb in your language?

People who live in glass houses shouldn't throw stones.
You can lead a horse to water, but you can't make it drink.
You can't teach an old dog new tricks.

2. The following proverbs contain the imperative form. Discuss the meaning of each proverb. Do you have a similar proverb in your language?

Don't put off until tomorrow what you can do today.
Don't look a gift horse in the mouth.
Look before you leap.
Don't count your chickens before they're hatched.
If at first you don't succeed, try, try again.

OUTSIDE ACTIVITY

If you have a driver's manual for this province, look for sentences in it that use modals. If you don't have it, go to a driver's licence testing facility and pick one up. Or look in the telephone directory, provincial government listings, or under Registry of Motor Vehicles, and call to ask for a book.

WRITING

Write about differences in traffic, driving regulations, or public transportation between your hometown and this city.

EDITING ADVICE

1. Don't use *to* after a modal.

   I must ~~to~~ go.

2. Use *to* between verbs.

   They like _∧ play.
   to

3. Always use the base form after a modal.

   He can swim~~s~~.

4. Use the base form in an infinitive.

   He wants to go~~es~~.

   I want to work~~ed~~.

5. Use *it* to introduce an infinitive before *be* + adjective.

   It i
   _∧ ~~I~~s important to get exercise.

6. Don't put an object between the modal and the main verb.

   understand the lesson.
   She can ~~the lesson understand.~~

SUMMARY OF LESSON TEN

1. Imperatives

    Sit down. *Don't* be late.

2. *Let's*

    Let's go to the movies. *Let's* not be late.

3. Infinitive Patterns

    He wants *to go*.
    It's necessary *to learn* English.
    I'm afraid *to stay*.

4. Meaning of Modals

Modal	Example	Explanation
can	He can swim. An 18-year-old can vote. Can I borrow your car?	He has the ability to swim. He has permission. I'm asking for permission.
can't	You can't park at a bus stop. I can't help you later. I have to work.	It is not permitted. It is not possible.
should	You should drive slowly when it is raining.	It's a good idea.
may	If you drive too fast, you may get a ticket. May I borrow your car?	Maybe this will happen. I'm asking for permission.
might	If you drive too fast, you might get a ticket.	Maybe this will happen.
must	A driver must have a licence. I'm late. I must hurry.	This is the law. It's necessary.
must not	You must not drive without a licence.	It's against the law.
will	We will have a test next week.	This is in the future.
would	Would you help me move?	I'm asking a favour.
would like	I'd like to help you.	I want to help you.
could	Could you help me move?	I'm asking a favour.
have to	She has to leave.	It's necessary.
not have to	He doesn't have to wear a suit to work.	It's not necessary.

LESSON TEN TEST/REVIEW

Part 1   Fill in the first blank with *to* or nothing (*X*). Then write a negative form in the second blank.

EXAMPLE: **I'm ready** _____*to*_____ **study Lesson Eleven. I** _*'m not ready to*_ **study Lesson Twelve.**

1. I need _____ learn English. I _____ Polish.

2. You must _____ stop at a red light. You _____ on the highway.

3. The teacher expects _____ pass most of the students. She _____ all of the students.

4. We want _____ study grammar. We _____ literature.

5. The teacher has _____ give grades. He _____ an A to everyone.

6. We might _____ have time for some questions later. We _____ time for a discussion.

7. It's important _____ practise Canadian pronunciation now. It _____ British pronunciation.

8. It's easy _____ learn one's native language. It _____ a foreign language.

9. Let's _____ speak English in class. _____ our native languages in class.

10. _____ be here at six o'clock, please. _____ late.

Part 2   Change each sentence to a question.

> **EXAMPLES: I'm afraid to drive.**
>
> **Why** *are you afraid to drive?*
>
> **He can help you.**
>
> **When** *can he help me?*

1. You should wear a seat belt.

   Why _____

2. I want to buy a car.

   Where _____

3. He must appear in court.

   When _____

4. She needs to drive to Vancouver.

   When _____

5. You can't park at a bus stop.

   Why _____

6. It's necessary to follow the rules.

   Why _____

7. She has to buy a car.

   Why _____

8. They'd like to see you.

   When _____

Part 3   In the following conversation, find the problems related to modals and
infinitives, and correct them.

   A. I have a problem. Can you ~~to~~ help me?

   B. What's your problem?

A. I need appear in court.

B. What I can do for you?

A. You know that my English is not very good. I afraid go to court alone.

B. Why do you have to go to court?

A. I had a traffic accident. I hit another car. Nobody was hurt, but I damaged a car. I wanted pay the other driver, but she decided called the police.

B. What happened after the police came?

A. The police officer wanted to saw my driver's licence, but I didn't have it with me.

B. Is necessary have your licence with you at all times.

A. I know. That's the reason I must to appear in court.

B. This is very serious. You might lose your licence. I'll give you the name of my lawyer. Call him. He's Canadian, but he can our language speak.

A. Thanks.

B. Good luck! And don't to drive without your licence again.

A. I won't.

Part 4   This is a conversation between two friends about going to court. Fill in each blank with *can, should, may, might, would, could,* or *have to* and other necessary words. (In some cases, more than one answer is possible.)

EXAMPLE: **A. I** ____*have to*____ **go to court a week from Friday.** *Can*_____
you go with me?

B. Why ___*do you have to*___ **go to court?**

A. I got a ticket for speeding.

B. That's terrible. You (not) _____ drive so fast.
                                    (1)

A. I know. I _____ lose my driver's licence if I get three speeding
                    (2)

tickets.

B. I'm not just talking about your licence. You _____ have an accident.
                                                                (3)

A. You're right. I _____ be more careful. Anyway, _____
                          (4)   (5)
    go to court with me?

B. Why do you need me?

A. You _____ speak English much better than me.
              (6)

B. Maybe you _____ get a lawyer.
                     (7)

A. I _____ like to, but I (not) _____ afford one. So
           (8)   (9)

    _____ you go with me, please?
         (10)

B. When is your court date?

A. A week from Friday.

B. I'm not really sure. I _____ have to work on that Friday.
                                  (11)

A. Maybe I can change the date.

B. That's impossible. You (not) _____ change the court date. You
                                        (12)

    _____ appear on the appointed date.
         (13)

A. I don't want to go alone.

B. Why _____ you ask my brother-in-law? He speaks English well.
              (14)

    He _____ help you, if he has the time.
            (15)

A. _____ I have his phone number, please?
          (16)

B. Sure. 123-9876.

LESSON ELEVEN

Lesson Focus   Count and Noncount Nouns; Quantifiers

- To talk about the definite and indefinite articles and quantity, we need to classify nouns into two groups: count nouns and noncount nouns.

    A **count noun** is something we can count. It has a singular form and a plural form.

one egg	five eggs	one Canadian	a thousand Canadians
one book	six books	a child	six children

    A **noncount noun** is something we don't count. It has no plural form.

bread	sugar	cheese
milk	oil	rice

- We use *quantifiers* to tell how much there is of something, when we count or measure.

    I bought *a few* apples   I bought *a lot of* rice.

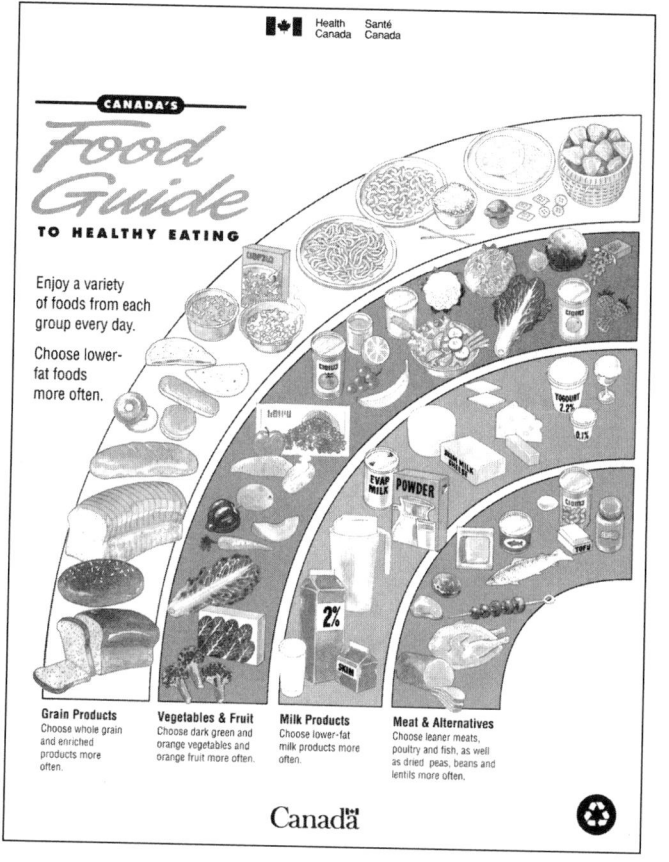

R
E
A
D

N
G

Before you read:

1. What kind of food do you like to eat? What kind of food do you avoid?
2. Do you eat the same kind of food in Canada as you did in your country?

Read the following article. Pay special attention to count and noncount nouns.

A HEALTHY DIET

Good **nutrition** is extremely important. Eating the right **kinds** of **food** can keep you healthy. It is important to get enough **vitamins** and **minerals**.

According to the Canada Food **Guide**, there are four different food **groups**. It is important to eat a **variety** of food from each **group** daily. The **amount** of food you eat depends on your **age**, body **size**, activity **level**, and **sex**. The first group includes **bread**, **cereal**, **rice**, and **pasta**. You should eat more **foods** from this group than from any other group. Choose whole **grain** and enriched **products** such as multi-grain **breads**, brown rice, oatmeal cereal, and enriched pasta. They are high in **starch** and **fibre**, and are a good source of **vitamins** and **minerals**. The second group includes **vegetables** and **fruit**. Dark green and orange vegetables such as **broccoli**, **spinach**, **carrots**, **squash** and orange fruits such as **cantaloupes** and **oranges** are higher in certain important **nutrients** than other **choices**. The third group consists of dairy products, including **milk**, **cheese**, and **yogurt**. The fourth group consists of protein products, including **meat**, **poultry**, **eggs**, and **fish**, and vegetarian **alternatives** such as **beans**, **lentils**, and **tofu**.

You should also limit your **consumption** of certain foods. Most **Canadians** eat more **oil** and **fat** than they need. **Scientists** believe that a low-fat **diet** helps prevent heart **disease**, high blood **pressure**, and some **forms** of **cancer**. Health **professionals** recommend that no more than 30 percent of your food **energy** come from fat. Also avoid foods that are high in **cholesterol**.

Cholesterol is a **substance** made by the body and obtained from animal **products** in the diet. A little cholesterol is good for the body, but high **levels** of cholesterol can be bad for the **heart**. Red meat, egg **yolks**, cheese and whole milk contain a lot of cholesterol, and large **quantities** of these foods are not good for you. Foods from **plants** don't contain any cholesterol. However, palm oil and coconut oil, which don't contain any cholesterol, can raise the cholesterol **level** in your **blood**. **Doctors** recommend that we take in less than 200 **milligrams** of cholesterol a day.

Foods that contain a lot of **salt** and **sugar** should be eaten only occasionally. Most Canadians eat 10 to 20 **times** as much salt as they need, often in the **form** of snack foods such as potato **chips**, salted **nuts**, and many fast food products. Too much salt causes high blood pressure in many people. Sweet **snacks** such as **cookies**, chocolate **bars**, and soft **drinks** contain high levels of sugar. Sugar makes food taste good, but too many **sweets** can lead to tooth **decay**. Many of these processed foods are not only high in salt or sugar, but are also often high in fat and low in **nutrients**. There are many **reasons** to cut back on these foods.

Many Canadians are changing their eating **habits**. They are eating more **chicken, turkey**, and fish as well as beans, lentils, and tofu because these foods have less fat and cholesterol than red meat. By law, all packaged food must list the **ingredients** used in the product. Many Canadians are reading the **labels** on **packages** to determine if a certain kind of food is nutritious.

The chart below shows how many grams (g) of fat and how many milligrams (mg) of cholesterol there are in certain foods:

Food	Serving Size	Fat (g)	Cholesterol (mg)	Calories
Lean ground beef	85 grams	3.4	58	140
Chicken breast	85 grams	3.5	45	131
Cod fish	85 grams	4.3	43	139
Boiled egg	1 (large)	5.6	312	79
Whole milk	250 millilitres	8.9	31	157
Butter	15 grams	12.3	35	108
Olive oil	15 grams	13.5	0	119
Cheese	30 grams	18.8	27.5	228

11.1 Noncount Nouns

There are several types of noncount nouns.

Group A: Nouns that have no distinct, separate parts. We look at the whole.

milk	yogurt	soup
oil	air	bread
water	pork	meat
coffee	cholesterol	butter
tea	paper	poultry[1]

Group B: Nouns that have parts that are too small or insignificant to count.[2]

rice	snow	hair
sugar	sand	grass
salt	corn	popcorn

---

[1]*Poultry* includes domestic birds, such as chickens, turkeys, and ducks.

[2]Count and noncount are grammatical terms, but they are not always logical. Rice is very small and is a noncount noun. Beans and peas are also very small but are count nouns.

Group C: Nouns that are classes or categories of things. The members of the category are not the same.

money (nickels, dimes, dollars)
food[3] (vegetables, meat, spaghetti)
furniture (chairs, tables, beds)
clothing (sweaters, pants, dresses)
mail (letters, packages, postcards)
fruit[3] (cherries, apples, grapes)
makeup (lipstick, rouge, eye shadow)
homework (compositions, exercises, reading)

Group D: Nouns that are abstractions.

love	advice	happiness
life	knowledge	education
time	nutrition	experience
truth	intelligence	crime
beauty	unemployment	music
luck	patience	art
fun	noise	work
help	information	health

11.2 Specific Quantities with Nouns

We can put a number before a count noun, but not before a noncount noun. With a noncount noun, we use a unit of measure, which we can count:

Count:		
1 potato	1 apple	1 peach
5 potatoes	7 apples	2 peaches

---

[3]You sometimes see the plural forms *foods* and *fruits*. For example: *Foods* that contain high levels of cholesterol are not good for you. Oranges and lemons are *fruits* that contain vitamin C. *Foods* means *kinds of food*. *Fruits* means *kinds of fruit*.

Noncount:

a cup of coffee   a jar of coffee
5 cups of coffee   5 jars of coffee

a bowl of sugar   a spoon of sugar
2 bowls of sugar   2 spoons of sugar

These are some units of measure that we use to count noncount nouns:

a loaf of bread   a piece of fruit
a piece (slice) of bread   a piece of mail
a bottle of wine   a piece (or sheet) of paper
a glass of wine   a piece of advice
a cup of tea   a piece of chalk
a bowl of soup   an ear of corn
a can of soup   a head of lettuce
a roll of film   a bar of soap
a pound of meat   a can of beer
a piece of meat   a six-pack of beer
a carton of milk   a tube of toothpaste
a litre of milk   a piece of furniture
a glass of milk   a homework assignment

EXERCISE 1   Think of a logical measurement for each of these noncount nouns.

EXAMPLES: She bought _____*two kilograms of*_____ **coffee.**

She drank _____*two cups of*_____ **coffee.**

1. She ate _____ meat.

2. She bought _____ meat.

3. She bought _____ bread.

4. She ate _____ bread.

5. She bought _____ rice.

6. She ate _____ rice.

7. She bought _____ sugar.

8. She put _____ sugar in her coffee.

9. She bought _____ gas for her car.

10. She put _____ motor oil into her car's engine.

11. She used _____ paper to do her homework.

12. She took _____ film on her vacation.

13. She ate _____ soup.

11.3 *A Lot of, Much, Many*

We use *a lot of, much,* and *many* to describe a large quantity of a noun.

	Count (plural)	Noncount
Affirmative	He baked *many* cookies. He baked *a lot of* cookies.	He baked *a lot of* bread.
Negative	He didn't bake *many* cookies. He didn't bake *a lot of* cookies.	He didn't bake *much* bread. He didn't bake *a lot of* bread.
Question	Did he bake *many* cookies? Did he bake *a lot of* cookies? How *many* cookies did he bake?	Did he bake *much* bread? Did he bake *a lot of* bread? How *much* bread did he bake?

Language Notes

1. We can use *a lot of* with noncount nouns and plural count nouns.

2. We use *much* with noncount nouns only.

3. We use *many* with plural count nouns only. We usually use it with questions and negatives. In affirmative statements, we use *a lot of*.

4. When the noun is omitted, we say *a lot*, not *a lot of*.

   Did he bake *a lot of* bread?
   No, he didn't bake *a lot* because he didn't have time.

EXERCISE 2   Fill in each blank with *much, many,* or *a lot of*.

    EXAMPLES: She doesn't eat _____*much*_____ **pasta.**

          He ate _____*a lot of*_____ OR _____*many*_____ **grapes.**

1. I eat _____ cherries.

2. Do you drink _____ alcohol?

3. I drink coffee only about once a week. I don't drink _____ coffee.

4. Asians eat _____ rice.

5. Canadians don't eat _____ rice.

6. It is good to eat _____ vegetables.

7. If you eat _____ eggs, you might have a problem with cholesterol.

8. How _____ cholesterol is there in an egg?

9. How _____ calories are there in an egg?

10. How _____ apples did you eat this week?

11. How _____ fruit did you eat this week?

11.4 *A Few, A Little*

We use *a few* with count nouns. We use *a little* with noncount nouns.

    I bought *a few* bananas.
    I spent *a little* money.

EXERCISE 3   Fill in each blank with *a few* or *a little*.

    EXAMPLES: He has _____*a few*_____ **good friends.**

          He has _____*a little*_____ **time to help you.**

1. Every day we study _____ grammar.

2. We do _____ exercises in class.

3. The teacher gives _____ homework every day.

4. We do _____ pages in the book each day.

5. _____ students always get an A on the tests.

6. It's important to eat _____ fruit every day.

7. It's important to eat _____ pieces of fruit every day.

8. I receive _____ mail every day.

9. I receive _____ letters every day.

10. I use _____ milk in my coffee.

11.5 *Some, Any,* and *A*

We can use *some, any,* and *a* before nouns.

	Singular Count	Plural Count	Noncount
Affirmative	I ate *an* apple.	I ate *some* grapes.	I ate *some* rice.
Negative	I didn't eat *an* apple.	I didn't eat *any* grapes.	I didn't eat *any* rice.
Question	Did you eat *an* apple?	Did you eat *any* grapes?	Did you eat *any* rice?

Language Notes

1. We use *a (an)* with singular count nouns only.

2. We use *some* for affirmative statements, with both noncount nouns and plural count nouns.

3. We use *any* for questions and negatives, for both noncount nouns and plural count nouns.[4]

4. To make a negative statement, we can use *a (an)* or *any* with a negative verb, or we can use *no* with an affirmative verb.

Compare:
   There isn't *an* elevator in my building.
   There's *no* elevator in my building.
   I don't have *any* money today.
   I have *no* money today.

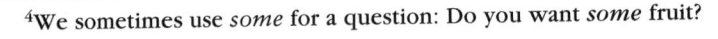

[4]We sometimes use *some* for a question: Do you want *some* fruit?

EXERCISE 4   Fill in each blank with *a, an, some,* or *any.*

> **EXAMPLE: I ate**_____*an*_____**apple.**

1. I ate _____ corn.

2. I didn't buy _____ potatoes.

3. Did you eat _____ watermelon?

4. I don't have _____ sugar.

5. There are _____ apples in the refrigerator.

6. Do you want _____ orange?

7. Do you want _____ cherries?

8. I ate _____ banana.

9. I didn't eat _____ strawberries.

EXERCISE 5   Take something from your purse, pocket, or book bag. Say, "I have _____ with me." Then ask the person next to you if he or she has this.

> **EXAMPLES: I have some keys in my pocket. Do you have any keys in your pocket?**
>
> **I have a picture of my daughter in my purse. Do you have any pictures of your family in your purse?**

EXERCISE 6   Practise count nouns. Make a statement about people in this class with the words given and an expression of quantity.

> **EXAMPLE: Vietnamese student(s)**
> **There are a few Vietnamese students in this class.**
> OR
> **There aren't any Vietnamese students in this class.**
> OR
> **There's one Vietnamese student in this class.**

1. Polish student(s)

2. Russian-speaking student(s)

3. Canadian(s)

4. child(ren)

5. woman/women

6. man/men

7. teacher(s)

8. Canadian citizen(s)

9. senior citizen(s)

10. teenager(s)

11. _____

12. _____

EXERCISE 7   Practise noncount nouns. Make a statement with the words given and an expression of quantity.

> EXAMPLES: **cholesterol/in liver**
> **There's a lot of cholesterol in liver.**
>
> **cholesterol/in an apple**
> **There's no cholesterol in an apple.**

1. cholesterol/in egg yolks
2. cholesterol/in fruit
3. cholesterol/in red meat
4. fat/in fish
5. fat/in pork

6. sugar/in candy
7. sugar/in a cracker
8. salt/in a cookie
9. salt/in a potato chip
10. salt/in a soft drink

EXERCISE 8   Practise noncount nouns. Ask a question with *much* and the words given. Use *eat* or *drink.* Another student will answer.

> EXAMPLE: **candy**
> A. **Do you eat much candy?**
> B. **Yes. I eat a lot of candy.**
> OR
> **No, not much.**
> OR
> **No. I don't eat any candy.**

Eat
1. rice
2. fish
3. chicken
4. pork
5. bread
6. cheese

Drink
7. beer
8. wine
9. milk
10. tea
11. coffee
12. fruit juice

EXERCISE 9   Ask a question with "Do you have ... " and the words given. Another student will answer. Practise both count and noncount nouns.

> EXAMPLES: **Canadian friends**
> A. **Do you have any Canadian friends?**
> B. **Yes. I have many (OR a lot of) Canadian friends.**
> OR
> **No. I don't have many Canadian friends.**
> OR
> **No. I don't have any Canadian friends.**

free time
A. **Do you have any free time?**
B. **Yes. I have a lot of free time.**
OR
Yes. I have some free time.
OR
No. I don't have any free time.

1. money with you now
2. credit cards
3. bread at home
4. bananas at home

5. beer in your refrigerator
6. plants in your apartment
7. _____
8. _____

EXERCISE 10   Fill in each blank. Choose an appropriate word from the words in parentheses ( ).

EXAMPLE: **There are** _____*many*_____ **stores in a big city.**
                                (many/much)

1. A small town doesn't have _____ factories.
                                        (many/much)

2. At 8:00 a.m., there is _____ traffic.
                              (much/many/a lot of)

3. At 4:00 a.m., there isn't _____ traffic.
                                  (much/many)

4. _____ people have car phones.
   (Any/A little/Some)

5. We don't like homework, but sometimes the teacher gives _____.
                                                              (much/a lot of/ a lot)

6. The teacher gives _____ homework every day.
                          (some/a/any)

7. Do you need _____ help with this exercise?
                  (any/a few)

8. Black coffee doesn't contain _____ calories.
                                    (some/any/no)

9. _____ cholesterol isn't good for you.
   (Many/Much/A lot of)

10. Do you have _____ money with you?
                    (any/a)

11. It takes _____ seconds to fill in the blank.
                (a little/a few)

12. There's _____ telephone in the classroom.
    (no/any/no a)

13. There's _____ chalkboard in the classroom.
    (a/any)

14. There are _____ public phones in the hall.
    (a/some/any)

15. Is there _____ elevator in your building?
    (a/an/any)

EXERCISE 11 Fill in each blank. Be careful to use a count noun or noncount noun appropriately. Discuss your answers in a small group.

1. I don't own a _____ , but I'd like to.

2. I have/don't have _____ time because _____ .

3. I don't have _____ in my apartment.

4. There are _____ in my country.

5. I don't eat much _____ .

6. In my country, there isn't much _____ .

EXERCISE 12 Fill in each blank in this conversation between a husband (H) and wife (W) with a quantity word. (In some cases, more than one answer is possible.)

> **EXAMPLE: H. Where were you today? I called you from work ___*many*___ times, but there was no answer.**

W. I went to the supermarket today. I bought _____ things.
                                                      (1)

H. What did you buy?

W. There was a special on coffee, so I bought _____ coffee. I didn't buy
                                                  (2)

_____ fruit, because the prices were very high.
   (3)

H. How _____ money did you spend?
       (4)

W. I spent _____ money because of the coffee. I bought 20 2-kilogram
            (5)

bags. But I saved _____ money because the coffee was so cheap.
                  (6)

H. It took you a long time.

W. Yes. The store was very crowded. There were _____ people in the store.
                                                        (7)

And there was _____ traffic at that hour, so it took me _____ time
                        (8)   (9)

to drive home.

H. There's not _____ time to cook.
                      (10)

W. Maybe you can cook today and let me rest?

H. Uh ... I don't have _____ experience. You do it better. You have
                              (11)

_____ experience.
    (12)

W. Yes. I have _____ because I do it all the time!
                      (13)

11.6 *Too, Too Many, Too Much, A Lot Of*

too much	+	noncount noun
too many	+	count noun
too	+	adjective or adverb

Language
Notes

1. *A lot of* shows a large quantity. *Too much* and *too many* show that the quantity is excessive for a specific purpose.

  I eat *a lot of* fruit.
  If you eat *too much* sugar, you might get cavities in your teeth.
  Last night I had *too many* drinks at the party, and I got drunk.

2. *Too much* and *too many* come before nouns. *Too* comes before adjectives and adverbs.

  I don't eat ice cream. It has *too many* calories. It has *too much* sugar. It is *too* fattening.

3. *Too much* can be at the end of a sentence.

  I need to lose 10 kilograms. I weigh *too much*.
  I can't afford a new car because it costs *too much*.

EXERCISE 13 Fill in each blank with *much* or *many,* and complete each statement.

   EXAMPLE: If I drink too ___*much*___ **coffee,** *I won't be able to sleep tonight.*

  1. If the teacher gives too _____ homework, _____

  2. If I take too _____ classes, _____

  3. If I eat too _____ candy, _____

  4. If I'm absent too _____ days, _____

  5. Too _____ cholesterol _____

EXERCISE 14   Fill in each blank with *too*, *too much*, or *too many*.

Situation A. Some students are complaining about the school cafeteria. They are giving reasons why they don't want to eat there.

EXAMPLE: It's _____*too*_____ noisy.

1. The food is _____ greasy.

2. There are _____ students. I can't find a place to sit.

3. The lines are _____ long.

4. The food is _____ expensive.

5. _____ people are playing loud music.

6. There's _____ noise.

Situation B. Some students are complaining about their class and school.

1. The classroom is _____ small.

2. There are _____ students in one class.

3. The class periods are _____ short.

4. The teacher gives _____ homework.

5. There are _____ tests.

EXERCISE 15   Write a few sentences to complain about something: your apartment, your roommate, this city, this institution, etc. Use *too, too much,* or *too many* in your sentences.

> **EXAMPLE:**   **My roommate spends too much time in the bathroom in the morning. He's too messy.⁵**

EXERCISE 16   Fill in the blanks with *too, too much,* or *too many* if a problem is present. Use *a lot of* if no problem is present.⁶

> **EXAMPLE:**   **Most people can't afford to buy a Mercedes because it costs**
> _*too much*_ **money.**

1. There are _____ noncount nouns in English.

2. "Rice" is a noncount noun because the parts are _____ small to count.

---

⁵A *messy* person does not put his or her things in order.

⁶In some cases, *too much/too many* and *a lot of* are interchangeable.

3. If this class is _____ hard for you, you should go to a lower level.

4. Good students spend _____ time doing their homework.

5. If you spend _____ time watching TV, you won't have time for your homework.

6. It takes _____ time to learn English, but you can do it.

7. Oranges have _____ vitamin C.

8. If you are on a diet, don't eat ice cream. It has _____ calories and _____ fat.

9. Babies drink _____ milk.

10. If you drink _____ beer, you'll get drunk.

EXPANSION ACTIVITIES

DISCUSSION   Cross out the phrase that doesn't fit and fill in each blank with an expression of quantity to make a true statement about your country. Find a partner from another country, if possible, and compare your answers.

     EXAMPLE: **There are/There aren't __*many*__ English-speaking people in my country.**

1. There's/There isn't _____ in my country.

2. There's/There isn't _____ opportunity to make money.

3. People eat/don't eat a lot of _____ because _____.

4. There are/There aren't _____ single mothers.

5. Most people have/don't have _____ education.

6. Parents give/don't give their children _____ advice.

7. People drink/don't drink _____ tea.

8. There are/There aren't _____ English-speaking people in my country.

OUTSIDE ACTIVITY   Bring to class a package of a food or drink you enjoy. Read the label for "Nutrition Facts." Look at calories, grams of fat, cholesterol, sodium, protein, vitamins, and minerals. Do you think this is a nutritious food? Why or why not?

EDITING ADVICE

1. Don't put *a* or *an* before a noncount noun.

   I want to give you ~~an~~ *some* advice.

2. Noncount nouns are always singular.

   My mother gave me ~~many~~ *a lot of* advice~~s~~.

   He received three ~~mails~~ *pieces of* mail today.

3. Don't use a double negative.

   He doesn't have ~~no~~ *any* time. OR   *He has no time.*

4. Don't use *much* with an affirmative statement.

   Uncommon: There was much rain yesterday.

   Common: There was a lot of rain yesterday.

5. Use *a* or *an,* not *any,* with a singular count noun.

   Do you have ~~any~~ *a* computer?

6. Don't use *a* or *an* before a plural noun.

   She has ~~a~~ blue eyes.

7. Use the plural form for plural count nouns.

   He has a lot of friend*s*.

8. Omit *of* after *a lot* when the noun is omitted.

   In my country, I have a lot of friends, but in Canada. I don't have a lot ~~of~~.

9. Use *of* with a unit of measure.

   I ate three pieces *of* bread.

SUMMARY OF LESSON ELEVEN

1. Words that We Use before Count and Noncount Nouns

Word	Count (singular) Example: *book*	Count (plural) Example: *books*	Noncount Example: *tea*
a	x		
one	x		
two, three, etc.		x	
some (affirmatives)		x	x
any (negatives and questions)		x	x
a lot of		x	x
much (negatives and questions)			x
many		x	
a little			x
a few		x	
the	x	x	x

2. *Too Much/Too Many/A Lot Of/Too*

   A lot of indicates a large quantity. *Too* indicates that the large quantity causes a problem.

   - *A lot of* + count or noncount noun
       He's a lucky man. He has *a lot of* friends.
       He has *a lot of* free time.
   - *Too much* + noncount noun
       There's *too much* noise in the cafeteria. I can't study there.
   - *Too many* + count noun
       There are *too many* students in the class. I can't find a seat.
   - *Too* + adjective or adverb
       She's *too* young to get a driver's licence.
       You came *too late*. The movie is over already.

LESSON ELEVEN TEST/REVIEW

Part 1   Read the following composition. Add an appropriate quantity word or an indefinite article before the noun. In some cases, more than one answer is correct.

I had ____*some*____ problems when I first came to Canada. First, I didn't have

_____ money. _____ friends of mine lent me _____ money, but I
   (1)   (2)   (3)

didn't feel good about borrowing it.

Second, I couldn't find _____ apartment. I went to see _____
               (4)   (5)

apartments, but I couldn't afford _____ of them. For _____ months, I
                           (6)   (7)

had to live with my uncle's family, but the situation wasn't good.

Third, I started to study English, but soon found _____ job and didn't
                                            (8)

have _____ time to study. As a result, I was failing my course.
     (9)

However, little by little my life started to improve, and I don't need

_____ help from my friends and relatives anymore.
  (10)

Part 2   Fill in each blank with an appropriate measurement of quantity.

EXAMPLE: a _____*cup*_____ of coffee

1. a _____ of wine   6. a _____ of advice

2. a _____ of sugar   7. a _____ of bread

3. a _____ of milk   8. a _____ of paper

4. a _____ of furniture   9. a _____ of meat

5. a homework _____   10. a _____ of medicine

Part 3   Find the mistakes with quantity words, and correct them. Not every sentence has a mistake. If the sentence is correct, write **C**.

EXAMPLES: **She found a good job, and now she is ~~too~~ *very* happy.**

You can be happy if you have a few good friends. *C*

1. He doesn't have no money with him.

2. He's a lucky man. He has too many friends.

3. There are a lot of tall buildings in a big city. There aren't a lot of in a small town.

4. I don't have much time to help you.

5. A 14-year-old person is too much young to get a driver's licence.

6. A few students in this class are from Pakistan.

7. I don't have some time to help you.

8. I don't have any car.

9. Did we have many snow last winter?

10. Many people would like to have a lot of money in order to travel.

11. He doesn't have any time to study.

12. I'd like to help you, but I have too many things to do this week. Maybe I can help you next week.

13. She drinks two cups of coffee in the morning.

14. I drink four milks a day.

15. He bought two kilograms sugar.

16. How much bananas did you buy?

17. How much money did you spend?

18. This building doesn't have a basement.

19. I have much time to read.

20. She gave me a good advice.

21. The piano is too much heavy. I can't move it.

22. I have a lot of cassette.

23. I don't have much experience with cars.

LESSON TWELVE

GRAMMAR

Adjectives
Noun Modifiers
Adverbs

CONTEXT

Christmas in Canada
Buying a Used Car
The Aging of the Canadian
Population

Lesson Focus   Adjectives; Noun Modifiers; Adverbs

- An adjective can describe a noun.
  They have a *beautiful* tree.

- A noun can also describe a noun.
  They have a *Christmas* tree.

- An adverb can describe a verb.
  They decorated the tree *beautifully*.

Before you read:

1. Does your family celebrate Christmas? How?
2. What is an important religious holiday that you celebrate? How do you celebrate it?

Read the following article. Pay special attention to the description words before nouns.

CHRISTMAS IN CANADA

The December holidays are a very **special** time in Canada. It is a **happy** time for children and a **busy** time for adults. It is also a very **religious** time for many people. People from many religions celebrate many **special** occasions in December. **Jewish** people celebrate Hanukkah. Christian people celebrate Christmas. Christmas is a celebration of the birth of Christ.

Many people buy a **Christmas** tree. Some people use a **natural** tree. Others use an **artificial** tree. People decorate the tree with **bright** ornaments. They usually put **colourful** lights on the tree.

Santa Claus

People buy gifts for their family and friends. They wrap the gifts in **colourful** paper and put them under the tree. Parents often tell their **small** children that Santa Claus brings the gifts. Santa Claus is a **fat**, **old** man with a **long**, **white** beard. He wears a **red** suit. He lives at the **North** Pole. Parents tell children that if they are **good**, they will get gifts. Children are very **excited** on Christmas Eve as they wait for Santa to bring the gifts.

Christmas is also a very **commercial** time for **shop** owners. They depend on Christmas for **heavy** business. **Store** windows often have **Christmas** decorations, and TV and magazines have many ads to attract **Christmas** shoppers. Some people complain that Christmas is too **commercial** because people forget about the **religious** meaning of the holiday. People begin to shop for **Christmas** presents after Thanksgiving and are usually very **tired** by the time Christmas arrives. After Christmas, the stores are **full** of people returning gifts.

12.1   Using Adjectives

We can use adjectives before nouns (subjects or objects) or after the verbs *be,*
look, seem, and other sense-perception verbs.

(Adjective)	Subject	Verb	(Adjective)	Object
Jewish	people I	celebrate prefer	 a natural	Hanukkah. tree.

Subject	Be/Seem/Look		Adjective
The children The tree	are looks		happy. beautiful.

1. We do not make adjectives plural.

   The gift is *expensive.*
   The gifts are *expensive.*

2. Sometimes we put two adjectives before a
noun.

   Santa Claus is a *fat, old* man.
   He has a *long, white* beard.

3. We can put *very* before an adjective to make
it stronger.

   Some people are *very* religious.

4. Some words that end in *-ed* are adjectives:
*married, divorced, excited, worried, finished,
located, tired, crowded.*

   Children are *excited* about Christmas.
   Stores are *crowded* before Christmas.

EXERCISE 1   Add an adjective to each of these sentences. Change *a* to *an* if your
adjective begins with a vowel sound.

   EXAMPLE: Christmas is a ___*religious*___ holiday.

   1. Santa Claus is a _____ man.

   2. Santa has a _____ beard and wears a _____ suit.

   3. We use _____ paper to wrap our gifts.

   4. _____ children believe in Santa Claus.

   5. Some people use a natural tree. Other people use a _____ tree.

   6. Christmas lights are _____ .

   7. Children are _____ on Christmas Eve.

   8. Children believe they will gets presents from Santa Claus if they are _____ .

Language Notes

1. After an adjective, we can substitute the noun with *one* (singular) or *ones* (plural).

> Some people prefer a real Christmas *tree,* but others use an artificial *one.*
> Big *children* don't believe in Santa Claus, but small *ones* do.

2. After *this* and *that* we can substitute *one* for the noun.

> *This tree* is artificial. *That one* is natural.

3. After *these* and *those,* we omit *ones.*

> I'm going to wrap *these presents.* You can wrap *those.*

EXERCISE 2   Ask a question of preference with the words given. Follow the example. Use *one* or *ones* to substitute for the noun. Another student will answer.

> EXAMPLES: **an easy exercise/hard**
> **A. Do you prefer an easy exercise or a hard one?**
> **B. I prefer a hard one.**
>
> **funny movies/serious**
> **A. Do you prefer funny movies or serious ones?**
> **B. I prefer funny ones.**

1. a big city/small
2. an old house/new
3. a cold climate/warm
4. a small car/big
5. a soft mattress/hard

6. green apples/red
7. red apples/yellow
8. strict teachers/easy
9. noisy children/quiet
10. an artificial Christmas tree/natural

EXERCISE 3   Complete each statement with *one* or *X* for no pronoun.

1. These presents are under the tree.

   Those _____ are on the table.

2. This tree is natural.

   That _____ is artificial.

3. Those houses have Christmas decorations.

   This _____ doesn't have any decorations.

undecorated   decorated

4. These people are Jewish. They celebrate Hanukkah.

5. Those _____ are Christian. They celebrate Christmas.

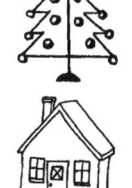

12.2 Noun Modifiers

An adjective describes a noun. One noun can also be described by another noun.

We see many *Christmas* trees in December.
Shop owners decorate their *store* windows.

Adjective	+	Noun	Noun	+	Noun
tall		tree	Christmas		tree
new		owner	shop		owner
clean		window	store		window
colourful		paper	wrapping		paper

Language Notes

1. An *-ing* form (gerund) can also describe a noun. It shows the purpose of the noun.

   A *shopping* cart is a cart for shopping.
   Wrapping paper is paper for wrapping.
   Running shoes are shoes for running.

2. When two nouns come together, the second noun is more general than the first.

   Wrapping paper is paper.
   A *paper plate* is a plate.

3. Sometimes we write the two nouns separately.

   orange juice   desk lamp   vegetable garden

   Sometimes we write the two nouns as one word.

   flashlight   ashtray   motorcycle

4. The first noun is always singular.

   A tray for ashes is an *ashtray*.
   A store that sells shoes is a *shoe* store.
   A garden of roses is a *rose* garden.

5. Sometimes a possessive form describes a noun. It tells who uses the noun.

   A driver uses a *driver's* licence.
   An owner of a VCR uses the *owner's* manual.

6. When a noun describes a noun, the first noun usually receives the greater emphasis in speaking. Listen to your teacher pronounce the following.

   I need a wínter coat.
   He works in a shóe store.

EXERCISE 4   Fill in each blank by putting the two nouns in the correct order. Remember to take the *s* off the plural nouns.

EXAMPLES: People need a ___*winter coat*___ **in December.**
                                     (coat/winter)

We buy groceries in a ___*grocery store.*___
                                     (groceries/store)

1. A _____ delivers the mail.
       (letters/carrier)

2. We use _____ to wrap presents.
       (wrapping/paper)

3. We use a _____ to paint the walls.
                (brush/paint)

4. If you want to drive, you need a _____.
                                        (driver's/licence)

5. A lot of woman like to wear _____.
                                    (rings/ears)

6. A married woman usually wears a _____ on her left hand.
                                        (wedding/ring)

7. Please put your garbage in the _____.
                                    (can/garbage)

8. Many people have a _____ in December and January.
                        (Christmas/tree)

9. The school is closed during _____.
                                (vacation/Christmas)

Before you read

1. Do you have a car? Did you buy it new or used? Are you happy with it?
2. Do you plan to buy a car soon? What are some important things to look for when you buy a used car?

Read the following article. Pay special attention to adverbs of manner.

BUYING A USED CAR

You should be very careful before you buy a used car.

Take the car for a test drive. Check to see if the brakes are working **well**. Take it to the highway and drive it **fast** to see if the engine is running **smoothly** and **quietly**. Drive the car when it is cold to see if it runs **well** with a cold engine.

See the car in the daytime so that you can see the body **clearly**. Check the car **completely**, inside and out. Inspect it **carefully** to see if it was ever in a serious accident.

Notice how many kilometres the car has. Ask if the owner drove in the city or on the highway. City cars wear out[1] more **quickly** than highway cars. A city-driven car with 80,000 kilometres is usually in worse shape[2] than a highway-driven car. The brakes and other parts wear out more **quickly**.

It is a good idea to take the car to a mechanic and have it checked over **thoroughly**.[3] It may cost some money to get a mechanic's opinion, but it is better to lose a few hundred dollars than a few thousand dollars. You don't want to spend your money **foolishly**.

---

[1]When something *wears out*, it gets old little by little as you use it.

[2]*Shape*, in this sentence, means condition.

[3]*Thoroughly* means completely.

12.3   **Adverbs of Manner**

An **adverb of manner** tells how or in what way the subject does something. It describes the action of the sentence.

> The teacher spoke *clearly.*
> The students listened *attentively.*

We form most adverbs of manner by putting *-ly* at the end of an adjective.

Adjective	Adverb
smooth	smoothly
quiet	quietly
quick	quickly

Adverbs of manner usually follow the verb phrase.

Subject	Verb Phrase (Verb + Complement)	Adverb
You	should inspect the car	carefully.
You	don't want to spend your money	foolishly.
He	arrived	early.

1. Observe the spelling rules for *-ly* adverbs:

   A. For adjectives that end in *-y* we change *y* to *i*, then ad *-ly*.

   easy/easi*ly*   happy/happi*ly*
   lucky/lucki*ly*

   B. For adjectives that end in *-e*, we keep the *e* and add *-ly*.

   nice/nice*ly*   free/free*ly*

   Exception: true/tru*ly*

   C. For adjectives than end in a consonant + *-le*, we drop the *e* and add *-ly*.

   simple/simp*ly*   comfortable/comfortab*ly*
   double/doub*ly*

2. Some adverbs of manner do not end in *-ly*.

   A. Some adjectives and adverbs have the same form: *fast, late, early, hard.*

   He has a *fast* car. (adjective)
   He drives *fast.* (adverb)

   She has a *late* class. (adjective)
   She arrived *late* last night. (adverb)
   He has a *hard* job. (adjective)
   He works *hard.* (adverb)

   B. *Good* is an adjective. *Well* is the adverb form.

   He is a *good* driver.   He drives *well.*

3. *Very* can come before an adjective or adverb. Never put *very* before a verb.

   WRONG: He *very* works hard. He *very* likes his job.[4]

   RIGHT: He works *very* hard. He's *very* tired. He likes his job *very much.*

4. Don't put the adverb between the verb and the complement.

   WRONG: He drove *carefully* the car.
   RIGHT: He drove the car *carefully.*
   WRONG: She *late* came home.
   RIGHT: She came home *late.*

---

[4]In informal conversation, you will hear, *he works really (or real) hard. He really likes his job.*

EXERCISE 5   Fill in each blank with the correct form of the word in parentheses ( ) to give advice about driving.

　　　　EXAMPLE: **It is important to drive** ＿＿＿*carefully*＿＿＿ .
　　　　　　　　　　　　　　　　　　　　(careful)

1. Don't follow the car in front of you ＿＿＿＿＿＿＿＿ .
　　　　　　　　　　　　　　　　　　　(close)

2. Make sure your brakes are working ＿＿＿＿＿＿＿＿ .
　　　　　　　　　　　　　　　　　　(good)

3. Check your rearview mirror ＿＿＿＿＿＿＿＿ .
　　　　　　　　　　　　　　　(frequent)

4. Drive ＿＿＿＿＿＿＿＿ on a curve.
　　　　　(slow)

5. Don't use your horn ＿＿＿＿＿＿＿＿ .
　　　　　　　　　　(unnecessary)

6. Don't drive ＿＿＿＿＿＿＿＿ in rain or snow.
　　　　　　(fast)

7. If you have an accident, stop ＿＿＿＿＿＿＿＿ .
　　　　　　　　　　　　　　(immediate)

EXERCISE 6   Tell how you do these things.

　　　　EXAMPLE: **write**
　　　　　　　　　　I write a composition carefully and slowly.

1. speak English　　　　　　　　6. do your homework
2. speak your native language　　7. drive
3. dance　　　　　　　　　　　　8. sing
4. walk　　　　　　　　　　　　 9. type
5. study　　　　　　　　　　　 10. work

EXERCISE 7   Name something.

　　　　EXAMPLE: **Name some things you do well.**
　　　　　　　　　　I speak my native language well.
　　　　　　　　　　I swim well.
　　　　　　　　　　I sing well.

1. Name some things you do well.
2. Name some things you don't do well.
3. Name some things you do quickly.
4. Name some things you do slowly.
5. Name something you learned to do easily.

R
E   ## Before you read:
A
D   1. What are some things you can do to have a longer, healthier life?
          2. Who is the oldest member of your family? Is he or she in good health?
N
G   Read the following article. Pay special attention to *very, too,* and *enough* used
          with adjectives and adverbs.

THE AGING OF THE CANADIAN POPULATION

The elderly population of Canada is increasing rapidly. At the beginning of the century, only 4.3 percent of the population was over 65. Today, 13.5 percent is over 65. By the year 2021, we can expect 20 percent of the population to be over 65. A person born in the year 1900 could expect to live only 45 years. Today, life expectancy at birth is 81.2 years for women and 74.9 years for men. The median age today is 34.6 years old. This means that half the population is over 34.6, and half is under. By the middle of the 21st century, we can expect the median age to be about 44. The proportion of senior citizens[5] over the age of 75 increased by 22 percent from 1986 to 1996, and the proportion of seniors over the age of 85 grew by 31 percent over the same 10-year period. Twice as many women as men are over 85. By 2021, the over-85 group is expected to double in size, and increase to 5 times its size by the middle of the next century. The population of Canada will be **very** different from what it is now.

Why are people living so much longer? First, medical care is much better today. All Canadians have free access to health care, with the exception of dental services. Most people over 65 receive the majority of their prescription drugs free of charge. In addition, a lot of people are **very** careful about their personal habits. Many Canadians are taking **very** good care of themselves by not smoking, by eating a healthy diet, and by getting **enough** exercise. As a result, many older Canadians are healthy **enough** to lead independent and enjoyable lives. Many older people swim, play tennis, travel, and take classes. Some older Canadians are **very** active politically; they influence government decisions.

Unfortunately, not all senior citizens are so fortunate. Some seniors are **too** old and **too** sick to take care of themselves. If they live with their children, their children may be **too** busy to give them the care they need. About 3 percent of seniors spend their last years in a nursing home (29 percent of those over 85).

But as a whole, the quality of life for older Canadians is **quite** good. In recognition of the growth of the world's aging population and the contribution that seniors make to society, the General Assembly of the United Nations decided to observe 1999 as the International Year of Older Persons. The U.N. General Assembly encouraged governments to make it possible for seniors "to add life to the years that have been added to life."[6]

---

[5]*Senior citizens,* or *seniors,* is a more polite way to talk about elderly people.

[6]General Assembly resolution 46/91, 16 December 1991 (http://www.un.org/dpcsd/dspd/iyop.htm).

12.4 Intensifiers—*Too* vs. *Very*

Intensifiers (*too* and *very*) modify adjectives and adverbs. We put *too* and *very* in front of the adjective or adverb that we want to intensify.

1. *Very* shows a large degree. It doesn't indicate any problems.

> My grandfather is *very* old. He's in *very* good health.
> The quality of life for older Canadians is *very* good.

2. *Too* shows that there is a problem.

> A. Do you want to play tennis?
> B. I'm *too* tired. I just got home from a hard day at work.

3. *Too* + adjective or adverb is often followed by an infinitive.

> My grandmother is *too* sick *to take* care of herself. We had to put her in a nursing home.

4. Compare *very* and *too*.

> My grandmother is *very* old and *very* healthy.
> My grandfather is *too* old to take care of himself. He's in a nursing home.
> Race car drivers drive *very* fast.
> If you drive *too* fast in the city, you'll get a ticket.
> This wine is *very* old. It tastes delicious.
> This bread is *too* old. I can't eat it.

5. We can also put *quite* before an adjective or adverb.

> The quality of life for many older Canadians is *quite* good.

EXERCISE 8   Fill in the blanks with *very* or *too*.

EXAMPLES: **Basketball players are _____*very*_____ tall.**

I'm _____*too*_____ short to touch the ceiling.

1. In December, it's _____ cold to go swimming outside.

2. June is usually a _____ nice month.

3. Some old people are in _____ good health.

4. Some old people are _____ sick to take care of themselves.

5. It's _____ important to know English.

6. This textbook is _____ long to finish in three weeks.

7. The prime minister has a _____ important job.

8. The prime minister is _____ busy to answer all his letters.

9. Some Canadians speak English _____ fast for me. I can't understand them.

10. I can speak my own language _____ well.

11. When you buy a used car, you should inspect it _____ carefully.

12. A turtle moves _____ slowly.

13. If you drive _____ slowly on the highway, you might get a ticket.

turtle

12.5 *Too* and *Enough*

We use *too* to refer to something excessive. We use *enough* to refer to something sufficient. Compare the word order in sentences with *too* and *enough*.

My father is 65. He's *old enough* to retire.
My mother is 58. She's *too young* to retire.

Too Adjective *Too* Adverb	Adjective *Enough* Adverb *Enough*
too old *too* well *too* quickly	old *enough* well *enough* quickly *enough*

My mother isn't *old enough* to retire.
My father rides a bike every day. He gets *enough* exercise.

Adjective *Enough* Adverb *Enough*	*Enough* Noun
old *enough* big *enough* tall *enough* well *enough*	*enough* money *enough* room *enough* time

EXERCISE 9   Fill in each blank with *too* or *enough* plus the word in parentheses ( ).

EXAMPLES: My son is 12 years old. He's ____*too old*____ **to believe in**
                                                              (old)
Santa Claus.

My daughter is 18 years old. She's ___*old enough*___ **to get a**
                                                                         (old)
driver's licence.

1. I can't read Shakespeare in English. It's _____ for me.
                                                         (hard)

2. My brother is 19 years old. He's _____ to get a driver's licence.
                                                       (old)

3. My grandfather is 90 years old and in bad health. He's in a nursing home. He's _____ to take care of himself.
       (sick)

4. I saved $8000. I want to buy a used car. I think I have _____.
                                                                           (money)

5. I'd like to get a good job, but I don't have _____.
                                                              (experience)

6. She wants to move that piano, but she can't do it alone. She's not _____.
         (strong)

7. The piano is _____ for one person to move.
                       (heavy)

8. I work in an office, and I don't get _____.
                                                      (exercise)

EXPANSION ACTIVITIES

DISCUSSIONS   1. In a small group or with the entire class, discuss the situation of older people in your country. Who takes care of them when they are too old or too sick to take care of themselves? How does your family take care of its older members?

2. In a small group or with the entire class, discuss Christmas or another important holiday in your country. How do people celebrate this holiday?

WRITING   Describe how you celebrate an important holiday in your country.

EDITING ADVICE

1. Don't make adjectives plural.

   Those are important~~s~~ ideas.

2. Put the specific noun before the general noun.

   He is a ~~driver truck~~.
   truck driver

3. Some adjectives end in *-ed.*

   I'm finish with my project.
   ed

4. A noun modifier is always singular.

   She is a letter~~s~~ carrier.

5. Put an adjective before a noun.

   He had a meeting ~~very important~~.
   very important

6. Use *one(s)* after an adjective to substitute for a noun.

   He wanted a big wedding, and she wanted a small.
   one

7. Don't confuse *too* and *very. Too* indicates a problem.

   My father is ~~too~~ healthy.
   very

8. Don't confuse *too much* and *too. Too much* is followed by a noun.
   Too is followed by an adjective or adverb.

   It's too ~~much~~ hot today. Let's stay inside.

9. Put *enough* after the adjective.

   He's enough ~~old~~ to drive.
   old

10. Don't use *very* before a verb. *Very* is used only with adjectives and
    adverbs.

    He ~~very~~ likes Canada.
    very much

11. Put the adverb at the end of the verb phrase.

                 late
    He ~~late~~ came home∧.

                      slowly
    He opened ~~slowly~~ the door∧.

12. Use an adverb to describe a verb. Use an adjective to describe a noun.

                 ly
    He drives careful∧.

    That man is very nice~~ly~~.

SUMMARY OF LESSON TWELVE

1. Adjectives and Adverbs

Adjectives	Adverbs
She has a *beautiful* voice.	She sings *beautifully*.
She is *careful*.	She drives *carefully*.
She has a *late* class.	She arrived *late*.
She is a *good* driver.	She drives *well*.

2. Adjective Modifiers and Noun Modifiers

Adjective Modifier	Noun Modifier
a tall tree	a Christmas tree
a clean window	a store window
a new store	a shoe store
colourful paper	wrapping paper
warm coats	winter coats
a new licence	a driver's licence

3. *Very/Too/Enough*

He's *very* healthy.
He's *too* young to retire. He's only 55.
He's old *enough* to understand life.
He has *enough* money to take a vacation.

LESSON TWELVE TEST/REVIEW

Find and correct the mistakes with adjectives, adverbs, and noun modifiers. Not every sentence has a mistake. If the sentence is correct, write **C**.

very important decision

EXAMPLES: I had to make a ~~decision very important~~ about her health.

She drives very carefully.   *C*

1. I took my olds shoes to a shoes repair shop.

2. It's too much cold outside. Let's stay inside today.

3. Basketball players are too tall.

4. I got my licence driver's last year.

5. My brother is only 15 years old. He's not enough old to drive.

6. The very rich woman bought an expensive Christmas present for her beautiful daughter.

7. She is only 16 years old. She's too young to get married.

8. I found a wonderful job. I'm too happy.

9. My father is only 50 years old. He is too much young to retire.

10. He speaks English very good.

11. You came home late last night. I was very worry about you.

12. I very like my new apartment.

13. He early woke up this morning.

14. He worked very hard last night.

15. He counted the money very carefully.

16. She opened slowly the door.

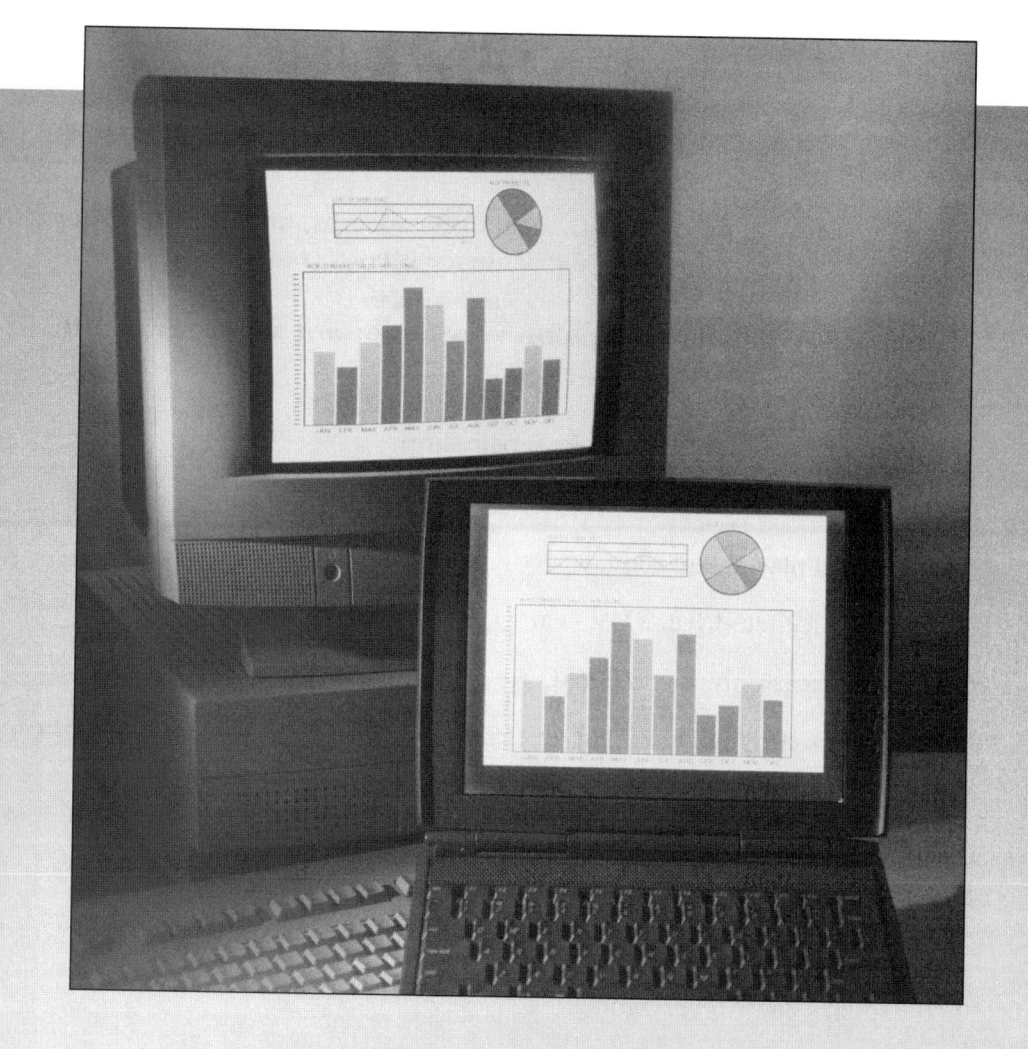

LESSON THIRTEEN

GRAMMAR

Comparatives
Superlatives

CONTEXT

Consumer Decisions
Facts About Canada

Lesson Focus Comparatives and Superlatives

Adjectives and adverbs have three forms: simple form, comparative form, and superlative form. Compare these sets of adjectives.

	Short Adjectives	Long Adjectives
Simple	A horse is a *big* animal.	She is *intelligent.*
Comparative	An elephant is *bigger than* a horse.	She is *more intelligent than* her sister.
Superlative	A whale is *the biggest* animal in the world.	She is *the most intelligent* person in her family.

Before you read:

1. Do you plan to buy something expensive soon? (examples: a TV, a computer, a VCR) What do you plan to buy?
2. Is it easier or harder to make a shopping decision in Canada or in your country? Explain.

Read the following article. Pay special attention to comparative forms.

CONSUMER DECISIONS

There are many choices of products to buy. You might be confused when you go to a store and have to decide from such a wide range of choices. You can use consumer magazines such as *Canadian Consumer* or *Consumer Reports* to help you make a smart decision. Ask friends for advice about a similar product they have bought. Ask them if they are satisfied with their purchase, and why. You can also do some comparison shopping[1] yourself, either by visiting a number of different stores or by making a list of the features you require and phoning several reputable stores.

For example, you need a computer, but you cannot decide whether to buy a desktop model or a laptop. You should consider the following:

A laptop is usually **much more expensive than** a desktop computer.

A desktop computer has a **larger screen than** a laptop. It may be **better** for your eyes.

Desktop computers are usually **more powerful than** laptop computers, and many have **more** memory.

The larger keyboard of the desktop computer may be **more comfortable** to use **than** the laptop keyboard.

---

[1]*Comparison shopping* involves visiting a number of stores to compare the prices and features of a particular product before you decide to buy it.

A laptop computer is **more convenient than** a desktop computer if you do a lot of travelling.

You can store a laptop **more easily than** a desktop computer when you aren't using it.

You can replace or upgrade components for a desktop computer **more cheaply than** you can for a laptop.

Before you shop, you need to decide what is **more important** for you: a **more portable** but expensive laptop computer or a **larger**, **more versatile** desktop model. Next, you need to decide which brand to buy.

When you are in the store, you might want to ask the salesperson questions such as the following, which will help you decide:

1. Which product has a **better** or **longer** warranty?

   Some products have a one-year warranty for parts and labour. After one year, only certain parts have a warranty for two or three years. Look for a product that has at least a two-year warranty for both parts and labour.

2. Which one has **more** features?

   Decide which features you need. There's no reason to pay for features that you don't need.

3. If I find this product in another store at a **lower** price, will you refund the difference in price?

   Many stores will match the price of another store.

Talk to friends who have a new computer and ask for their advice. Visit several well-known computer stores and do some comparison shopping. Consult consumer magazines for information about the price and features of specific brands.

Consumer magazines help us to be smarter consumers. These magazines can be found in the reference section of the library.

 **13.1** **Comparative and Superlative Forms**

The chart below shows comparative and superlative forms. Fill in the last examples.

	Simple	Comparative	Superlative
One-syllable adjectives and adverbs	tall	taller	the tallest
	fast	*faster*	*the fastest*
Exceptions	bored	more bored	the most bored
	tired	more tired	the most tired

	Simple	Comparative	Superlative
Two-syllable adjectives that end in *-y*	easy	easier	the easiest
	happy	happier	the happiest
	pretty	_____	_____
Other two-syllable adjectives	frequent	more frequent	the most frequent
	active	_____	_____
Some two-syllable adjectives have two forms.	simple	simpler more simple	the simplest the most simple
	common	_____	_____

(Other two-syllable adjectives that have two forms are *handsome, quiet, gentle, narrow, clever, friendly, angry.*)

	Simple	Comparative	Superlative
Adjectives with three or more syllables	important	more important	the most important
	difficult	_____	_____
-ly adverbs	quickly	more quickly	the most quickly
	brightly	_____	_____
Irregular adjectives and adverbs	good/well	better	the best
	bad/badly	worse	the worst
	far	farther	the farthest
	little	less	the least
	a lot	more	the most

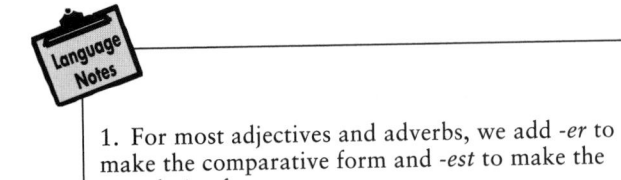

Language Notes

1. For most adjectives and adverbs, we add *-er* to make the comparative form and *-est* to make the superlative form.

    old—older—oldest
    tall—taller—tallest

2. For adjectives that end in *-y*, change the *y* to *i* before adding *-er*.

    happy—happier—happiest
    healthy—healthier—healthiest
    sunny—sunnier—sunniest

Remember: Use *more* and *most* for *-ly* adverbs.

    quickly—more quickly—most quickly

3. If the word ends in *-e*, just add *r*.

    nice—nicer—nicest
    fine—finer—finest

4. For one-syllable words that end in consonant-vowel-consonant, we double the final consonant before adding *-er*.

    big—bigger—biggest
    sad—sadder—saddest
    hot—hotter—hottest

Exception: Do not double the final *w*.

    new—newer—newest

EXERCISE I Give the comparative and superlative forms of the word.

EXAMPLES: **fat** _____*fatter*_____ _____*the fattest*_____

important _____*more important*_____ _____*the most important*_____

1. interesting _____ _____

2. young _____ _____

3. beautiful _____ _____

4. good _____ _____

5. common _____ _____

6. thin _____ _____

7. carefully _____ _____

8. pretty _____ _____

9. bad _____ _____

10. famous _____ _____

11. lucky _____ _____

12. simple _____ _____

13. high _____ _____

14. delicious _____ _____

15. far _____ _____

16. foolishly _____ _____

13.2 Comparisons with Adjectives

We use the comparative form to compare two items. We use *than* before the
second item we are comparing.

X	Be	Comparative	Than	Y
A desktop computer	is	cheaper	than	a laptop computer.
A laptop computer	is	more expensive	than	a desktop computer.

Language Notes

1. Omit *than* if the second item of comparison is not included.

   A desktop computer is larger than a laptop computer, but a laptop is *better* for travellers.

2. *Much* or *a little* can come before a comparative form.

   A laptop computer is *much* more convenient if you do a lot of travelling.
   The keyboard of a desktop is *a little* easier to use.

3. In a question, we use *or* instead of *than*.

   Which is better, a desktop *or* a laptop computer?

4. When a pronoun follows *than*, the most correct form is the subject pronoun. Sometimes an auxiliary verb follows.

   She is taller than *he* (is).
   She is older than *I* (am).

Informally, many Canadians use the object pronoun after *than*. An auxiliary verb does not follow.

   She is taller than *him*.
   She is older than *me*.

EXERCISE 2   Fill in each blank with the comparative form of the word in parentheses ( ). Add *than* when necessary.

   EXAMPLE: **Warranty A is** ___*longer than*___ **warranty B.**
                                    (long)

   1. A laptop computer is _____ a desktop computer.
                              (small)

   2. A desktop computer is usually _____ a laptop computer.
                                         (cheap)

   3. The screen of a desktop computer is _____ the screen of a laptop
                                              (large)
      computer.

   4. A laptop computer is _____ a desktop computer in terms of portability.
                              (good)

   5. A desktop computer is expensive, but a laptop computer is _____.
                                                                   (expensive)

EXERCISE 3   Compare yourself to another person, or compare two people you know using these adjectives:

   EXAMPLES: **tall**
                My father is taller than I am. (OR **than me.**)

                talkative
                My mother is more talkative than my father.

   1. tall   5. thin   9. successful
   2. educated   6. quiet   10. strong
   3. friendly   7. stubborn   11. _____
   4. lazy   8. patient   12. _____

EXERCISE 4   Compare men and women. Give your own opinion. Talk in general terms.

       EXAMPLE: **intelligent**
                 Women are more intelligent than men.
                 OR
                 Men are more intelligent than women.

1. polite	5. kind	9. romantic
2. strong	6. friendly	10. sensitive
3. tall	7. talkative	11. _____
4. intelligent	8. patient	12. _____

EXERCISE 5   Compare where you live now to your hometown.

       EXAMPLES: big
                Tokyo is bigger than Winnipeg.

                crowded
                Tokyo is more crowded than Winnipeg.

1. crowded	5. beautiful
2. modern	6. interesting
3. big	7. cold in winter
4. noisy	8. _____

 **13.3**   **Comparisons with Adverbs**

We use adverbs to compare verbs.

X	Verb	Complement	Comparative Adverb	*Than*	Y
I	can read	this computer screen	more easily	than	that one.
I	can operate	a computer	better	than	my brother can.

We can also use *more* and *less* to compare verbs.

X	Verb	More/Less	*Than*	Y
This computer	costs	less	than	that one.
I	paid	more	than	you did.

EXERCISE 6 Compare men and women. Give your own opinion. Talk in general terms.

EXAMPLES: **work hard**
Men work harder than women.
OR
Women work harder than men.

talk a lot
Women talk more than men.

1. run fast
2. gossip a lot
3. work hard
4. drive foolishly
5. drive fast
6. spend a lot on clothes

7. take care of children well
8. worry a lot
9. drink a lot (alcohol)
10. live long
11. get old fast
12. _____

13.4 Comparisons with Nouns

We can make comparisons with nouns.

X	Verb	Better Worse More	Noun	*Than*	Y
A desktop computer	has	more	features	than	a laptop computer.
Which computer	has	a better	warranty?		

EXERCISE 7 Compare where you live now to your hometown. Use *better, worse,* or *more.*

EXAMPLES: **factories**
Toronto has more factories than Siena.

public transportation
Moscow has better public transportation than Calgary.

1. traffic
2. climate
3. rain
4. crime
5. pollution

6. job opportunities
7. factories
8. tall buildings
9. people
10. _____

EXERCISE 8   Work with a partner or in a small group. Make comparisons with the following words. Give your opinions and reasons.

> EXAMPLE: **men/women—have an easy life**
> **In my opinion, men have an easier life than women. Women have to work two jobs—in the office and at home.**

1. men/women—have an easy life
2. men/women—live long
3. Canadian women/women in my country—have an easy life
4. Canadian couples/couples in my country—have children
5. married men/single men—are responsible

EXERCISE 9   Work with a partner. Find some differences between the two of you. Then write five sentences that compare you and your partner.

> EXAMPLES: *I'm taller than Anita.*
>
> *Anita is thinner than I am.*

1. _____
2. _____
3. _____
4. _____
5. _____

**R
E
A
D
I
N
G**

Before you read:

1. What is the biggest city in your country? Do you like where you live now?
2. In your opinion, what is the most interesting city in your country? Why is it interesting?
3. What cities or regions in your country have the best climate?

Read the following list of facts. Pay special attention to superlative adjectives.

FACTS ABOUT CANADA

1. **The biggest city** in Canada is Toronto.
2. The Canada-U.S. boundary is **the longest** undefended border in the world. It has a total length of 8890 kilometres.
3. **The tallest** building is the CN Tower. It's in Toronto.

4. St. John's, Newfoundland, has **the greatest number** of days per year with fog (121 days). It is also the city with **the most wind** and **the most** freezing **precipitation**[2] (38 days).
5. The Trans-Canada Highway is **the longest** national highway in the world.
6. Prince Edward Island is **the smallest** province in Canada in area.
7. Ontario is **the most populated** province.
8. The Northwest Territories has **the highest** proportion of Aboriginal people: more than 60 percent of its population is of Aboriginal descent.
9. Yellowknife is **the coldest** city, but it also has **the sunniest** summers.
10. Estevan, Saskatchewan, gets **the most sunshine** per year. It has an annual average of 2500 hours of sunshine.
11. Prince Rupert, British Columbia, gets **the least** sunshine. It has an average of 6123 hours of overcast skies. It also has **the most precipitation**.
12. Corner Brook, Newfoundland, gets **the most snow**.
13. **The lowest** temperature recorded in Canada is –63°C at Snag, Yukon Territory, on February 3, 1947.
14. Mount Logan is **the highest** mountain in Canada (5959 metres). It is in Yukon Territory.
15. **The most common** cause of death for Canadians is cancer. Heart disease is **the** second **most common**.

13.5 Superlatives

We use the superlative form to point out the number-one item of a group of three or more items. We use *the* before a superlative, and we usually put a prepositional phrase after it.

X	Verb	*the*	Superlative	Noun	Prepositional
Toronto	is	the	biggest	city	in Canada.
Tokyo	is	the	most populated	city	in the world.

Language Notes

1. We often say "one of the" before a superlative form. Then we use a plural form.
   Quebec city is *one of the most beautiful cities* in Canada.
   Canada has *one of the highest standards of living* in the world.

2. When the verb is *be*, there are two possible word orders.
   Ivan *is* the youngest student in the class.
   The youngest student in the class *is* Ivan.

3. Omit *the* after a possessive form.
   My best friend lives in London.
   Jack's oldest son got married.

---

[2]*Precipitation* includes both rain and snow.

EXERCISE 10   Talk about the number-one person in your family for each of these adjectives.

> EXAMPLES: **interesting**
> **My aunt Rosa is the most interesting person in my family.**
>
> **tall**
> **The tallest person in my family is my brother Stavros.**

1. intelligent
2. kind
3. handsome/beautiful
4. stubborn
5. lazy
6. tall

7. serious
8. hard working
9. strong
10. funny
11. _____
12. _____

EXERCISE 11   Name the person in your family who is the superlative in each of the following activities.

> EXAMPLES: **cook well**
> **My mother cooks the best in the family.**
>
> **eat a lot**
> **My brother eats the most in the family.**

1. talk a lot
2. drive well
3. walk fast
4. speak English well
5. stay up late

6. get up early
7. speak softly
8. eat a lot
9. spend a lot
10. _____

EXERCISE 12   Write a superlative sentence, giving your opinion about each of the following items. Find a partner. Compare your answers to your partner's answers.

> EXAMPLES: **big problem in my country today**
> *The biggest problem in my country today is the civil war.*
> OR
> *The biggest problem in my country today is the economy.*

1. good pet

2. bad war

_____

3. big tragedy in the world or in Canada

_____

4. important invention of the 20th century

_____

5. interesting city in the world

_____

6. big problem in Canada today

_____

7. bad job

_____

8. good job

_____

9. hard teacher at this school

_____

EXERCISE 13   Fill in each blank with the comparative or superlative form of the word in parentheses ( ). Include *than* or *the* where necessary.

     EXAMPLES: July is usually _____*hotter than*_____ **May.**
                                       (hot)

            January is usually _____*the coldest*_____ **month of the year.**
                                          (cold)

1. A lion is _____ a dog.
                (big)

2. A whale is _____ animal in the world.
                   (big)

3. A dog is _____ a bird.
               (intelligent)

4. A dolphin is one of _____ animals in the world.
                          (intelligent)

5. Toronto is _____ Vancouver.
    　　　　　　(crowded)

6. Mexico City is one of _____ cities in the world.
    　　　　　　　　　　　(crowded)

7. Toronto is a crowded city, but Tokyo is _____ .
    　　　　　　　　　　　　　　　　　　　　(crowded)

8. Quebec City is one of _____ cities in Canada.
    　　　　　　　　　　(beautiful)

9. _____ distance between two points is a straight line.
    　　(short)

10. Line A is _____ line B.
    　　　　　(short)

EXPANSION ACTIVITIES

DISCUSSIONS　1. Work with a partner from the same country, if possible. Compare Canadian men and men from your country. Compare Canadian women and women from your country. Report some of your ideas to the class. Do you think generalizations about groups of people are accurate?

2. In a small group or with the entire class, discuss how you choose a product when you shop. Talk about inexpensive items like shampoos or toothpaste. Talk about expensive items like televisions and microwave ovens.

PROVERBS　1. The following proverbs contain the comparative form. Discuss the meaning of each proverb. Do you have a similar proverb in your language?

Two heads are better than one.
It's better to give than to receive.
Easier said than done.
Better late than never.
The grass is always greener on the other side of the fence.

2. The following proverbs contain superlative forms. Discuss the meaning of each proverb. Do you have a similar proverb in your language?

The best things in life are free.
Experience is the best teacher.

WRITING   1. Choose one of the topics below to write a comparison:

a. Compare your present car with your last car.
b. Compare two cities you know well.
c. Compare Canadian women and women in your country.
d. Compare Canadian men and men in your country.
e. Compare soccer and football.
f. Compare a word processor and a typewriter.
g. Compare two pets (a dog and a cat) or two types of dogs.
h. Compare your life as a child and your life as an adult.
i. Compare the place where you lived in your country with the place where you live now.

2. Write about the biggest problem in the world (or in your country, or in Canada) today. Why is this a problem? How can we solve the problem?

OUTSIDE   1. Go to the library. Look for a consumer magazine or book that tells
ACTIVITIES   about used cars. Look at information about two cars that interest you. Compare the prices and features of these cars. Report something interesting to the class.

2. If you are planning to buy something new soon, find product information in a consumer magazine or book. Use this information to help you make a decision.

3. Interview a Canadian. Get his or her opinion about the superlative of each of the following items. Share your findings with the class.

Sample Question for a Canadian:

good car: What do you think is the best car?

1. good car

2. famous celebrity

3. good prime minister in the last 25 years

4. beautiful city in Canada

5. good university in Canada

6. popular movie at this time

7. terrible tragedy in Canadian history

8. big problem in Canada today

9. popular singer in Canada

EDITING ADVICE

1. Don't use a comparison word when there is no comparison.

   Ontario is a big~~ger~~ province.

2. Don't use *more* and *-er* together.

   My new car is ~~more~~ better than my old one.

3. Use *than* before the second item in a comparison.

   than
   He is younger ~~that~~ his wife.

4. Use *the* before a superlative form.

   the
   China has ∧biggest population in the world.

5. Use a plural noun after the phrase "one of the."

   s
   Jim is one of the tallest boy∧in the class.

6. Use the correct word order.

   drives faster
   She ~~faster drives~~ than her husband.

   more
   I have ∧responsibilities ~~more~~ than you.

SUMMARY OF LESSON THIRTEEN

1. Simple, Comparative, and Superlative Forms

   Short words:

   > Vancouver is a *big* city.
   > Vancouver is *bigger than* Winnipeg.
   > Toronto is *the biggest* city in Canada.

   Long words:

   > Computer A is *expensive.*
   > Computer B *is more expensive* than computer A.
   > Computer C is *the most expensive* of the three.

   Comparison with adverbs:

   > Product A works *efficiently.*
   > Product B works *more efficiently* than Product A.
   > Product C works *the most efficiently* of all three.

   Comparison with nouns:

   > He has a *good* accent.
   > He has a *better* accent *than* his sister.
   > He has *the best* accent of anyone in his family.

2. Word Order

   Verb Phrase + Comparative Adverb

   > She *speaks English more fluently* than her husband.

   More + Noun

   > She has *more experience* than her husband.

LESSON THIRTEEN TEST/REVIEW

Part 1   Fill in each blank with the comparative or the superlative of the word in parentheses ( ). Add *the* or *than* if necessary.

EXAMPLES: **Toronto is** _____*bigger than*_____ **Montreal.**
                                (big)

Toronto is _____*the biggest*_____ **city in Canada.**
                                (big)

1. Mount Everest is _____ mountain in the world.
                              (high)

2. A D grade is _____ a C grade.
                        (bad)

3. Smith is one of _____ last names in Canada.
                            (common)

4. Tokyo is _____ Toronto.
                  (populated)

5. June 21 is _____ day of the year.
                      (long)

6. The teacher speaks English _____ I do.
                                          (well)

7. Quebec is _____ province in Canada.
                      (large)

8. Children learn a foreign language _____ adults.
                                                (quickly)

9. A lot of people think that Japanese cars are _____ North
                                                          (good)
   American cars.

10. A dog is _____ a cat.
                      (friendly)

11. Women drive _____ men.
                        (carefully)

12. Who is _____ student in this class?
                    (good)

13. The teacher speaks English _____ I do.
                                          (fluently)

14. A dog is intelligent, but a monkey is_____.
                                              (intelligent)

Part 2   Find the mistakes with comparative and superlative forms, and correct them. Not every sentence has a mistake. If the sentence is correct, write **C**.

EXAMPLES: **I am taller _than_ my father.**

I am tall, but my father is taller.   *C*

1. Paul is one of the youngest student in this class.

2. I have problems more than you.

3. She is more older than her husband.

4. I'm the most tall person in my family.

5. I earlier woke up than you.

6. My father is more educated my mother.

7. She more fluently speaks English than her mother.

8. She is the most intelligent person in her family.

9. I faster type than you do.

10. Toronto is biggest city in Canada.

LESSON FOURTEEN

GRAMMAR

Auxiliary Verbs

CONTEXT

Football and Soccer

Lesson Focus Auxiliary Verbs

To avoid repetition of the main verb, we use the auxiliary verbs *do/does/did,* modal verbs, and *be.*

> I speak French, and the teacher *does* too.
> You went to Paris on your vacation, *didn't* you?

Before you read:

1. What's your favourite sport? Do you like to play it or watch it?
2. Do you ever watch a football game on TV in Canada?

Read the following conversation between a student from Ecuador (E) and his Canadian friend (C). Pay special attention to auxiliary verbs.

FOOTBALL AND SOCCER

E. My favourite sport is football. In my country, Ecuador, everyone likes football.

C. I think you mean soccer, **don't** you?

E. In Ecuador we say football, but football means something different for you, **doesn't** it?

C. Yes.

E. What exactly is the difference between football and soccer?

C. Well, for one thing, the ball is different. A soccer ball is round. A football **isn't**. A football player can carry or throw the ball, but a soccer player **can't**.

E. A football team has the same number of players as a soccer team, **doesn't** it?

C. That's true for American football. They both have 11 players, but an American football team really has 22 players. There are only 11 players on the field at one time.

E. Canadian football and American football are the same, **aren't** they?

C. Not exactly. Canadian football has one extra player. There are 12 players on a Canadian football field at one time, and 24 players on the team. Also, a Canadian football field is 10 yards[1] longer than an American one.

E. That's very confusing, **isn't** it? Are the rules of the game different too?

C. No, they're the same.

E. There are other differences, between soccer and football, **aren't there**?

C. Oh, yes. A soccer game lasts 90 minutes, but a football game **doesn't**. A football game lasts 60 minutes.

E. I don't like football very much.

C. I **don't** either.

E. I prefer soccer.

C. I **do** too.

E. That's strange. I thought all Canadians love football.

C. Maybe most **do**, but I **don't**.

---

[1]Although Canada uses metric measurement, a football field is still calculated in yards. A Canadian football field is 110 yards long and an American one is 100 yards long.

14.1   Auxiliary Verbs with *Too* and *Either*

Sometimes two statements have the same verb phrase. We can use *and* to combine two sentences with the same verb phrase.

A soccer team *has 11 players*.		An American football team *has 11 players*.
A soccer team *has 11 players*,	and	an American football team *does too*.
Football *isn't popular in Ecuador*.		Baseball *isn't popular in Ecuador*.
Football *isn't popular in Ecuador*,	and	baseball *isn't either*.

Language Notes

1. We can use the auxiliary verb (same tense) plus *too* to combine two affirmative sentences in conversation.

   A. A soccer team *has 11 players*.
   B. An American football team *does too*.

   A. Football *is popular in Canada*.
   B. Hockey *is too*.

2. We can use the auxiliary verb (same tense) plus *either* to combine two negative sentences in conversation.

   A. I *don't like football*.
   B. I *don't either*.

   A. I *didn't see the soccer game last night*.
   B. I *didn't either*.

   A. I *can't play tennis very well*.
   B. I *can't either*.

3. In informal speech, Canadians often use the forms *me too* and *me neither*.

   A. I like soccer.
   B. *Me too*.

   A. I don't like football.
   B. *Me neither*.

4. When *have* is a main verb, Canadians use *do*, *does*, or *did* as a substitute.

   CANADIAN:

   A. I have tickets to the game.
   B. I *do* too.

   BRITISH:

   A. I have tickets to the game.
   B. I *have* too.

EXERCISE 1   Sylvie and Ilya have some things in common. Finish each affirmative statement with an auxiliary verb (the same tense as the main verb) + *too*.

   EXAMPLES: Sylvie plays volleyball, and Ilya _____*does too.*_____

   Sylvie went to a soccer game last night, and Ilya _____*did too.*_____

1. Sylvie is interested in football, and Ilya _____

2. Sylvie likes to play tennis, and Ilya _____

3. Sylvie went bowling last week, and Ilya _____

4. Sylvie will watch a football game on TV next Sunday, and Ilya _____

5. Sylvie can play chess, and Ilya _____

EXERCISE 2   Sylvie and Ilya have some things in common. Finish each negative statement with an auxiliary verb (the same tense) + *either*.

> **EXAMPLES: Sylvie doesn't play the guitar, and Ilya** ____*doesn't either.*____
>
> **Sylvie didn't go to the hockey game, and Ilya** ____*didn't either.*____

1. Sylvie doesn't know how to swim, and Ilya _____

2. Sylvie can't ski, and Ilya _____

3. Sylvie won't go to the game next Sunday, and Ilya _____

4. Sylvie isn't interested in baseball, and Ilya _____

5. Sylvie didn't play tennis last summer, and Ilya _____

Language Notes

1. We can use the auxiliary verb to make a short opposite statement when the two verb phrases are the same.
   - A. I like football.
   - B. I *don't*.
   - A. I didn't see the soccer game.
   - B. I *did*.

2. We can use *but* to connect an affirmative statement and a negative statement.
   - I didn't see the soccer game, *but* my friend *did*.
   - Football players can carry the ball, *but* soccer players *can't*.

EXERCISE 3   Sylvie and Ilya are different in some ways. Finish each statement with an auxiliary verb.

> **EXAMPLES: Sylvie works downtown, but Ilya** _____*doesn't.*_____
>
> **Sylvie isn't interested in classical music, but Ilya** _____*is.*_____

1. Sylvie likes to cook, but Ilya _____

2. Sylvie doesn't play the guitar, but Ilya _____

3. Sylvie can't speak Russian, but Ilya _____

4. Sylvie went to Bermuda for vacation, but Ilya _____

5. Sylvie won't work next Sunday, but Ilya _____

EXERCISE 4   Fill in each blank to compare Canada and your country. Use *and ... too* or *and ... either* for similarities between Canada and your country. Use *but* for differences. Use an auxiliary verb in all cases.

> **EXAMPLE: Canada is a big country,** *and Russia is too.* _____
>
> OR
>
> **Canada is a big country,** *but the United Arab Emirates isn't.* _____

1. Canada has more than 29 million people, _____

2. Canada is in North America, _____

3. Canada has a prime minister, _____

4. Canada doesn't have a socialist government, _____

5. Canada fought in World War II, _____

6. Canada is a member of the British Commonwealth, _____

7. Canadians like hockey, _____

8. Canadians don't celebrate Labour Day in May, _____

9. Canadian schools are closed on December 25, _____

10. Canada has a federal election at least every five years, _____

_____

EXERCISE 5   Complete each statement. Then find a partner and compare yourself to your partner by using an auxiliary verb.

> **EXAMPLES: A. I speak** _____ *Chinese.* _____
>
> **B. I do too.**   OR   **I don't.**
>
> **A. I don't speak** _____ *Spanish.* _____
>
> **B. I don't either.**   OR   **I do.**

1. I speak _____

2. I don't speak _____

3. I can _____

4. I have _____

5. I don't have _____

6. I'm _____

7. I usually drink _____ every day.

8. I'm going to _____ next week.

9. I come from _____

10. I'm wearing _____ today.

11. I bought _____ last week.

12. I went _____ last week.

13. I don't like _____

14. I brought _____ to Canada.

15. I don't like to eat _____

16. I can't _____ very well.

17. I should _____ more.

EXERCISE 6   Fill in each blank in the conversation below. Use an auxiliary verb and *too* or *either* when necessary.

A. I'm moving on Saturday. Maybe you and your brother can help me. Are you working on Saturday?

B. My brother is working on Saturday, but I *'m not*_____. I can help you.

A. I need a van. Do you have one?

B. I don't have one, but my brother _____. I'll ask him if we can use
                                                (1)

it. Say, why are you moving?

A. There are a couple of reasons. I don't like the apartment, and my husband

_____. He says it's too small for two people.
        (2)

B. How many rooms does your new apartment have?

A. The old apartment has two bedrooms, and the new one _____.
                                                                        (3)

The rooms are much bigger in the new one, and there are more closets. Also, we'd like to live near the lake.

B. I _____, but apartments there are very expensive.
(4)

A. We found a nice apartment that isn't so expensive. Also, I'd like to own a dog, but my present landlord doesn't permit pets.

B. Mine doesn't _____. What kind of dog do you plan to get?
(5)

A. I like big watchdogs. Maybe a German shepherd or a doberman. I don't like small dogs.

B. I _____. They just make a lot of noise.
(6)

A. So now you know my reasons for moving. Can I count on you for Saturday?

B. Of course you _____.
(7)

EXERCISE 7   Find a partner. List some things you have in common. List some differences too. Report a few interesting sentences to the class.

EXAMPLE: *Alex plays the violin, and I do too.*

                  Alex is majoring in chemistry, but I'm not.

                  Alex doesn't have a computer, and I don't either.

_____

_____

_____

14.2   Auxiliary Verbs in Tag Questions

A tag question is a short question that we put at the end of a statement. Use a tag question to ask if your statement is correct or if the listener agrees with you. Observe the statements and tag questions below:

Statement	Tag Question	Answer
A Canadian football team has 24 players,	doesn't it?	Yes, it does.
You can play football,	can't you?	Yes, I can.
Football and soccer aren't the same,	are they?	No, they aren't.
You didn't play soccer last week,	did you?	No, I didn't.

Language Notes

1. Use *be*, a modal verb, or an auxiliary verb in a tag question. Use the same tense as the main verb.

   You're interested in soccer, *aren't you?*
   You went to the game, *didn't you?*

2. An affirmative statement uses a negative tag question. A negative statement uses an affirmative tag question.

   You saw the game, *didn't you?*
   You didn't see the game, *did you?*

3. A tag question always uses a subject pronoun. If the subject is *this* or *that*, use *it* in the tag. If the subject is *these* or *those*, use *they*. If *there* introduces the subject, use *there* in the tag.

   Your brother plays soccer, doesn't *he?*
   This is a soccer ball, isn't *it?*
   There are many differences between soccer and football, aren't *there?*

4. *Am I not?* is a very formal tag. We often say *aren't I?*

   FORMAL: I'm right, *am I not?*
   INFORMAL: I'm right, *aren't I?*

5. Compare the Canadian and British use of the main verb *have*.

   CANADIAN: You have tickets to the game, *don't you?*

   BRITISH: You have tickets to the game, *haven't you?*

EXERCISE 8   Add a tag question. All the statements are affirmative and have an auxiliary verb.

   EXAMPLE: **This class is large,** *isn't it?*

   1. You're a hardworking student, _____

   2. You can understand English, _____

   3. We'll have a test soon, _____

   4. We should study, _____

   5. There's a library at this school, _____

   6. You'd like to improve your English, _____

   7. This is an easy lesson, _____

   8. I'm asking too many questions, _____

EXERCISE 9   Add a tag question. All the statements are negative and have an auxiliary verb.

   EXAMPLE: **You can't speak Italian,** *can you?*

   1. You aren't a Canadian citizen, _____

   2. The teacher can't speak your language, _____

   3. We shouldn't talk in the library, _____

4. You weren't absent yesterday, _____

5. There aren't any Swiss students in this class, _____

6. This exercise isn't hard, _____

EXERCISE 10   Add a tag question. All the statements are affirmative and have a main verb.

   EXAMPLE: You have the textbook, _____*don't you?*_____

   1. English has a lot of irregular verbs, _____

   2. You want to speak English well, _____

   3. You understood the explanation, _____

   4. A soccer team has 11 players, _____

   5. They went to a soccer game last week, _____

   6. We had a test last week, _____

EXERCISE 11   Add a tag question. All the statements are negative.

   EXAMPLE: We don't have class on Saturday, _____*do we?*_____

   1. The teacher doesn't pronounce your name correctly, _____

   2. Your brother didn't take the last test, _____

   3. You didn't bring your dictionary today, _____

   4. We don't always have homework, _____

   5. I don't have your phone number, _____

   6. Your mother doesn't speak English, _____

EXERCISE 12   This is a conversation between two acquaintances, Bogdan (B) and Stan (S). Stan can't remember where he met Bogdan.

   B. Hi, Stan.

   S. Uh, hi ...

   B. You don't remember me, _____*do you?*_____

S. You look familiar, but I can't remember your name. We were in the same

chemistry class last semester, _____
                                              (1)

B. No.

S. Then we probably met in math class, _____
                                              (2)

B. Wrong again. I'm Linda Karasek's brother.

S. Now I remember you. Linda introduced us at a party last summer,

_____ And your name is Bogdan, _____
              (3)   (4)

B. That's right.

S. How are you, Bogdan? You graduated last year, _____
                                                 (5)

B. Yes. And I've got a good job now.

S. You majored in computers, _____
                                   (6)

B. Yes. But I decided to go into real estate.

S. And how's your sister Linda? I never see Linda anymore. She moved back to

Manitoba, _____
                       (7)

B. No. She's still here. But she's married now, and she's expecting a baby.

S. That's wonderful. Give my regards to Linda when you see her. It was great
seeing you again, Bogdan.

EXERCISE 13 A mother (M) is talking to her daughter (D). Fill in the blanks with a tag
question.

M. You didn't get your scholarship, _____*did you?*_____

D. How did you know?

M. Well, you look very disappointed. You can apply again next year,

_____ ?
                (1)

D. Yes. But what will I do this year?

M. There are government loans, _____?

(2)

D. Yes.

M. And you don't have to pay them back until you graduate, _____?

(3)

D. No.

M. And your professors will give you letters of recommendation,

_____?

(4)

D. I'm sure they will.

M. So don't worry. Just try to get a loan, and you can apply again next year for a scholarship.

14.3 Answering a Tag Question

When we use a tag question, we expect the listener to agree. When we add a negative tag question, we expect an affirmative answer. When we add an affirmative tag question, we expect a negative answer. Notice how we answer these tag questions.

Right Information	Agreement
British Columbia is in the West, isn't it?	Yes, it is.
Prince Edward Island isn't a big province, is it?	No, it isn't. It's small.

When the listener does not agree with the statement, notice how he answers the tag question.

Wrong Information	Correction
British Columbia is in the East, isn't it?	No, it isn't. It's in the West.
Quebec isn't a big province, is it?	Yes, it is. It's very big.

EXERCISE 14   Read a statement to another student, and add a tag question. The other student will tell you if this information is correct or not.

EXAMPLES: **You speak Polish,** _____*don't you?*_____

No, I don't. I speak Ukrainian.

You aren't from Poland, _____*are you?*_____

No, I'm not. I'm from Ukraine.

You came to Canada two years ago, _____*didn't you?*_____

Yes, I did.

1. You're married, _____

2. You have children, _____

3. You didn't study English in your country, _____

4. You have a car, _____

5. You don't live alone, _____

6. You'll take another English course next term, _____

7. You won't return to your country, _____

8. You took the last test, _____

9. You have to work on Saturdays, _____

10. The teacher doesn't speak your language, _____

11. You can type, _____

12. This class isn't too hard for you, _____

13. There was a test last Friday, _____

14. You don't speak German, _____

15. I'm asking you a lot of personal questions, _____

EXERCISE 15   Fill in each blank with a tag question and an answer that tells if the information is true or not.

A. You come from Russia, _____don't you?_____

B. _____ I come from Ukraine.

(1)

A. They speak Polish in Ukraine, _____

(2)

B. _____ They speak Ukrainian and Russian.

(3)

A. Ukraine isn't part of Russia, _____

(4)

B. _____ Ukraine and Russia are different. They were both part of

(5)
    the former Soviet Union.

A. You come from a big city, _____

(6)

B. _____ I come from Kiev. It's the capital of Ukraine.

(7)

A. Your parents aren't here, _____

(8)

B. _____ We came together two years ago. I live with my parents.

(9)

A. You studied English in your country, _____

(10)

B. _____ I only studied Russian and German. I never studied English

(11)
    there.

A. You're not going to go back to live in your country, _____

(12)

B. _____ I'm a permanent resident here. I plan to become a

(13)
    Canadian citizen.

EXPANSION ACTIVITIES

DISCUSSIONS   1.   Find a partner. Tell your partner some things that you think you know about him or her and about his or her country. Your partner will tell you if you are right or wrong.

EXAMPLES: **The capital of your country is New Delhi, isn't it?**

Hindus don't eat meat, do they?

You're studying engineering, aren't you?

2.   Tell the teacher what you think you know about Canada or Canadians. The teacher will tell you if you're right or wrong.

EXAMPLES: **Most Canadians don't walk to work, do they?**

Quebec is the largest province, isn't it?

WRITING   Choose two sports, religions, countries, people, or stores, and write sentences comparing them.

EXAMPLE: **my mother and my father**

My father speaks English well, but my mother doesn't.

My father isn't a Canadian citizen, and my mother isn't either.

My father was born in 1942, and my mother was too.

SUMMARY OF LESSON FOURTEEN

Uses of Auxiliary Verbs

1. To avoid repetition of the same verb phrase

Affirmative Sentence	*and*	Shortened Affirmative Sentence + *Too*
I *like football*,	and	my friend *does too.*
Football *is* fun,	and	soccer *is too.*

Negative Sentence	*and*	Shortened Negative Sentence + *Either*
I *don't like* baseball,	and	she *doesn't either.*
I *didn't watch* the game,	and	she *didn't either.*

Negative Sentence	*but*	Shortened Affirmative Sentence
I *didn't watch* the game,	but	you *did.*
I *can't go* to the game,	but	you *can.*

Affirmative Sentence	*but*	Shortened Negative Sentence
My brother *likes* hockey,	but	I *don't.*
I *have* tickets to the game,	but	my friend *doesn't.*

2. To form tag questions

Affirmative Sentence	Negative Tag
Soccer *is* fun,	*isn't* it?
You *like* soccer,	*don't* you?

Negative Sentence	Affirmative Tag
He *can't* swim,	*can* he?
She *didn't* go,	*did* she?

LESSON FOURTEEN TEST/REVIEW

Part 1   This is a conversation between two students who meet for the first time. Fill in each blank with an auxiliary verb to complete this conversation. Use *either* or *too* when necessary.

B.   Hi. My name is Boris. I'm a new student.

I.   I _____*am too*_____. My name is Irena.

B.   I come from Russia.

I.   Oh, really? I _____. I come from a small town in the southern
           (1)

part of Russia.

B.   I come from Moscow. I love big cities.

I.   I _____. I prefer small towns.
           (2)

B.   How do you like living here in Montreal?

I.   I don't like it much, but my sister _____. She has a good job. But
                                                          (3)

I _____. I miss my life back home.
        (4)

B.   I love it here. And my family _____. The climate is similar to the
                                                    (5)

climate of Moscow.

I.   What about the long winters? Moscow doesn't have a long summer, and
Montreal _____, so you probably feel right at home.
                    (6)

B.   Ha! You're right about the winters, but there are many nice things about
Quebec. Do you want to get a cup of coffee and continue this conversation? I
don't have any more classes today.

I.   I _____, but I have to go home. I enjoyed our talk.
           (7)

B.   I _____. Maybe we can continue some other time. Well,
          (8)

see you in class tomorrow.

Part 2   In this conversation, a new student is trying to find out information about the school and class. Add a tag question.

A. There's a parking lot at the school, _____*isn't there?*_____

B. Yes. It's east of the building.

A. The teacher's Canadian, _____
$$(1)$$

B. Yes, she is.

A. She doesn't give hard tests, _____
$$(2)$$

B. Not too easy, not too hard.

A. We'll have a day off for Christmas, _____
$$(3)$$

B. We'll have a whole week off.

A. We have to write compositions, _____
$$(4)$$

B. A few.

A. And we can't use a dictionary when we write a composition,

_____
$$(5)$$

B. Who told you that? Of course we can. You're very nervous about school,

_____
$$(6)$$

A. Yes, I am. It isn't easy to learn a new language, _____
$$(7)$$

B. No.

A. And I should ask questions about things I want to know, _____
$$(8)$$

B. Yes, of course. You don't have any more questions, _____
$$(9)$$

A. No.

B. Well, I'll see you in the next class. Bye.

LESSON FIFTEEN
VERB REVIEW

15.1 Comparison of Tenses

Compare the four tenses presented in this book.

SIMPLE PRESENT	We usually *study* hard.
PRESENT CONTINUOUS	We *are studying* four tenses now.
SIMPLE PAST	We *studied* the simple past last week.
FUTURE	We *are going to study* Book 2 next term.
FUTURE	We *will study* Book 2 next term.

15.2 Statements and Questions

Simple Present

Base Form	-*S* Form
They *live* in Saint John.	He *lives* in Saint John.
They *don't live* in Moncton.	He *doesn't live* in Moncton.
Do they *live* in the city?	*Does* he *live* in the city?
Yes, they *do.*	Yes, he *does.*
Where *do* they *live*?	Where *does* he *live*?
Why *don't* they *live* in a suburb?	Why *doesn't* he *live* in a suburb?
How many people *live* with them?	Who *lives* with him?

Present Continuous

They're *speaking* English now.	She's *making* dinner.
They *aren't speaking* French.	She *isn't making* lunch.
Are they *speaking* fast?	*Is* she *making* a pie?
Yes, they *are.*	No, she *isn't.*
Why *are* they *speaking* fast?	What *is* she *making*?
Why *aren't* they *speaking* slowly?	Why *isn't* she *making* a pie?
How many people *are speaking*?	Who's *making* dessert?

Future

Will	Be Going to
He'*ll buy* a car.	He's *going to buy* a car.
He *won't buy* a Honda.	He *isn't going to buy* a Honda.
Will he *buy* a Volkswagen?	*Is* he *going to buy* a Volkswagen?
No, he *won't.*	No, he *isn't.*
What kind of car *will* he *buy*?	What kind of car *is he going to buy*?
Why *won't* he *buy* a Honda?	Why *isn't* he *going to buy* a Honda?
Who *will buy* a Toyota?	Who *is going to buy* a Toyota?

Simple Past	
<u>Regular Verb</u>	<u>Irregular Verb</u>
He *opened* the door.	She *found* a wallet.
He *didn't open* the window.	She *didn't find* money.
Did he *open* the front door?	*Did* she *find* identification?
Yes, he *did*.	No, she *didn't*.
When *did* he *open* the door?	Where *did* she *find* the wallet?
Why *didn't* he *open* the window?	Why *didn't* she *find* money?
Who *opened* the window?	Who *found* the money?

Be	
<u>Present</u>	<u>Past</u>
She*'s* in Alberta.	You *were* late.
She *isn't* in Calgary.	You *weren't* on time.
Is she in Edmonton?	*Were* you very late?
No, she *isn't*.	Yes, I *was*.
Where *is* she?	Why *were* you late?
Why *isn't* she in Calgary?	Why *weren't* you on time?
Who *is* in Edmonton?	Who *was* late?

15.3 Uses of the Tenses

Simple Present Tense

1. Use the simple present for habits, customs, regular activities, and facts.

   Thanksgiving *is* a Canadian holiday.
   Canadians *celebrate* Thanksgiving in October.
   They usually *eat* turkey on Thanksgiving.
   The teacher often *tells* us about Canadian holidays in class.

2. Use the simple present for nonaction verbs.

   We *know* a lot about Canadian customs.
   We *need* more information about grammar now.

3. In a future sentence, use the simple present in a time clause or an *if* clause.

   When we *finish* this review, we will do an exercise on tenses.
   If we *don't understand* tenses, the teacher will review them.

Present Continuous Tense

Use the present continuous tense for actions that are happening now or in a present period of time.

> We*'re reviewing* verb tenses now.
> We*'re studying* verbs this week.

EXCEPTIONS: Do not use the continuous tense with nonaction verbs: *have, need, want, know, like, love,* etc.

Future Tense

Use the future tense for actions that will happen at a later time.

> The term *will end* in May.
> *We're going to have* a test at the end of the term.

Do not use the future tense in a time clause or an *if* clause. Use the simple present.

> When the term *ends,* we*'ll have* a party.

Simple Past Tense

Use the simple past tense to talk about an action that is completely past. It usually refers to a specific past time.

> We *studied* the present tense four weeks ago.
> I *bought* my book at the beginning of the term.
> John Lennon *died* in 1980.

The Verb *Be*

Use *be* for classification, description, location, origin, with *born,* and with *there.*

> John Lennon *was* a singer.
> He *was* popular.
> He *was* from Liverpool.
> Liverpool *is* in England.
> He *was* born in 1940.
> There *are* many good songs on a Beatles album.

EXERCISE 1   Jane, her husband, Ed, and their two children are on vacation now. Jane is writing a letter to her friend Rosemary. Fill in each blank with the correct tense of the verb in parentheses ( ) to complete this letter. Use the simple present, the present continuous, the future, or the simple past.

Dear Rosemary,

We _____*arrived*_____ in Mexico last Monday. Our flight
       (arrive)

_____ smooth and comfortable. We _____ at a
   (1 be)   (2 stay)

beautiful hotel in Cancun this week. It _____ a big swimming pool
                                         (3 have)

and tennis courts. Ed _____ tennis every morning. I usually
                         (4 play)

_____ late in the morning. In the afternoon, we usually
   (5 sleep)

_____ to the beach or to the pool. The children _____
   (6 go)   (7 love)

to swim. Sometimes I _____ shopping in the early evening. At night
                     (8 go)

we usually _____ at a restaurant. Last night we _____
            (9 eat)   (10 have)

dinner in a lovely Mexican restaurant. The dinner _____
                                      (11 be)

delicious. Tomorrow we _____ another restaurant.
                  (12 try)

Now I _____ on the beach. I _____ a good suntan.
         (13 sit)   (14 get)

The children _____ in the water. Ed _____ the
            (15 play)   (16 read)

newspaper in the shade. He always _____ the shade, but I usually
                           (17 like)

_____ the sun.
   (18 prefer)

Next week we _____ to another city, Merida. We
             (19 go)

_____ at seven o'clock on Friday morning. We _____ there
   (20 leave)   (21 be)

for three days. After that, we _____ home. I _____
                      (22 return)   (23 call)

you when I _____ home. I _____ you all about our
(24 get) (25 tell)

vacation.

Take care,

Jane

EXERCISE 2 Fill in each blank with the negative form of the underlined verb.

> EXAMPLE: **They <u>ate</u> in a Mexican restaurant. They** ____*didn't eat*____ **in a French restaurant.**

1. They <u>went</u> to Mexico. They _____ to Bermuda.

2. They'<u>re staying</u> in a hotel. They _____ with friends.

3. The hotel <u>has</u> tennis courts. It _____ a golf course.

4. They'<u>re</u> at the beach now. They _____ at the hotel.

5. Ed <u>plays</u> tennis every day. Jane _____ tennis.

6. They'<u>ll be</u> home in a few weeks. They _____ home this week.

7. Jane <u>likes</u> the sun. Ed _____ the sun.

8. They'<u>re going</u> to Merida. They _____ to Acapulco.

9. They'<u>re going to spend</u> three days in Merida. They _____ a week there.

EXERCISE 3 Read each statement. Then write a *yes/no* question about the words in parentheses ( ). Write a short answer.

> EXAMPLE: **Jane went to Mexico. (her husband)**
>
> *Did her husband go to Mexico? Yes, he did.*

1. Jane likes to swim. (her husband)

2. Jane's getting a suntan now. (her husband)

_____

3. Jane prefers the sun. (her husband)

_____

4. Ed gets up early every day. (Jane)

_____

5. They ate dinner at a restaurant. (at a French restaurant)

_____

6. The hotel has a pool. (tennis courts)

_____

7. The flight was smooth. (comfortable)

_____

8. They'll visit Merida. (Acapulco)

_____

EXERCISE 4   Read each statement. Then write a _wh-_ question about the words in parentheses ( ). Answer with a complete sentence.

EXAMPLE: **Ed plays tennis. (when)**

  A. _When does he play tennis?_ _____

  B. _He plays tennis in the morning._ _____

1. They went to Mexico. (how)

  A. _____

  B. _____

2. Ed isn't sitting in the sun. (why)

  A. _____

  B. _____

3. They ate dinner last night. (where)

    A. _____

    B. _____

4. Jane will call Rosemary. (when)

    A. _____

    B. _____

5. The children are playing now. (where)

    A. _____

    B. _____

6. They're going to leave on Friday. (what time)

    A. _____

    B. _____

7. Someone plays tennis every morning. (who)

    A. _____

    B. _____

8. Jane doesn't go shopping in the morning. (why)

    A. _____

    B. _____

EXPANSION ACTIVITIES

INTERVIEW Find a partner. Use the words below to ask and answer questions with your partner. Practise the simple present, the present continuous, the future, and the simple past.

EXAMPLES: **you/from Asia**
A. Are you from Asia?
B. Yes, I am. OR **No, I'm not.**

where/you/from
A. Where are you from?
B. I'm from Pakistan.

1. when/you/leave your country
2. how/you/come to Canada
3. you/come to Canada alone
4. where/you/born
5. what language(s)/you speak
6. you/return to your country next year
7. you/have a job now
8. you/have a job in your country
9. how many brothers and sisters/you/have
10. your country/big
11. your country/have a lot of petroleum
12. you/live in an apartment in your country
13. you/study English in your country
14. what/you/study this term
15. what/you/study next term
16. you/like this class
17. the teacher/speak your language
18. this class/hard for you
19. who/your teacher last term
20. who/your teacher next term
21. _____
22. _____
23. _____

OUTSIDE ACTIVITY

Use the words below to interview a Canadian student at this institution. Practise the simple present, the present continuous, the future, and the simple past. Report something interesting to the class about this student.

1. you/study another language now (what language)
2. you/live alone (who ... with)
3. your family/live in this city
4. you/like this city (why/why not)
5. you/go to high school in this city (where)
6. what/your major
7. you/graduate soon (when)
8. what/you do/after/you/graduate
9. you/like to travel (when ... your last vacation) (where ... go)
10. you/own a computer (what kind) (when ... buy it)
11. you/eat in a restaurant/last week (where)
12. you/buy something new/in the near future (what)
13. you/do something interesting/last weekend (what ... do)
14. you/plan to do something interesting/next weekend (what ... do)
15. _____
16. _____

Invite the Canadian to interview you. Write down the questions that he or she asks you.

Appendix A
The Verb *GET*

Get has many meanings. Here is a list of the most common ones:

- get something = receive
  I got a letter from my father.

- get + (to) place = arrive
  I got home at six. What time did you get to school?

- get + object + infinitive = persuade
  She got him to wash the dishes.

- get + past participle = become

get accustomed to	get hurt
get acquainted	get lost
get bored	get married
get confused	get scared
get divorced	get tired
get dressed	get used to
get drunk	get worried
get engaged	

  They got married in 1989.

- get + adjective = become

get angry	get old
get dark	get rich
get fat	get sleepy
get hungry	get upset
get nervous	get well

  It gets dark at 6:30.

- get an illness = catch
  While I was travelling, I got malaria.

- get a joke or an idea = understand
  Everybody except Tom laughed at the joke. He didn't get it.
  The boss explained the project to us, but I didn't get it.

- get ahead = advance
  He works very hard because he wants to get ahead in his job.

- get along (well) (with someone) = to have a good relationship
  She doesn't get along with her mother-in-law.
  Do you and your roommate get along well?

- get around to something = find the time to do something
  I wanted to write my brother a letter yesterday, but I didn't get around to it.

- get away = escape
  The police chased the thief, but he got away.

- get away with something = escape punishment
  He cheated on his taxes and got away with it.

- get back = return
  He got back from his vacation last Saturday.

- get back at someone = get revenge
  My brother wants to get back at me for stealing his girlfriend.

- get back to someone = communicate with someone at a later time
  I can't talk to you today. Can I get back to you tomorrow?

- get by = have just enough but nothing more
  On her salary, she's just getting by. She can't afford a car or a vacation.

- get in trouble = be caught and punished for doing something wrong
  They got in trouble for cheating on the test.

- get in(to) = enter a car
  She got in the car and drove away quickly.

- get out (of) = leave a car
  When the taxi arrived at the theatre, everyone got out.

- get on = to seat yourself on a bicycle, motorcycle, horse, etc.
  She got on the motorcycle and left.

- get on = enter a train, bus, airplane, boat, etc.
  She got on the bus and took a seat in the back.

- get off = leave a bicycle, motorcycle, horse, train, bus, airplane
  They will get off the train at the next stop.

- get out of something = escape responsibility
  My boss wants me to help him on Saturday, but I'm going to try to get out of it.

- get over something = recover from an illness or a disappointment
  She has the flu this week. I hope she gets over it soon.

- get rid of someone or something = free oneself of someone or something undesirable
  My apartment has cockroaches, and I can't get rid of them.

- get through (to someone) = to communicate, often by telephone
  She tried to explain the dangers of drugs to her son, but she couldn't get through to him.
  I tried to call her many times, but her line was busy. I couldn't get through.

- get through with something = finish
  I can meet you after I get through with my homework.

- get together = to meet with another person
  I'd like to see you again. When can we get together?

- get up = to arise from bed
  He woke up at 6:00 a.m., but he didn't get up until 6:30.

Appendix B
MAKE and *DO*

Some expressions use *make*. Others use *do*.

Make

      make a date/an appointment
      make a plan
      make a decision
      make a telephone call
      make a reservation
      make a meal (breakfast, lunch, dinner)
      make a mistake
      make an effort
      make an improvement
      make a promise
      make money
      make noise
      make the bed

Do

      do (the) homework
      do an exercise
      do the dishes
      do the cleaning, laundry, ironing, washing, etc.
      do the shopping
      do one's best
      do a favour
      do the right/wrong thing
      do a job
      do business
      What do you do for a living? (asks about a job)
      How do you do? (said when you meet someone for the first time)

Appendix C
Questions

1. Statements and Related Questions with a Main Verb

(Wh- Word)	Do/Does/Did(n't)	Subject	Verb	Complement
		She	watches	TV.
When	does	she	watch	TV?
		My parents	live	in Peru.
Where	do	your parents	live?	
		Your sister	likes	someone.
Who(m)	does	she	like?	
		They	left	early.
Why	did	they	leave	early?
		She	found	some books.
How many books	did	she	find?	
		He	bought	a car.
What kind of car	did	he	buy?	
		She	didn't go	home.
Why	didn't	she	go	home?
		He	doesn't like	tomatoes.
Why	doesn't	he	like	tomatoes?
		Someone	has	my book.
		Who	has	my book?
		Someone	needs	help.
		Who	needs	help?
		Someone	took	my pen.
		Who	took	my pen?
		One teacher	speaks	Italian.
		Which teacher	speaks	Italian?
		Some people	have	a car.
		Which people	have	a car?
		Some boys	saw	the movie.
		How many boys	saw	the movie?

2. Statements and Related Questions with the Verb *Be*

Wh- Word	*Be*	Subject	*Be*	Complement
		She	is	in Nova Scotia.
Where	is	she?		
		They	were	hungry.
Why	were	they		hungry?
		He	isn't	tired.
Why	isn't	he		tired?
		He	was	born in England.
When	was	he		born?
		One student	was	late.
		Who	was	late?
		Which student	was	late?
		Some kids	were	afraid.
		How many kids	were	afraid?
		Which kids	were	afraid?

3. Statements and Related Questions with an Auxiliary (Aux) Verb and a Main Verb

Wh- Word	Aux	Subject	Aux	Main Verb	Complement
		She	is	running.	
Where	is	she		running?	
		They	will	go	on a vacation.
When	will	they		go	on a vacation?
		He	should	do	something.
What	should	he		do?	
		You	can	take	a pill.
How many pills	can	you		take?	
		You	can't	drive	a car.
Why	can't	you		drive	a car?
		Someone	should	answer	the question.
		Who	should	answer	the question?

Appendix D
Alphabetical List of Irregular Past Forms

Base Form	Past Form	Base Form	Past Form
arise	arose	drink	drank
awake	awoke	drive	drove
be	was/were	eat	ate
bear	bore	fall	fell
beat	beat	feed	fed
become	became	feel	felt
begin	began	fight	fought
bend	bent	find	found
bet	bet	fit	fit
bind	bound	flee	fled
bite	bit	fly	flew
bleed	bled	forbid	forbade
blow	blew	forget	forgot
break	broke	forgive	forgave
breed	bred	freeze	froze
bring	brought	get	got
broadcast	broadcast	give	gave
build	built	go	went
burst	burst	grind	ground
buy	bought	grow	grew
cast	cast	hang	hung[1]
catch	caught	have	had
choose	chose	hear	heard
cling	clung	hide	hid
come	came	hit	hit
cost	cost	hold	held
creep	crept	hurt	hurt
cut	cut	keep	kept
deal	dealt	kneel	knelt
dig	dug	know	knew
do	did	lay	laid
draw	drew	lead	led

[1]*Hanged* is used as the past form to refer to punishment by death.

Base Form	Past Form	Base Form	Past Form
leave	left	slit	slit
lend	lent	speak	spoke
let	let	speed	sped
lie	lay	spend	spent
light	lighted, lit	spin	spun
lose	lost	spit	spit
make	made	split	split
mean	meant	spread	spread
meet	met	spring	sprang
mistake	mistook	stand	stood
pay	paid	steal	stole
prove	proved	stick	stuck
put	put	sting	stung
quit	quit	stink	stank
read (/rid/)	read (/rɛd/)	strike	struck
ride	rode	strive	strove
ring	rang	swear	swore
rise	rose	sweep	swept
run	ran	swim	swam
say	said	swing	swung
see	saw	take	took
seek	sought	teach	taught
sell	sold	tear	tore
send	sent	tell	told
set	set	think	thought
shake	shook	throw	threw
shed	shed	understand	understood
shine	shone	upset	upset
shoot	shot	wake	woke
show	showed	wear	wore
shrink	shrank	weave	wove
shut	shut	weep	wept
sing	sang	win	won
sink	sank	wind	wound
sit	sat	withdraw	withdrew
sleep	slept	wring	wrung
slide	slid	write	wrote

INDEX

COPYRIGHT ACKNOWLEDGMENTS

Lesson Four
Reading: Facts About Canadians, p. 81: Statistics Canada, "Canadian Statistics: The People." http://www.statcan.ca/english/Pgdb/People/popula.htm

Statistics Canada, "1996 Census." http://www.statcan.ca/english/english/census96/list.htm

Lesson Nine
Reading: Standard Time, p. 203–4: The CRB Foundation Heritage Project: A Heritage Minute, "Sandford Fleming Makes Trains Run on Time." http://www.nmarcom.com/heritage/minutes/min21.htm

"Sir Sandford Fleming." http://fleming0.flemingc.on.ca/techlaw/comptech/theman.htm

Lesson Eleven
Reading: A Healthy Diet, pp. 262–63: Publications Health and Welfare Canada, "Using the Food Guide." http://www.hc-sc.gc.ca/main/hppb/nutrition/pube/foodguid/food1.htm

The Minister of National Health and Welfare, *Canada Food Guide.*

"Towards Healthier Eating." *Vimy Park Health Magazine.* http://www.vimy-park.mb.ca/eat.html

Lesson Twelve
Reading: The Aging of the Canadian Population, pp. 288: Statistics Canada, "Canadian Statistics: The People." http://www.stat.can.ca/english/Pgdb/People/Population/demo10a.htm

"We're Not Getting Any Younger." *Canadian Issues: The Aging Population.* http://www-nais.ccm.emr.ca/schoolnet/issues/agepop/eaging.html

"Age Pattern of the Potential for Instutionalization." *Info-Âge,* Issue No. 17, December 1996 (published by the National Advisory Council on Aging). http://www.hc-sc.gc.ca/datahpsb/seniors/seniors/pubs/info17e.htm

United Nations Department for Policy Coordination and Sustainable Development, "International Year of Older Persons." http://www.un.org/dpcsd/dpcsd/iyop.htm

Lesson Thirteen
Reading: Facts About Canada, pp. 303–4: *Government of Canada Primary Internet Site* (National Atlas on SchoolNet), "Interactive Geography Quiz." http://www-nais.ccm.emr.ca/schoolnet/quiz2/english/html/Home.html

PHOTO CREDITS

Lesson One chapter opener (Montreal) © Photodisc, Inc.
Lesson One internal photo (Parliament) © CP Photo
Lesson Two chapter opener (CN Tower) © CP Photo
Lesson Three chapter opener (schoolchild) © Photodisc, Inc.
Lesson Four chapter opener (real estate) © Hemingway: Photographs
Lesson Five chapter opener (St. Patrick's) © CP Photo
Lesson Six chapter opener (family) © Photodisc, Inc.
Lesson Seven chapter opener (sledding) © Photodisc, Inc.
Lesson Eight chapter opener (repair) © Dick Hemingway: Photographs
Lesson Nine chapter opener (ice storm) © Robert Del Tredici
Lesson Nine internal photo (Beatles) © CP Photo
Lesson Ten chapter opener (moving) © Photodisc, Inc.
Lesson Eleven chapter opener (shopping) © CP Photo
Lesson Twelve chapter opener 1 (couple) © Photodisc, Inc.
Lesson Twelve chapter opener 2 (walker) © Photodisc, Inc.
Lesson Thirteen chapter opener (computers) © Photodisc, Inc.
Lesson Fourteen chapter opener (football) © CP Photo
Lesson Fifteen chapter opener (beach) © Photodisc, Inc.

CANADA

Arctic Circle

Yukon

(Northwest Territories)

treeline

Nunavut

British Columbia

Alberta

Manitoba

Saskatchewan

Ontario

Quebec

Newfoundland

Prince Edward Island

Nova Scotia

New Brunswick

Abbreviation	Province/Territory	Capital	Population[1]
NF	Newfoundland	St. John's	564,929
PE	Prince Edward Island	Charlottetown	137,715
NS	Nova Scotia	Halifax	945,839
NB	New Brunswick	Fredericton	762,760
QC	Quebec	Quebec	7,413,944
ON	Ontario	Toronto	11,361,578
MB	Manitoba	Winnipeg	1,148,251
SK	Saskatchewan	Regina	1,025,086
AB	Alberta	Edmonton	2,828,189
BC	British Columbia	Victoria	3,915,898
YT	Yukon Territory	Whitehorse	31,627
NT	Northwest Territories	Yellowknife	45,057
NV	Nunavut (April 1, 1999)	Iqaluit	22,000 (approx.)
CA	Canada	Ottawa	30,202,873

[1]Statistics Canada population figures are postcensus estimates, as of April 1, 1997.

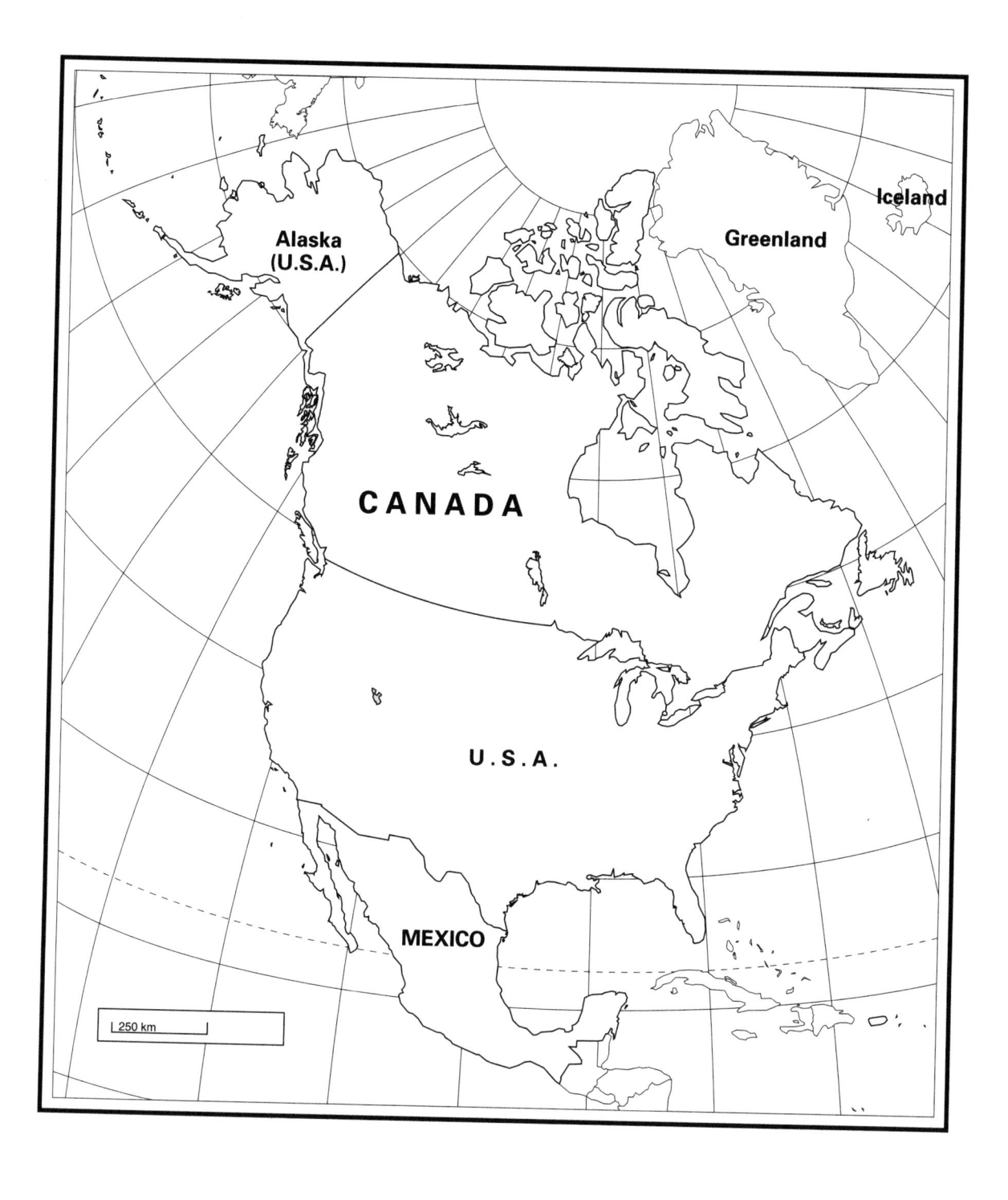

Alaska
(U.S.A.)

Greenland

Iceland

CANADA

U.S.A.

MEXICO

250 km

NOTES

NOTES

NOTES

NOTES

To the owner of this book

We hope that you have enjoyed *Grammar in Context, Book 1,* and we would like to know as much about your experiences with this text as you would care to offer. Only through your comments and those of others can we learn how to make this a better text for future readers.

School _____   Your instructor's name _____

Course _____   Was the text required? _____   Recommended? _____

1. What did you like the most about *Grammar in Context, Book 1?*

_____

_____

_____

2. How useful was this text for your course?

_____

_____

_____

3. Do you have any recommendations for ways to improve the next edition of this text?

_____

_____

_____

4. In the space below or in a separate letter, please write any other comments you have about the book. (For example, please feel free to comment on reading level, writing style, terminology, design features, and learning aids.)

_____

_____

_____

Optional

Your name _____   Date _____

May ITP Nelson quote you, either in promotion for *Grammar in Context, Book 1* or in future publishing ventures?

Yes _____   No _____

Thanks!

You can also send your comments to us via e-mail
at **college_arts_hum@nelson.com**

FOLD HERE

MAIL POSTE

Canada Post Corporation
Société canadienne des postes

Postage paid   Port payé
if mailed in Canada   si posté au Canada
Business Reply   Réponse d'affaires

0066102399   01

0066102399-M1K5G4-BR01

ITP NELSON
MARKET AND PRODUCT DEVELOPMENT
PO BOX 60225 STN BRM B
TORONTO ON M7Y 2H1